Plays By
Michael McGuire

Broadway Play Publishing Inc
New York
BroadwayPlayPub.com

Plays By Michael McGuire
© Copyright 1999 Michael McGuire

All rights reserved. This work is fully protected under the copyright laws of the United States of America. No part of this publication may be photocopied, reproduced, stored in a retrieval system, or transmitted, in any form or by any means, electronic, mechanical, recording, or otherwise, without the prior permission of the publisher. Additional copies of this play are available from the publisher.

Written permission is required for live performance of any sort. This includes readings, cuttings, scenes, and excerpts. For amateur and stock performances, please contact Broadway Play Publishing Inc. For all other rights please contact the author c/o B P P I.

Cover photo: Greg Erf

First printing: June 1999
I S B N: 978-0-88145-160-3

Book design: Marie Donovan
Copy editing: Liam Brosnahan
Typeface: Palatino

CONTENTS

About the author v
THESE FLOWERS ARE FOR MY MOTHER 1
HOLD ME 71
HELEN'S PLAY 137

For Bill & Eva

ABOUT THE AUTHOR

Michael McGuire has had plays produced by the New York Shakespeare Festival (with Kevin McCarthy and Bob Balaban) and the Mark Taper Forum (with Ken Mars and Nan Martin) among others, including the American Theatre of Actors in New York, the Source in Washington, DC, The Changing Scene in Denver, the Actor's Workshop of San Francisco and at theatres in Frankfurt and Stuttgart, Germany. THE SCOTT FITZGERALD PLAY was published by the University of Missouri Press. BACKPACKER was grand prize winner and produced at the 9th Annual Great Platte River Playwrights' Competition in 1997. There have been many staged readings, including ones at N Y U, the Living Theatre, Lamb's with Tammy Grimes and Bob Stattel, the Public, the Hudson Guild, the Organic in Chicago, the Odyssey in Los Angeles, and two at Lincoln Center with Tammy Grimes, Richard Merrill, and Michael Zaslow.

Mr. McGuire's fiction has appeared in *The Paris Review, New Directions in Prose & Poetry*, and the *Hudson Review*. A collection of his stories, *The Ice Forest* (Marlboro Press), was named one of "the best books of 1991" by *Publisher's Weekly*.

He has been writer-in-residence at several universities and directed a creative writing program; he has had residencies at Yaddo and the Virginia Center for the Creative Arts, been aided in his work by the National Endowment for the Humanities, named an Individual Artist Fellow by the Oregon Arts Commission, and awarded the Oregon Arts Foundation Theatre Award. He is a member of the Dramatists Guild.

THESE FLOWERS ARE FOR MY MOTHER

CHARACTERS & SETTING

ADAM, *husband and father, mid-thirties, tall, manly; a lawyer, he is rarely out of his well-tailored business suit. Though often imaginative and playful, he does not always succeed in understanding his wife. He is separated from her, and she has temporary custody of their son.*

EDEN, *wife and mother, a lovely woman in her mid-thirties; stunning short blonde hair; she is always exquisitely dressed, favoring black dresses that display her figure and shoes that are elegantly feminine. A woman of great perception and sensibility. Though still young, she does not feel she will ever do what she feels she ought to be capable of. Prone to depression, sleeplessness, and alcohol.*

ALAN, *the son, age twelve, the present focus of his mother's hopes. Though bright, he doubts he will ever achieve all his mother would like him to.*

DR WRIGHT, *a child psychologist in his fifties, somewhat overweight; his dress is slatternly while engaged in his private practice; on the other hand, he is brisk and hygienic at the clinic. Sometimes appears as an expert witness in domestic cases involving children.*

(Locales are marked by islands of light in a sea of darkness; a door unit might be useful, an occasional piece of furniture.)

ACT ONE

Scene One

(The boy, lit from above, stands dwarfed in a child-size pool of light. The psychologist stands looking down at him; if possible, he is lit from underneath, and his features appear outsize, grotesque. The boy, hurt, hesitant to speak, looks at the floor much of the time in this scene. The closed door to the waiting room is behind ALAN. *A moment passes.)*

DR WRIGHT: *(Very softly)* And stillness was upon the face of the earth. *(Inhaling deeply, puffing himself up)* You know who I am?

ALAN: *(Barely audible)* ...You're Dr Wright....

DR WRIGHT: Tell the truth now. Just for a moment, didn't you think I might be God Almighty?

ALAN: ...No...

DR WRIGHT: Well, we can't always be right, but if I am Wright, Dr Wright, and I am, you must be Alan... *(With an imperious finger pointing into the distance)* ...the boy about to be banished. Right?

ALAN: ...Right...

DR WRIGHT: And how do you feel about your impending exile from what must appear—looking back over your young shoulder, as it were—as God's green garden itself?

ALAN: I...

DR WRIGHT: You do know what I'm talking about, don't you? Biblical references seem to go the way of Classical these days. God give them ears to....

ALAN: I know.

DR WRIGHT: *(Somewhat concealing the fact that he is impressed)* You do? *(Aside)* Good lord, I hope we haven't got a smarty-pants here. They're the worst kind. Hm. Now what can I...? Ah, yes.

(No longer looking down at the boy from his full height, the psychologist exhales and turns to the desk behind him. He faces ALAN *with a tray spread with several toy soldiers of American wars gone by. One of the figurines, the Indian Brave, outclasses all the others; it is clearly the most desirable toy.)*

DR WRIGHT: Now, young man, before we send you off—Mom or Dad does have that one-way, half-price ticket in his/her pocket, hasn't he/she?—we'll want to conduct a little experiment in the name of pure science. *(Quickly)* Here we go now./Ready?/Which soldier would you like?/Alan?/You can have any one. *(Beat. Smiling sincerely)* Really.

(ALAN *hesitates, looks up at* DR WRIGHT, *then chooses the best, the Indian Brave, for himself, lifting it in the air where he can get a good look at it.*)

DR WRIGHT: *(Watching him closely, speaking with precision)* That is, any one but that one, Alan. I should have made that clear. *(Normally)* Yes, that is my hero, my Brave Indian, my Indian Brave. When one of my nuts misses an appointment and I have half an hour to get down on the carpet and play war, that is my centerpiece, that one I group the others about...

ALAN: *(Softly)* "...that, that..."

DR WRIGHT: *(Gently)* Pardon me? Did you say something? I thought I heard you. No? Well, put the Brave Indian back, Alan. That's right. Choose another. This time I mean it. Any one. Any one at all. One who can fight back, of course, achieve something in this life, not some loser all ready to slump over his horse and die.

(ALAN *does as indicated.*)

DR WRIGHT: Very good, Alan. Are you sure that's the one you want?

(ALAN *nods.*)

DR WRIGHT: Good. *(Replacing the tray)* That's yours to keep. Now let's see... *(Bending towards the boy)* Which one have you chosen? Hm. Are you sure? That's an unusual choice. Odd. Strange. Look. See. This Wounded Warrior has something missing, broken off. Yes, I'd be a little worried about myself if I'd chosen that one. Tell me, Alan, are you a little worried about yourself? *(Without giving him a chance to answer)* But perhaps you're still sulking over the fact you didn't get your first choice, that that one happened to be my Indian Brave...?

ALAN: "...that, that..."

DR WRIGHT: Are you mocking me?

ALAN: Yes.

DR WRIGHT: Good. Good for you! God knows we doctors of drivel and drool, we mumbo jumbo men, need to be mocked once in a while. *(Quickly)* Tell me./Alan./Quickly./You didn't get your first choice./Disappointed?

ALAN: *(Interrupting)* No.

DR WRIGHT: Good. Very good. Extremely good. Because, smart aleck— or was it Alan?—regardless of our acquaintance with Genesis, even with Sophocles—with Freud!—not getting the toy we want is only one of a rather long, might I say endless, stream of disappointments...beginning with the loss of our mothers...and you'd better get used to *them*, the disappointments that is, because we tend to think when something goes wrong; when, just to pick a miserable *vita*, a sordid case history out of my hat, we're sent off—far, far away, against our will—we tend to think that there's something wrong with *us*, that's *when* we realize we've been deeply, I might say irremediably, hurt. Wounded. Like your Wounded Warrior, the one you chose, damaged beyond repair. Yes, Alan, these tiny exiles who transit my office on their way to God knows where—Boarding School, just to seize an example— can never, never be mended. Their cases are hopeless. They will always be in pain. *(Sitting informally on the edge of his desk)* Good. Now that you have a little perspective on the case. *(Slowly, drawing it out for clarity's sake)* Who brought you here today, Alan...your mother...or your father...? *(Too quickly)* Quick now./Who's just the other side of that door./ Who's poisoning the air of my waiting room?

ALAN: *(Having taken in much of what was said, looking down, his voice smaller than ever)* ...My mother...

DR WRIGHT: ...Your mother... Yes, well, there are terrors in our lives, my boy, holy terrors we just have to... *(Peeking out the eyehole into his waiting room)* Hm...! Not much wrong with that holy terror. God, what skin! Have you noticed her skin, Alan? Her hair? *(Raising a pocket telescope to the eyehole, extending it)* Those little blonde hairs on her neck.... *(Turning from the eyehole, snapping his telescope shut)* You can't have missed them, not if you have eyes to see. *(Rubbing his hands together)* Yes, if I were just a little nuttier myself, that is just the kind of nut that I... *(To himself)* Get a hold of yourself, Wright. *(Calmly)* But you don't want to hear my problems, do you?

ALAN: No.

DR WRIGHT: No, of course not. However, it's best you be aware, Alan, of certain undeniable...uh, qualities possessed by a certain unnamed knockout now gracing a chair in my waiting room... By the way, Alan, what is her name?

ALAN: *(Reluctantly)* ...Eden...

DR WRIGHT: Eden, Eden! I'm in love with her already. *(Unable to keep himself from peeking again)* God, those waiting room eyes! *(Tearing himself away, speaking with authority)* But, and here comes Disappointment #1: they, the eyes, my boy, along with the skin, the hair, etc, and anything else you may have noticed or failed to notice, are for the lucky paterfamilias—in short, your father—you understand, not for you.

ALAN: I understand.

DR WRIGHT: Not for me. But if only one—not both of your parents— has dragged you here for your first...and possibly last...visit, before your imminent exile, your impending and probably permanent exclusion from the warm lap, the protecting arms, the nurturing breast, my guess would be, the last time those two were seen together on God's earth has already come and gone. Am I right, Alan? Have Mom and Dad packed their separate afflictions and gone their separate ways?

ALAN: Yes.

DR WRIGHT: Yes, if I were you, young man, I'd remember that moment, the last time I saw Mom and Dad together. That's a snapshot for the mind's eye, an engraving to carry to your grave. Understand?

ALAN: Yes, sir.

DR WRIGHT: Well, Alan. No need to keep you. *(Smiling in a kindly fashion)* I'm sure your calendar is as chock full as mine: innocent games of tag, carefree bouts of sandlot ball, the old swimming hole.... *(To himself)* How well I know the children of today. *(To ALAN)* That's enough before Mom or Dad thrusts that one-way, half-price ticket deep into a little hand already damp with despair. Remember that unfortunate couple, Alan, standing only a foot or two apart; the threshold, as it were, between them; each with a hand on the handle of the door to nowhere—there's a picture for you now—for this is their tragedy as much as yours, and their last scene together might as well play in your mind as well as any, for only you were there—in a pint-size, nonspeaking part, you'll be the first to admit, but with eyes as big as your head and the tears afraid to fall. Am I right? Such grief, Alan, in a blameless child, such unadulterated....

ALAN: You're right.

DR WRIGHT: That's right. I'm right. Dr Wright. Good. Now get out of here. I've got all the patients I can bear to look at, much less listen to. Have you noticed, Alan? I'm not much of a listener. Anyway, you're on your own now, as if you didn't know it in the soles of your feet, as if those little boy's legs aren't just waiting to run so fast we can't even see them. No, there's nothing I can do for you. Hopeless, hopeless.

(As the boy begins to move away)

DR WRIGHT: So long, Alan. Hop the train to Boarding School. Ride the rails forever. Say hello to the future for me. May you hold your own children close, may their laughter fill your days. *(Barely opening the oversize door)* Goodbye. Goodbye. Just leave me wondering how it all began. How they ever hit on Boarding School. It works every time, you know. Crushes the little so-and-sos forever. Don't tell me. Let me guess. Did your father suggest it to your mother? Did his lawyer suggest it to him? Never mind. Who cares? I can live in ignorance. It hasn't bothered me yet. *(Bowing his farewell)* Until you find yourself somewhere even worse then, at a charming little enterprise of my own, for example. *(Raising his eyebrows)* Mystery/mystery. *(Suddenly)* Goodbye.

ALAN: *(Squeezing into the doorway)* Goodbye.

DR WRIGHT: *(Trapping him with the door, leaning close)* Uhhh, run down the hall a moment, won't you, Alan? It's pee-pee time. There's a good boy. Nurse will give you the key. I'd just like to take a closer look at that hair-raiser, that holy terror of yours.

(Exit ALAN. DR WRIGHT, *closes the door, immediately peeks through the eyehole, grabs his wall phone, speaks softly.)*

DR WRIGHT: ...Nurse...just send Mrs...uh, uh...the boy's mother... I don't care whose turn it is! I don't care if he's crying into my *New Republic*! Just send...whatever her... The one with the legs, goddamn it! No, no. On your right. The skin, the skin! The hair! That's it. *(Hanging up, leaning back against the door, rolling his eyes)* God give them eyes to see. *(Embracing the door)* ...Eden, Eden... To think I've lived long enough to catch a glimpse of Eden in my own waiting room! *(Heading toward his desk, all business)* Thank God I'm no longer subject to those embarrassingly sudden infatuations....

(The light fades on DR WRIGHT *as* ALAN, *in light that lingers only a moment longer, looks in opposite and quietly addresses the audience.)*

ALAN: Ladies and gentlemen, Dr Wright. There's probably very little we can do for Dr Wright. Very, very little. But perhaps you'd like a glimpse of Eden yourself. And... *(Making a magic sign in the air)* ...Pepto-Bismol: It's night, this night, or the next. Ladies and gentlemen: a lady named Eden.

Scene Two

*(*EDEN, *at home, stands in a pool of light, in a black nightgown, her stunning blonde hair holding the light like a golden helmet. She laughs.)*

EDEN: I told you. I'm still married. These things don't happen overnight. Let me... *(Correcting herself)* Let it cool down a little. *(Gasping)* Oh, you're awful. I can't say anything to you. I don't know if I want... *(She laughs.)* Seriously, my friend. This is talk—understand?—one word after another. But that's it. And that's enough now. This is not my night for worthwhile causes; I'm not up to anything else you might have in...

*(*ALAN, *in the shadows, carefully picks up an extension phone, listens.)*

EDEN: Are you there? I thought you'd hung up. *(She listens.)* That's not you breathing. Is your wife listening in? You don't have a...? *(Listening; then, her voice changed...)* Yes, my voice may be sad. Sad because something is ending, has ended. You ought to understand that. I don't want to talk about it. To you or anybody else. In fact I need a long silence...beginning now. *(She hangs up, speaks with both hands on the receiver.)* Sorry. My apologies to all to who need...whatever it is...when I have not one ounce of...whatever it is...to give. *(Loosening her gown)* Because I'm not going anywhere tonight. Tonight... Tonight is for my son.

(ALAN *hangs up softly, watches. The light on* EDEN *dims as she goes to a cabinet, takes a fine wine glass into which she pours about two inches of fine red wine and holds it up to the light.* EDEN *sniffs, but does not sip; she sits, one long bare arm extended on the table, one hanging at her side. She lowers her head onto the arm outstretched on the table which still holds the stem of the glass of wine. Awake, she is a painting of grace resting.*)

ALAN: *(Facing downstage)* Ladies and gentlemen, my mother. *(Softly, to her)* And believe me, Mom, if there were only one life we could save, it wouldn't be mine.

(EDEN, *on cue, raises her head, turns slowly, gracefully, without releasing her glass, to look at* ALAN. *Their eyes lock. She smiles coolly as the light fades on her and* ALAN *faces downstage.*)

ALAN: And before we know it, ladies and gentlemen, the night that Eden has willed to her son has passed. It's morning, or nearly; the next morning.

Scene Three

(*Before dawn.* ADAM, *standing erect, suited for the office and about to leave, talks to his lawyer on the telephone. The steaming mug of coffee on the table is ignored.*)

ADAM: Listen, Lawless, I don't need to be told what juries need to be told at any time—not even before breakfast. I know: wine-tasting is no sin, and she may be tasting in the best of taste...*but*...she's savoring the fruitiness, the *nuttiness*, to the point where she not only can't care for the boy, she can't even talk to him. Her tongue thickens, her gaze wanders. Those park bench eyes rise from a glass of *Chateau Neuf du Pape* and fix on my son. His image wavers in its bouquet. Understand? I want him out of her line of sight! *(Listens briefly)* Anywhere! *(Interrupting)* I know I can't take care of him. *(Listening, interrupting)* I know he's different. I'm not raising little lawyers. That's right. He's like her, only he's not a lovely lush with park bench eyes. *(Listening)* Send him where neither of us...? *(Beat)* Good. My friend, you may have hit on it. I know you'll get busy on your end, that's what I pay you to do. Suggest it myself? To Eden? You don't know the lady. *(Dismissing his lawyer's mild attempt at humor)* Very funny. Trust you to see the lighter side of custody. I'll think about it. *(He hangs up, starts towards the door, returns to the table, sits, puts his hand on the mug of coffee, withdraws it to look at his watch.)* Oh, what the hell! *(He goes to the cabinet, gets the whiskey, pours a shot into his coffee, puts away the bottle, sits, raises the mug, sets it down without a sip, speaks to himself.)* Watch your breath, old man. The image of an image mustn't waver, air on air heated like an empty room. Husband, father, friend... Solid as a tree that isn't there one day: an empty place against the sky, a pile of leaves. Now where did I learn to talk like that? Oh yes, I remember. *(Turning to the phone)* You taught me. *(He draws the phone closer, hesitates, walks around, returns to the stand by the phone, dials, listens as the ringing in his ear stops and he hears a familiar voice. After a moment, half smiling, echoing her lovely voice on his name)* Adam? Yes, it's Adam. Still know the sound of my breathing. What? *(Looking at his watch)* Nearly seven. Listen. What are you doing? Reading what? *(Listens)* At your age? I mean our age. I guess I may have seen it or read it in childhood. Maybe I never finished it. Say, mmm... how's Alan? What's he...? *(He reaches for his mug, leaves it where it is as he responds to her.)* You think he's reading—Is that wise? I mean: before breakfast?—or writing his memoirs? Now I know you're... Listen... Can we talk? Yes, I know we're not supposed to. Damn the court. One o'clock. I'll extend my lunch. The park. Where we.... Yes, as you say: once upon a time... Thank you, Ede... *(Realizing she has hung up, he hangs up gently, remains with both hands on the downed receiver.)* I know your breathing too, wife, mother of my child; my teacher. I'd know it anywhere. *(He reaches for the spiked coffee, raises it almost to his lips, sets the mug down.)* Since when did a man with a date with a lady with eyes like that need a pick-me-up?

(He picks up his briefcase, goes to work. ALAN *wanders into the fading light, picks up the mug, sniffs it, faces downstage.)*

ALAN: Ladies and gentlemen, my father. A not-unintelligent man. No one ever asked him to be extraordinary. Or didn't they? "They?" She. Maybe she did. "She?" You. *(His hand on the phone)* Did you whisper in his ear: "Adam, just for once: Be extraordinary?" I don't know, Mom. Did you? Was that wise? I mean: before breakfast? *(Fading)* Ladies and gentlemen, it's the same day. One o'clock.

Scene Four

(The park, the fountain, a pile of leaves. EDEN, *statuesque, motionless, one of the Graces at wait—black slacks, exquisite shoes, a sweater that might have been stolen from a Mondrian—waits on the bench. Enter* ADAM, *moving quickly.)*

EDEN: *(Looking at her watch)* Adam...you know how I feel about women waiting for men.

ADAM: *(Looking at his)* Eden...you know how I feel about men running to meet women. *(Sitting, still in a hurry)* I couldn't get away. *(Breathing, leaning back)* Strange place. *(Looking at* EDEN*)* Must be the center of the known world. *(When she raises her eyebrows inquisitively)* Because everything else seems to turn around it. *(With a sweeping gesture)* Look, you can see it all from here, all tumbling about in a great wind: our house, the lawyers; the school where they taught you to smile your smile, to walk across the room the way you walk across the room; your parents, mine, the boy...

EDEN: *(Softly)* The boy.

ADAM: You're still beautiful, Eden.

EDEN: *(Beat. Her voice cooler)* What do you want, Adam? Oh, I know what you want.

ADAM: *(Laughing warmly)* You couldn't possibly.

EDEN: *(With an almost warm half-smile)* Tell me then.

ADAM: *(Leaning slightly towards her)* I came here with something in mind.

EDEN: *(Ironically)* Oh, no! What? *(Opening her arms to him, leaning back enough to raise one leg subtly, gracefully)* Me reclining on our bench of yore?

ADAM: There's always that.

EDEN: *(Coolly)* Is there?

ADAM: That's only part of it.

EDEN: Oh? *(Singing softly to him)* ...Should old acquaintance be forgot... and never brought to mind... *(Straightening up)* What's the other part? My "book learnin'"?

ADAM: *(Standing, the pacing lawyer)* There's our conversations, the things I heard from you I'd never heard before. You taught me....

EDEN: I taught you to walk across the room without knocking anything over.

ADAM: You taught me to move through worlds I didn't know were there...

EDEN: I taught you to use the semicolon, to avoid those deadly run-on sentences...

ADAM: *(Still pacing)* More than that, you...

EDEN: Come off it, Adam. I'm not a jury. *(He faces her. Beat)*

ADAM: I still love you.

EDEN: *(Coolly)* We'll always love each other.

ADAM: Doesn't that make any difference?

EDEN: It makes the difference it makes, no more, no less. You want the boy, don't you?

ADAM: Not exactly.

EDEN: What do you want, exactly? Tell me how you and the boy...or me and the boy...how you see us exactly. Are we all whirling around in that great wind of yours? Is that it, exactly...more or less?

ADAM: *(Sitting at her side, leaning forward, hands together)* Eden... I've had an idea.

EDEN: You've had an idea or your lawyer has had an idea? Or shall we say you both had an idea...in the middle of a phone conversation perhaps...say at about seven this morning?

ADAM: You're always smarter than me, aren't you?

EDEN: That doesn't mean I don't respect you.

ADAM: Or love me.

EDEN: Or love you. Tell me then, what's your idea? *(As he opens his mouth to speak)* Yours and your lawyer's?

ADAM: *(Having intended to say more but suddenly settling on a couple of words)* Boarding School.

(They look at each other. EDEN looks away, shakes her head.)

ADAM: Think for a moment. It's not to get him away from you.

EDEN: Of course not.

ADAM: I mean it's not taking him. I won't have him either. He'll be on his own, equidistant from you, from me. There'll be vacations, his choice: Mom's, Dad's...or: everything set, Thanksgiving with his father, Christmas with his mother, summers half and half... *(Beat)* What do you think?

EDEN: I think it stinks.

ADAM: What's wrong with it? Wait a minute before you tell me. A moment ago I was going to tell you everything I had in mind, then just two words popped out: Boarding School.

EDEN: I believe I heard them.

ADAM: I wanted to say much more. I wanted to raise the question, hypothetically. *(Standing, walking away, but not as the lawyer)* What if...I was going to say...what if there were some way we could resolve the conflict, temporarily, without anybody, either of us, winning or losing, while we had a chance to get to know each other again, without the pressure of...

EDEN: What if?

ADAM: I still....

EDEN: You still love me. You said that. Just a couple of minutes ago. Remember?

ADAM: I used to say it twenty times a day.

EDEN: I didn't know you were keeping count. *(Standing)* Adam. *(He looks at her.)* I have an appointment. We'll talk about this another time.

ADAM: What kind of appointment?

EDEN: A doctor's appointment.

ADAM: Is something wrong?

EDEN: Not with me.

ADAM: *(Alarmed)* With Alan?

EDEN: Adam, there isn't anything wrong with our son. Not yet. I've been taking him to see someone highly recommended...well, so there won't be.

ADAM: So you'll seem like a responsible mother?

EDEN: You mean I'm not a responsible mother?

ADAM: It's just strange, isn't it, that girls raised by their fathers grow into lovely young women, while a boy raised by his mother is at risk...?

EDEN: "At risk." There's an interesting locution. Is it yours? *(Starting to leave, turning back)* I always think you're changing, that you're open... Then I spot the plot beneath the words, I realize it was always there.

ADAM: Eden, there was no plot. I came here...

EDEN: And you can stay here for all I care, floating gracelessly through worlds you never knew were there, hearing words you'd never heard before... Here are a couple you might want to remember. No more, Adam, understand? No more. Should I take a stick and scratch them in the dirt for you? "No. More." But here's what I had to say. Are you listening?

ADAM: I'm listening.

EDEN: What you want for the boy isn't wrong or evil. It's practical and levelheaded; it's solid...if not stolid. It's like you, Adam, earthbound; I wouldn't want to say "pedestrian." How about... *(With emphasis)* ...Prosaic?

ADAM: Meaning not poetic.

EDEN: Meaning not poetic. What you want isn't wrong for you and wouldn't be wrong for most. But it would be wrong for Alan, because Alan isn't Adam. He isn't you—or me. Don't you realize that? Don't you know your own son?

ADAM: I guess not. Well, tell me then. What's my son like?

EDEN: Oh, don't put it all onto me. Admit it, Adam. The court recorder isn't pecking away in the corner. This is just between you and me. Admit it.

ADAM: Admit what?

EDEN: Your son's, well, one of a kind. *(Beat)*

ADAM: I know he's intelligent, perceptive. But other people see things, *I* see things. Of course, he's not very good at sports, but that doesn't get him into the Special Olympics.

EDEN: What a wonderful sense of humor you...

ADAM: Eden, I never hit you or made fun of you. I only bored you. If I hear anyone laughing now, it isn't me. I just hope Alan isn't being encouraged to join in a good kindly laugh at the man who can't understand.

EDEN: We don't laugh at you. Ever. You're Alan's father.

ADAM: Is that the only reason? I'm myself. I'm your husband too. Still.

EDEN: That's about to change. *(Beat)*

ADAM: *(Stepping back, near defeat)* Yes, and that's why I'm suggesting a partial solution—I know it isn't perfect—one that will preclude a battle which can only harm....

EDEN: Adam, give him a chance at something beyond what any Boarding School can.

ADAM: A chance at what?

EDEN: Do I have to say it?

ADAM: For me. Yes.

EDEN: At, at...well—at being one who wrote the book.

ADAM: One who...? What book? Is Alan writing a...?

EDEN: Sure he is. The one he's in. We all...

ADAM: How's it going, Eden, this book? He doesn't discuss it with me.

EDEN: I think it's going well. His phrasing...

ADAM: I thought there was more to writing the book than avoiding those deadly run-on sentences.

EDEN: I'm asking you, Adam: Give him a chance, give him that chance.

(Beat) ADAM: You think that just being with you gives him this chance, don't you? Well, he is a great twelve year-old. I admit that. I've tried to be a great father. There was a time when we used to say we were great together. Isn't that enough greatness for this life?

EDEN: If you don't understand...

ADAM: One who wrote the book! Eden, he's twelve years old. Maybe claiming too much for a child is as bad as asking too little. Though you think you're making perfect sense, the way I hear it your words might as well be a little slurred. I don't know why drinking mothers all think their children are phenomenal. Is it because they realize how ordinary they are themselves? I see the day when you don't get up from your special vintages to go to the bathroom. I see a beautiful, well-dressed woman...with all her semicolons in the right place...so weak she's slipping down in her own doorway. I see her crawling under the table she's so fond of reading at. I see an early, pathetic death. Think about it. Is that where you want to drag your one-of-a-kind, extraordinary child? *(Beat)* I've had enough of this. We'll do just what I didn't want to do. We'll deal with this in the courts. Who will that be good for? Are you really going to stand up and argue that one of Alan's parents, his father, isn't really bad, he'd be good enough for most boys, he's just not good enough for this one?

EDEN: Oh, I'll probably come up with a better argument, but that is what I'll think, yes. Thank you for showing me how absurd what I really think would sound. I should never have told you.

ADAM: Pearls before swine.

EDEN: Worlds you still don't know are there.

ADAM: I may come up with a better argument myself.

EDEN: That's always a possibility. *(Beat)* What time is it?

ADAM: *(Looking at his watch)* Not yet two.

EDEN: Well, you'd better....

(They stare at each other a moment. Exit ADAM opposite the direction in which EDEN was about to leave. EDEN looks after him, her parting shot not fired, her mouth open a moment before she closes it, draws herself up and leaves as intended. A moment of empty stage. Enter ALAN. He looks briefly at the spaces where his mother and father stood. He looks downstage.)

ALAN: *(Shrugging)* Ladies and gentlemen, is this the unfortunate couple I'm supposed to remember, standing only a foot or two apart, the threshold "as it were" between them, each with a hand on the handle of the door to nowhere? *(As the light fades)* Well, that moment's past, that door might be swinging in the wind....as the afternoon goes wherever afternoons go. Exit the light of day. Enter night, that night. I don't know where my father is. *(Leaving)* My mother reads....

Scene Five

(EDEN alone at her table. Late night. A reading lamp. A glass of red wine. A book lies open on the table, though she isn't reading it. As usual, she is very attractively dressed, perhaps for an evening that isn't taking place. Her long neck is revealed; her earrings catch the light. A minute passes in which she does nothing at all, though she may have several impulses: to take up the book, for example. The fingertips of one hand caress the open pages, the fingers of the other rest on the base of her wine glass. ALAN appears behind her in the shadows, barefoot in robe and pajamas, watching her. Though he hasn't made a sound, EDEN leans back in her chair to look over her shoulder at him. She is statuesque, alluring, her legs long and revealed.)

EDEN: Just because I can't sleep doesn't mean you...

ALAN: I woke up.

EDEN: Come here, Alan.

(Releasing book and glass, she sits up straighter; he comes around in front of her.)

EDEN: This won't do, you know, lying awake, watching our shadows traverse the ceiling, watching our ghosts. Let them go. They have business, they're on errands of their own. You must sleep. You'll need your strength.

ALAN: For what?

EDEN: For the things you're going to do.

ALAN: What am I going to do?

EDEN: Only you know that.

ALAN: Am I going to sit all night with a glass in one hand and a book in the other?

EDEN: Alan, just because I haven't used my time well doesn't mean you... You may have been made for greater things.

ALAN: I may not have been made for anything at all. *(Beat)* What are you reading?

EDEN: *(Shrugging, smiling)* Peter Pan.

ALAN: *Peter Pan*!

EDEN: Don't mock what you don't know, Alan. *(Taking up the book)* Listen. "Peter Pan. Act I. The night nursery of the Darling family, which is the scene of our opening Act, is at the top of a rather depressed street in Bloomsbury. We have a right to place it where we will, and the reason Bloomsbury is chosen is that Mr Roget once lived there. So did we in days when his Thesaurus was our only companion in London; and we whom he has helped to wend our way through life have always wanted to pay him a little compliment. The Darlings therefore lived in Bloomsbury."

(Beat)

ALAN: So?

EDEN: So. M. Roget helped Mr Barrie wend his way through life.

ALAN: So what?

EDEN: Maybe that's where Wendy came from. Wendy is one of the characters.

ALAN: I know.

(EDEN and ALAN look at each other.)

ALAN: Why did you two go to all the trouble?

EDEN: What trouble?

ALAN: Of making me.

EDEN: It wasn't any trouble. *(Laughing)* It was fun. *(Serious)* We... Because... I don't remember.

ALAN: Did you ever ask Dad to be extraordinary?

(Beat)

EDEN: I may have, yes.

ALAN: Was it before breakfast?

EDEN: *(Laughing.)* I don't know. Why?

ALAN: I may not be who you want me to be.

EDEN: You may not. *(Smiling)* It's too soon to tell.

ALAN: I may be no one at all.

(EDEN *pats her lap. After a moment's hesitation,* ALAN *sits on it. She looks at him, he doesn't look at her. She speaks with gentle irony.)*

EDEN: You're someone. Someone who's already too heavy for me. *(Beat)* Sometimes you look just like your father.

ALAN: Does that bother you?

EDEN: Your father is a handsome man.

(ALAN *nods as if he is well aware of this. Then his stomach rumbles and he puts his hand on it. She smiles warmly, puts her hand on top of his.)*

EDEN: Did you get enough to eat?

ALAN: Did you get enough to drink?

(EDEN *closes her eyes briefly before answering.)*

EDEN: Don't be cruel, Alan.

ALAN: You can be cruel.

EDEN: Never to you. Let me tell you something I've learned: Cruelty is a waste of time.

ALAN: When did you learn that?

EDEN: This afternoon, I think.

ALAN: In the park?

EDEN: How did you...?

ALAN: Did you learn it too late?

EDEN: I think so.

ALAN: So you were wasting your time?

EDEN: Yes.

ALAN: Tomorrow will be wasted if you don't go to....

EDEN: Do you think, Alan, it's easier to waste time at night because...?

ALAN: You are beautiful.

EDEN: Sh.

ALAN: *(Looking at her)* I always knew about your eyes, but, as the doctor said... *(Touching them)* ...there's your skin, your hair...

EDEN: *(Drawing back)* The doctor? The doctor I took you to?

ALAN: Dr Wright. He said if he were just a little nuttier, you were just the kind of nut that he....

EDEN: *(Laughing)* He never....

ALAN: Don't believe me. Just write him a check.

EDEN: *(Dumping him off her lap)* I think it's off to bed with you.

ALAN: *(Rising from the floor, holding his hands over her glass of wine, looking into it as if it were a crystal ball)* Speaking of time, Mom, I wonder what's going to happen to that skin, that hair, those "waiting room eyes..."

EDEN: Is that what the doctor...?

ALAN: I don't know. I hear these voices lately...as if I'm someplace I shouldn't be, hearing things I shouldn't hear. Is that possible, Mom? To be places where I shouldn't be?

EDEN: I don't know.

ALAN: As if I were writing, not a poem before breakfast, but my memoirs...

(EDEN *glances up at him as* ALAN, *still looking into her glass, assumes something of his father's manner.*)

ALAN: "I see a woman so weak she's slipping down in her own doorway. I see her crawling under the table she's so fond of reading at."

(Beat)

EDEN: How...where did you hear that?

ALAN: I don't know.

EDEN: You know why I drink, Alan?

ALAN: *(Sniffing the wine)* No.

EDEN: To sleep.

ALAN: Does it help?

EDEN: Sometimes. At first. Then I wake up more awake than ever. I think of everything I should have done, or how I could have done what I did do better.

ALAN: That's no time to think of it.

EDEN: No.

(ALAN *raises her glass almost to his lips.*)

EDEN: Alan, don't.

ALAN: *(Lowering the glass)* Why not?

EDEN: I don't want you to.

(ALAN *raises the glass again, barely tastes the wine. Patiently)*

EDEN: Do you like it?

ALAN: No. *(He sips again.)*

EDEN: Then why...?

ALAN: Maybe I wonder what it's like to be you.

EDEN: That won't tell you. *(Beat)* Alan.

ALAN: What?

EDEN: May I tell you something?

(ALAN nods.)

EDEN: I haven't slept for three days.

(He looks at her.)

EDEN: Maybe I haven't really been awake either, but I haven't slept. You don't want to be like that.

ALAN: No.

EDEN: Tell me you'll never be like that.

(Beat)

ALAN: *(Putting down the glass)* I'll never be like that.

(EDEN nods, hangs her head.)

EDEN: *(Sleepily)* ...Thank you...Alan...thank...

(EDEN closes her eyes, slumps a little in her chair. ALAN, standing at her side, puts his arms around her shoulders. EDEN stiffens a little, then leans against him, emitting a small sound of relief. ALAN tightens his arms around her and opens his mouth to say something, then notices how deeply she is breathing. Looking down at her, he realizes she is asleep. He waits, at first not knowing what to do, then, seeing how deeply she sleeps, he arranges her arms on the table, lowering her head to rest on them. He places his robe over her shoulders. He stands looking down at her a moment before taking up the glass and moving some distance away. He speaks softly as the light fades.)

ALAN: And if I am someplace I shouldn't be, hearing things I'd rather not be hearing...? *(Looking into the glass he holds)* I too foresee an early, a pathetic death. *(Leaving with the glass)* I go to pour this down the drain. I go to sit on the side of my bed. *(He pauses at the door.)* Ladies and gentlemen: wasted or not... *(About to extinguish the light)* ...this night, as so many, falls....apart. *(Quickly, as the light quickly fades)* And suddenly: It's tomorrow, or the next day, or the next. My father is checking out this Dr Wright....

Scene Six

(ADAM *and* DR WRIGHT *face each other across his desk.*)

DR WRIGHT: You want to know what's going on?

ADAM: That's what I said. Since it appears to have official sanction, I assume it's relatively public.

DR WRIGHT: Very little goes on here, Adam. There are whole days when I wonder if it isn't really the preceding day playing itself out again...or the next day, having arrived without my knowledge.

ADAM: I didn't come here to listen to you philosophize.

DR WRIGHT: Suppose you tell me what you think is going on.

ADAM: Did you encourage Alan to hold his mother until she falls asleep?

DR WRIGHT: If you will recall, Adam, I'm not in your house at bedtime. I wasn't there, Adam. I didn't know it was going to happen.

ADAM: But you know it did happen. And it not only did happen, Dr Wright, it's happening. It's a practice, a habit. It's going on every night now.

DR WRIGHT: Is it? *(Carefully)* And just where is this...?

ADAM: As far as I know, it's at the table. He holds her, she falls asleep, he goes to bed. Since I left, she can only sleep at the table.

DR WRIGHT: I wish I could leave them shivering sleepless in chairs.

ADAM: Never mind what you wish. Alan told you about it. It happened to come out later in a conversation with me. My understanding is you told him you didn't see anything wrong in it. Is that true?

DR WRIGHT: Well, yes, yes, I suppose it is. You're not holding her. I, unfortunately, am in no position to. That leaves the boy. You don't want her breaking down, do you? That's how it can start, with sleeplessness; insomnia is a symptom, Adam, of the kind of wakefulness none of us can stand. After a while we break down. You don't want her institutionalized, do you?

(Beat)

ADAM: No.

DR WRIGHT: Are you sure?

ADAM: I'm sure.

DR WRIGHT: No, none of us does. That wouldn't do anyone any good, not the boy. Not you.

ADAM: No.

DR WRIGHT: Of course not. *(Quickly)* You don't want her dead, do you?/Never want to beat her brains out?/Quick, Adam./Quick./A woman smarter than you are./Your own wife.

(ADAM *will not move at* DR WRIGHT's *speed. A moment passes during which they confront, then:)*

ADAM: I think I've heard about enough of this.

DR WRIGHT: As you wish.

(ADAM *turns, begins to move towards the door.)*

DR WRIGHT: There's no chance of getting together again, is there?

ADAM: *(Stopping)* With Eden?

DR WRIGHT: Who else?

ADAM: We do not communicate.

DR WRIGHT: Really? But she expresses herself so well. I can almost hear her punctuation.

ADAM: She thinks Alan can only flourish in close association with her.

DR WRIGHT: Do you think it might be possible?

ADAM: I certainly did once consider her brilliant in her way.

DR WRIGHT: Only you didn't flourish...in such close association.

ADAM: For a while I... No, not in the long run.

DR WRIGHT: No, you drooped, you wilted. You decided one can only give so much to long walks, long talks, to one word after another. One day you turned away. You threw yourself into your work.

ADAM: Did she tell you?

DR WRIGHT: No. But you're afraid that—perhaps with reason—the boy will end up more fragile than ever, a hothouse flower, his mother asleep in his arms...that he'll carry that knockout wherever he goes from here, unable to put her down....that the man with his mother in his arms might not pass for any extraordinary, one-of-a-kind fella...and worse: that the sleeping beauty might just sleep forever. *(Putting his hands on an invisible crystal ball, tilting his head back)* I see an Alan stuck, afraid of moving, paralyzed with fear of disturbing his mother. Where am I? Ah yes, the family crypt, the "mummy chamber," as it were. I see a kind of bas-relief: mother and child so lightly, so eternally, carved upon the slimy limestone of our dreams.

ADAM: Doesn't sound too healthy.

DR WRIGHT: No. *(Whisking aside his crystal ball, making the sound of its crash)* Put like that, it doesn't.

ADAM: You're a bit of a case yourself, aren't you?

DR WRIGHT: That's right. Dr Wright. At your service.

ADAM: You're not working for me.

DR WRIGHT: No? Why, I might be working for...almost anyone, Adam, given the opportunity. *(Beat; then quickly)* What do you propose to do about the situation?

ADAM: I may sue, get her declared incompetent, no: not in need of institutionalization, just not qualified for the tasks of motherhood.

DR WRIGHT: I wouldn't try to take him away from her.

ADAM: Why not?

DR WRIGHT: If you fail, you'll poison all future relations where cooperation is to be desired. If you succeed, you'll just hurt her deeply. The boy will see her hurt. He'll know who did it. Another poison, but a poison nevertheless. I wouldn't touch it if I were you. Ah, yes... *(Taking another invisible crystal ball out of his desk drawer—he has an unlimited supply—looking into it)* I see a kind of bas-relief, on the surface, at ground level: yes, three figures—a man, a woman and a child—each with a glass of...of some concoction in hand, a mixture all would be better off without. See that one, Adam, graved upon the groaning granite of our nights?

ADAM: You're a frustrated stonecutter, Wright. I've got a few case histories myself, cases I've won. I have a feeling your days on this case are limited.

DR WRIGHT: *(Whisking this crystal ball off his desk, making the sound of its crash)* You may have forgotten: The court ordered...

ADAM: I don't care what the court ordered. I'm not helpless. *(Advancing)* There are professional organizations, as I'm sure both of us are aware, that keep an eye on their members. A man like you might have a bit of a past. A little research, and I might have them scratching your name off the member's list. *(With a motion at the door)* Off the door you hide behind.

(Close, they face each other.)

DR WRIGHT: *(Unflinching)* Very good, Adam. I think we can call this session a success. You got through to some elemental anger there, my boy. *(Smiling approvingly, gesturing towards an open door)* Until next week then.

(Smiling and nodding as ADAM leaves)

DR WRIGHT: Good, good... *(Closing the door behind ADAM, leaning back against it)* Sad, sad... I think you may have eyes to see, Adam, ears to hear... You may not be as ordinary as I've been led to expect. *(Crossing toward his desk)* I wonder if the mother is a reliable witness, as they say. I wonder what she has in mind for the boy...

Scene Seven

(ALAN *sits on a stool, his fingers resting on his laptop computer.* EDEN *stands downstage, her book in her hand. Her wine glass and bottle stand on the sideboard.*)

ALAN: *(Looking anywhere but at her)* Tell me, Mom: just what is it you have in mind for me?

EDEN: *(To herself)* Once, in a Chinese restaurant in San Francisco, I received a fortune in a cookie. "He who can handle a writing brush will never have to beg." And, in general, it's true. To be able to express oneself...

(*The moment* ALAN *begins to type,* EDEN *is moving towards him.*)

ALAN: *(Typing)* "...for this is their tragedy as much as yours," said the doctor, "and their last scene together might as well play in your mind as well as any, for you..."

(EDEN *having stepped up behind* ALAN, *looks over his shoulder, smiles, nods.*)

EDEN: Good, good... *(Leaning closer, eyes narrowing, stopping his typing with a word)* Wait a minute. First paragraph, last line, middle. "Such grief, Alan, in a child..." Are you sure you want "grief?" What's wrong with "heartache?" What's wrong with "woe?" Old words, but all of them older than you. Where's your thesaurus, Alan?

ALAN: *(Having reread while she spoke)* I think I'll stick with "grief." It seems right somehow.

EDEN: Seems? What's wrong with "is"? There's the right word and the wrong word. *(Leaning closer)* Alan, I hate to mention this, but have you checked your spacing? I see some ugly gaps. You're not ready for the printer, young man.

ALAN: I never said I was.

EDEN: *(Pointing out another typo)* And here...

ALAN: *(Interrupting)* I wonder if everyone who has his mother looking over his shoulder is destined for such extraordinary success...

EDEN: *(Straightening, moving away)* Never mind mothers looking over our shoulders. Some say there is some beauty though, a little off to the side, nodding or shaking her head, helping us all to sidestep imperfections. You know of whom I speak, don't you, Alan?

ALAN: Yes, mother.

EDEN: I don't have to name her?

ALAN: No, mother.

EDEN: It's simple. Keep *her* happy. *(Further away, not looking back)* That's all there is to it. Find the best of all possible words, Alan, put them in the best of all possible orders.

ALAN: Right away, mother. Best of all words coming up...

EDEN: *(Distant, shaking her head)* "Grief," "grieving..." Grieving is official now, you know; they do it in high schools with the pledge of allegiance. You don't have to look far for the dead words, Alan. They're all around us. People love them. Pick them up like seashells. Hold them to their ears. Hear a shifting sea of barbarisms, prosaicisms...

(Tasting a bad taste at about the same time ALAN's *attention returns to his work)*

EDEN: ...put them in their mouths. Alan, are you listening? Have you heard a word I...?

ALAN: *(Typing)* "Remember that unfortunate couple," said the doctor, "standing only a foot or two apart; the threshold, as it were, between them; each with a hand on the handle of the door to...to..."

EDEN: *(Not looking at him)* Don't stare at the keyboard, Alan. It isn't in the eyes. It's in the hands.

ALAN: *(Typing)* "...of the door to nowhere—there's a picture for you now..."

EDEN: *(Looking at one of her own hands in the light as* ALAN *turns to stare)* Yes, that's where it comes from, Alan, the fingertips....

ALAN: *(Typing; with conviction)* "Such...sadness, Alan, in a child..."

EDEN: *(In the process of picking up her bottle and wine glass, holding onto her book; to herself)* "Sadness?" I think I preferred "grief."

ALAN: *(Turning on her)* What's wrong with your fingertips, Mom?

EDEN: Mine? Yes, you're right. I don't know. There is something wrong with them, Alan. *(Leaving)* They're not like yours. But really, Alan. "Sadness." *(At the door, hand going to the knob)* You can do better than....

ALAN: Mom, don't touch that door! There's nothing on the other side of it. Darkness. Ropes and pulleys. A trap door. Nothing at all. A void. Grief!

(EDEN, *burdened with glass, bottle and book, opens the door and exits, swallowed by the darkness. Her reading light, off, comes on.)*

ALAN: Ladies and gentlemen, never mind the eyes. It's the hands, my mother's hands, my mother's fingertips. I'm surprised Dr Wright never noticed them. *(Raising his voice)* How did you miss them, Dr Wright, an astute observer of the human scene like yourself? *(More loudly)* Oh, Dr Wright...!

EDEN: *(Off)* Alan, please. You know how I hate to be disturbed when I'm reading.

ALAN: *(Turning on his stool to face downstage, more softly)* Ladies and gentlemen, as I said, my mother "reads." Oh, don't worry, she'll be back. To look over my shoulder. To leave again...distant, distracted, in another world...mumbling my mistakes as she goes. And I... I'll... *(Returning to his work)* I'll try again...as Dr Wright answers our call, and somewhere between Mom and Dad, equidistant "as it were," grasps some of the possibilities of his situation.

(ALAN remains perched over his laptop, typing in the gathering dark as DR WRIGHT is brilliantly highlighted.)

Scene Eight

(DR WRIGHT, dressed to give Expert Testimony, stands before the mirror.)

DR WRIGHT: "Dr Wright, oh, Dr Wright!" Did I hear someone calling? Let them call. Let them scream and tear their hair for all I... *(Returning to the practice of his Expert Testimony)* And, in conclusion, I would advise the court that the child is, at the least, in danger of...of, shall we say, uncustomary attention from his mother, that the child might therefore be removed from the mother's care while her own case is dealt with in a professional setting; I might mention one not inexpensive clinic in this context, though Long Hauls may not be as renowned for its cuisine as for its chief therapist. To the point: I do not propose there be anything permanent in this arrangement. It is simply an opportunity, for a while, to better observe the mother while the child and its father, as its father so succinctly put it one day, have a chance to get to know each other again, free from the pressure of, free from the pressure of....I'm sure the court understands... *(Loosening his collar)* ...free from the heat that, that, that Looker, that Dreamboat is sure to generate, even on the most sleepless of nights, perhaps especially on the most sleepless of.... *(Suddenly seeing himself in the mirror as the light fades)* My God! I'm awfully dressed up, aren't I? Why...? Oh, yes, they're delivering my Cadillac today. For once I'll be holding my head up with the best of them, right there in the parking lot at Presbyterian. In a recent copy of its journal, a certain organization assures its members, "Boys, There's Still Time to Make a Killing." Well, I'll tell you boys something. A PhD can do it too. We don't give nothing for free no more. *(Dancing joyfully)* Not even Expert Expert Testi-testi-testi-testimo-ony....

(As the light fades on DR WRIGHT, it rises to a low fitful level on ALAN, perched as before.)

ALAN: Carry on, Dr Wright. They haven't got you yet. *(Bending over his laptop, typing)* "And once more Alan bent over the keyboard—comma—once more attempting to stifle the 'sad'—the 'sad'—the 'lament' in his throat—semicolon—once more—comma—however—comma—the words themselves were somehow—dot-dot-dot—prosaic—comma—and Alan—comma—flinching deep within—comma—wondered if perhaps he didn't have more in common with his father after all—period."

Scene Nine

(ADAM *and* ALAN *at the zoo, the unseen cages downstage. The father stands before the unseen lion, reads the unseen sign, then looks up at the miserable animal.*)

ADAM: *Felis leo*...the lion...

(*Enter* ALAN, *holding a box of animal crackers, inspecting them as he eats.*)

ALAN: *(To himself)* ...the rhinoceros...the hippopotamus...the bear...

ADAM: *(Not hearing him)* We like to think that we're the king of beasts, but how long will it be before we're locked up, looking out through the bars, wishing we were somewhere else? What do you think, Alan?

ALAN: *(Mouth filling)* ...the elephant...the tiger...the buffalo, the giraffe, the seal, the panther, the sheep...the monkey... *(Offering one)* Want a monkey?

(When ADAM *hesitates)*

ALAN: They taste just as good, they all taste the same.

ADAM: Yes. Thank you, Alan. *(Eating the monkey)* Not bad. Alan, did you hear a word I was saying? What if...?

ALAN: "...what if..."

ADAM: Are you mocking me?

ALAN: No. But you do always say "what if."

ADAM: I suppose I do. But...what if one day we woke up to discover we had eaten all the animals, all the birds and all the fish? What if, one day, there weren't any animals left, except the ones who had our permission not to be eaten...and they all had numbers; and collars, radio collars. How would you feel then?

ALAN: Awful.

ADAM: Worse than you feel now?

ALAN: Much worse.

ADAM: Yes, scientists, watching their screens, would always know where every moose, every polar bear, every eagle, every whale was at that moment, perhaps also, what he was eating, or thinking of eating.

ALAN: Or thinking of thinking. Dad: Would they need hall passes when they wanted to go outside, that is, when they weren't needed for experiments?

ADAM: Yes. Of course. Hall passes would be strictly required. Well, Alan, if you think you'd feel bad then, what if, in the electronic future, all, practically all the children in the world, none of the girls and very few of the boys, could ever be lost because... *(His fingers gently closing on* ALAN's *throat)* ...they'd all be wearing...?

ALAN: *(Interrupting)* What if we went to visit Mom, Dad? What if she hasn't got a hall pass? What if she's lost her appetite and can't even eat the potatoes they plop on her plate? What if, Dad, they're experimenting... on her...painting her brain black and blue and...?

ADAM: *(Releasing him)* The doctor said....

ALAN: The doctor said Mom was a knockout. What if the doctor's saying what you want him to say? You pay him, don't you?

ADAM: Alan, that's not fair. I don't control the doctor. He's an independent human being. He only wants what's best... You see, we don't want your mother all excited about the prospect of going home. That would only make it harder for her after we leave. She should stay, don't you think, until she's better?

ALAN: Well...what if Mom wore a collar, a radio collar, or a radio necklace and bracelet? Would they let her out then? That way, the doctor would always know where she was and if she was lifting a glass... *(His fingers close on the stem of an invisible wine glass.)* ...or even thinking of lifting a...

ADAM: *(Interrupting)* Alan...

ALAN: What if...?

ADAM: Alan, that's enough. You talk too much. What if you had gone to boarding school? How would you feel then?

ALAN: Worse still.

ADAM: Maybe you will yet. If you're the pressure on her. She wants so much for you, maybe too much. Sometimes I think she forgets you're a child.

ALAN: *(Calmly)* Who said I was a child? I'm not a child. *(Throwing down his animal crackers, stomping on the box, crushing them in a frenzy)* I will not! not! not! go to boarding school! *(Calmly)* Did you get the point, dad? I don't think I will ever go to boarding school.

ADAM: Maybe, also, it would be best for you. Think, Alan: the other children, new friends, football... And then, when the year's over, they have wonderful Summer Camps now for little boys who can afford it. It's not just bows and arrows and sleeping in tents. Nope. Now it's Skydiving, Big Game Hunting, Space Travel... *(He shoves his son playfully to show he's kidding.)*

ALAN: *(Refusing to be amused)* Just because you got Mom locked up, doesn't mean you can lock me up.

(They face each other. Beat)

ADAM: I didn't get your mother locked up, Alan.

ALAN: I know there was a hearing. I know Dr Wright said what you wanted him to say. How did you get Dr Wright in your pocket, Dad, if it isn't the money you...?

ADAM: Alan, I...

ALAN: I know Dr Wright testified that Mom couldn't sleep unless I held her, that he was worried one thing might lead to another. What thing? What is the terrible thing might happen when you hold your mother so she can sleep and one thing leads to another?

(ADAM spreads his arms almost helplessly, opens his mouth with some reluctance.)

ADAM: Alan, if I...

ALAN: What if she can't sleep at all there? Have you thought of that? How did you get her to sleep when you were together? I know she slept then. Did you hold her?

ADAM: I don't think I have to answer that.

ALAN: Who's going to hold her when she can't sleep now? When the lights that never go off never go off...or when, suddenly, they do go off and the smell of soap or soup, or both, is drifting down the hall, and someone is singing one line over and over, or crying in her pillow? Or screaming? Who, Dad? Some hairy woman they keep strapped in bed, except when she's needed to hold Mom? Or will they let Mom hold a puppy for a few minutes before they take it away...a puppy who looks like me?

ADAM: Alan, you think too much. If I were home all day, I'd need a rest cure by the end of the week.

ALAN: Or a drink. Do you think, dad, mom drinks because of me? Is that what you're saying? Is that what they're all saying? Is that why she has to be where she is, why you're always talking about boarding school and sometimes summer camp? Why didn't she just put cotton in her ears? Why...?

(ADAM puts his hand over the boy's mouth. When ALAN grows silent, he walks him up and down, his hand on his shoulder.)

ADAM: Alan, I take all that back. Sometimes I forget you're a child myself. But you have been thinking too long about this. It's like a drug... You're thinking, and....

ALAN: ...and Mom's drinking.

ADAM: I doubt if she's drinking. They're probably not known for their cellar up there. Your mother would no more drink Carlo Rossi than eat Cheez Whiz. *(An encouraging attempt at friendliness)* Can you see your mother munching Cheez Whiz?

ALAN: I can't see her at all. You haven't let me visit her. It's been six weeks. Do you realize that? What if she's dead? What if she died last week and nobody told me? It's possible. Do you know? Are you keeping it a secret? What if they keep her in a dirty, filthy cage? What if it stinks? What if...Dad...what if Mom's in a zoo?

ADAM: Stop it, Alan. It isn't a...

ALAN: A zoo, Dad, or a prison ship like in *Great Expectations*, or an ark. What if it's rained all the time she was there, forty days and forty nights, and the doctors have taken two of everything aboard, so they won't run out of animals in the future, and that means they've got another mother just like my mother, who reads and drinks *Chateau Neuf du Pape* and can't sleep and worries about her only son, Alan, who can't be taken aboard because there's only one of him and that would be against the rules?

(ADAM *grabs* ALAN *by the shoulder, slaps his face though not too hard, then places him in one spot, and lets go.* ALAN *stands quietly looking up at him.*)

ADAM: Good. Just stand still for a moment. I want some stillness in that soul. And if it isn't there naturally, if you didn't inherit it from either one of us, you've got to make it there yourself, inside you. You have to move your hand...like this...'til the storm passes or the rain stops and the sun comes out and the waters are calm...

(ADAM *moves his hand once in a grand smoothing motion,* ALAN *does the same.*)

ADAM: Good. All this wasn't necessary. I was going to tell you before all this happened. We're going to visit your mother on Saturday. Would Saturday be convenient? We'll drive up Saturday morning. We'll have lunch with her, and we'll make up our own minds about whether she's being treated well, about whether she's getting any better, whether she's ready to be driven back to her place where you can stay with her, look out for her. Will that be all right? *(Beat)* Alan?

ALAN: That will be all right.

Scene Ten

(DR WRIGHT's *clinic, Long Hauls. A colorless light, a straight-backed chair,* EDEN, *paler, a gray, flowered hospital gown tied about her, gray tennis shoes on her feet, but as beautiful as ever. She is restless in her chair, stretching, her legs tending to reveal themselves as she strains to look out the oversize wired window through which the gray light descends. She speaks in a kind of daze, to no one in particular but, nevertheless, with focus.*)

EDEN: To touch my own....? *(Beat)* How could any but a lawyer come up with what that lawyer, Lawless, came up with? A crime I cannot even mention to myself. I could not be so heartless. If I have ever been cruel, it was only to my husband...and that doesn't count. *(Smiling at herself)* It was a limited cruelty with him, no more than I needed to hold my own. We cannot harm our children. We cannot even, ultimately, harm ourselves because of the harm that futile gesture would do to them. They'd never forget, always think it was because of them... *(Standing, seeing the place)* I do not even think Adam, my husband, could have come up with the idea of putting me here, not if he knew what this place was like. "Be Right, Turn Right, at Long Hauls, the Clinic for Loved Ones in General & Your Wife in Particular." There was...an influence. There are powers behind the scenes. Interests that profit from my situation. *(Carefully sitting)* But I shall outwait them. I can wait. Even without a good book, a good wine. *(With conviction)* I can wait till the sky falls. *(Suddenly she stands, rushes with a cry at the wired window, bounces off it, returns, stands by her chair.)* I don't think I've jumped up from a chair and run across the room since I was five. It seems I've always been so cool, so self-possessed, so blonde. With an effort, I spoke smoothly, evenly. I did not choke on my tongue or curl up, a sobbing bundle on the floor. My sentences were...careful, enunciated. Vintage. The right word is always there, right behind the wrong one. If you look, you'll see it peeking out at you. My Alan was beginning to, well, at least to look. My Alan would have been...what? He would have been calm, that's all I wanted for him. You're not screaming deep inside, not if you're looking for the right word. You have to be calm for that. What will happen to Alan now, with me out of the way? Nothing so terrible. *(Sitting, with deadliness)* Nothing out of the ordinary.

(Enter DR WRIGHT. *He is wearing a white jacket over his suit coat. He is much more formal, and more carefully dressed, than he is in his private practice, apparently a different man. He stands a moment, unseen by* EDEN, *looking at her.)*

DR WRIGHT: God, what beauty! *(Looking downstage but not addressing the audience)* If only they were all like her, but misery of the soul so often comes with bad skin, bad hair, a face that's falling apart... *(With the appropriate gesture)* ...eyes like lost marbles...

EDEN: Are you talking to me, Doctor? Or about me?

DR WRIGHT: To you, Eden. Yes, of course. Who else? You see someone else here? Another me? Another you?

*(*EDEN *doesn't answer. Aside)*

DR WRIGHT: Sometimes I get them with that. Schizophrenia 101. *(Coming around in front of her)* How's the appetite, Eden? Nurse tells me you've left your tray again.

EDEN: Do you eat here?

DR WRIGHT: Not if I can avoid it.

EDEN: Well...

DR WRIGHT: *(Aside)* And now the big one. *(To* EDEN, *casually, looking at his clipboard, pencil in hand)* Sleeping? How are you sleeping, my dear?

EDEN: Like a log.

DR WRIGHT: Come now, Eden. Do logs sleep...or do they just lie there torturing themselves with thoughts of what was and is no more...of empty places against the sky, of fallen leaves? Besides, I know such language is beneath you. You haven't been lying awake, now have you, as the headlights of those who are free to come and go play across the ceiling? You haven't been watching the shadows waver, assuming, perhaps, the shape of a glass of *Chateau Neuf du Pape*, say, or of a little boy who is forgetting how to read...and write...? *(Eyes gleaming)* Am I right?

EDEN: That's cruelty, Dr Wright. Are you being cruel?

DR WRIGHT: Only a little. And yes. Why not? *(Jabbing a finger lightly in her ribs)* You know what it is to be a little cruel, don't you, you dreamboat, you? *(Walking away from her)* Besides, sometimes a little cruelty snaps my patients right out of it. A person who won't let himself be mocked isn't completely lost.

EDEN: I am not completely lost.

DR WRIGHT: I didn't say you were.

EDEN: I am getting out of here. Soon.

DR WRIGHT: Yes, of course. There's no need to keep you. The tests are complete, there's not a damn thing wrong with your brain, you can clearly survive without a drink. There've been no charges filed. What are you hanging around for? You could have checked yourself out yesterday...last week.

EDEN: I could have?

DR WRIGHT: You signed yourself in, didn't you? You've always been free to leave.

EDEN: *(Standing, moving towards the door)* Well then, Doctor, if you don't mind, I think I'll just be on my...

DR WRIGHT: *(Letting her get most the way to the door, then...)* Uh, Eden?

EDEN: *(Stopping, not looking back)* Doctor?

DR WRIGHT: I'm afraid there's a little more to it than that. We don't just set you on the street with one good suit and a couple of bucks in your pocket. This isn't a prison.

EDEN: *(Facing him)* It isn't?

DR WRIGHT: No, no. You have to make arrangements, get a ride home. You can't just walk out like that.

EDEN: I can't?

DR WRIGHT: You know your phone number, don't you? Quick. No, it's not Northside 777. That was Barbara Stanwyck's number. I know. I often rang her up on a rainy...

EDEN: What the hell are you talking about?

DR WRIGHT: Nothing, nothing. The days run together sometimes, the old films. Sometimes I get a little disoriented, that's all.

EDEN: You're sure you're free to leave yourself?

DR WRIGHT: Oh, yes, yes, yes. Absolutely. Why, just last night...

EDEN: Who did you go home to? *(Taking a step towards him)* Who do you go home to, generally speaking, Dr Wright?

DR WRIGHT: Well, I...

EDEN: Is someone waiting for you; someone at the door with a dry martini, for example?

DR WRIGHT: Well, not ex...

EDEN: Children?

DR WRIGHT: What? Chil...? Uhh, well...

EDEN: A son? Does he talk like you? Does he look like you, Doctor?

DR WRIGHT: I wouldn't wish that on my son, even if I did have one.

EDEN: Then a little daughter who's in love with her daddy?

DR WRIGHT: No one's in love with me, Eden. I was hoping perhaps you...

EDEN: *(Laughing)* Me? Hm. I know what it's like to live without hope, Doctor. Meanwhile, if you wouldn't mind telling me. If you know nothing of wife, of home and child, how do you presume...? I mean, a priest doesn't know either, but then he hears this Voice, I suppose. Do you hear a Voice, Dr Wright?

DR WRIGHT: No, Eden. Let me be perfectly up front about that. I hear no Voice, not even voices. It's true, it's true, everything you say. *(Sitting in the chair)* I'm an ugly, middle-aged man. I talk like an idiot. I haven't got half your imagination, your wit. I'm not even very intelligent. I don't know how I got my degree. I suppose they wanted to get rid of me. You know... if you've got a moment, Eden...

EDEN: It seems I've got a moment.

DR WRIGHT: *(Gratefully)* Thank you, thank you. You know, we were doing studies on language at the university. Can you imagine that, people who talk like we do...about patients who are experiencing a little "discomfort," who are or are not "candidates" for this or that procedure...people like us studying language?

EDEN: I can imagine.

DR WRIGHT: And we even thought we were making discoveries, about language and the brain and all that...

EDEN: And all that.

DR WRIGHT: And you know we never once, I don't think it ever occurred to us, to talk to anyone who could really use language, who could speak any better than we could, who could, well, just to take an absurd example, could write a poem—or a play: hahaha—who—and this is the point—who had spent the long mornings, the years maybe, writing that poem—or play—and who must, after all that... *(Coming to a stop)* ...know something about, about...language...

EDEN: *(Encouragingly)* Yes? *(Beat)* Yes, Doctor?

DR WRIGHT: I'm sorry. Was I saying something?

EDEN: You thought you were.

DR WRIGHT: *(Standing, facing her)* Ah, yes, yes. I remember now. No, I wouldn't plan on leaving today, Eden, no, not today.

EDEN: And why not?

DR WRIGHT: Why not? Because, you lovely thing, I'm hopelessly in love with you. I'll never let you go. No, no, forget I said that. It's your husband and your son, Eden, your Adam and your Alan, they're coming up to see you tomorrow. In the morning. They'll stay for lunch. I've ordered a special menu. Then, in the afternoon, if you haven't had a fit of laughter describing your dear old Dr Wright to them, they might take you somewhere in the afternoon, yes. Home, for example. Would you like that?

EDEN: I'd like that.

DR WRIGHT: Yes, well, I thought you would. That was why I came here today before I got distracted with talk of eating and sleeping and...and whatever it was. Yes, and now you're wondering how to show your gratitude, your appreciation... *(Aside)* How well I know my patients. *(Holding open his arms)* How about a big kiss, Eden, for your Dr Wright? Oh, this is not a privilege granted to just any nuthouse case. Some of them, believe me, don't look like you, Eden. In fact, they look like hell.

EDEN: I believe you, Dr Wright. And it isn't that I'm not grateful...after all you've done for me. I'll just take a rain check on that big kiss, if you don't mind. And now... *(Leaving)* I think I'll take a bath. I think I'll get into my own clothes. I think I'll make myself beautiful. *(She exits.)*

DR WRIGHT: Yes, well, Eden, really, it isn't necessary, you're a knockout, even in hospital white, and besides... *(The sound of a very loud shower. Leaning up against the door)* Are you in the shower, Eden? Is the water hot and, well, wet...? *(Moving away)* What am I talking about? My God! What kind of a nut am I? *(Back at the door)* Eden, Eden, why bother with a shower? Why not just curl up on the cold floor? You haven't forgotten all that hopelessness...I hope? You might want to stay here a little longer, shall we say. Eden, Eden, they're not coming today, Eden, no not today at all, and between today and tomorrow, why anything might happen. Your son might forget you. Yes, Eden. Eden, I only made it up. Nobody's coming. Ever. You're never going home. Only one thing is certain, Eden, that tonight the headlights will play upon the walls, your shadows will dance, obscenely, like mine, they'll laugh, they'll cry, Eden, like me. Eden, Eden... *(Observing his shadow on the door)* I am a shadow of a man without you. *(Slipping down the door)* My dear, dear Eden...won't you stay...forever, shall we say?

Scene Eleven

(ADAM *and* ALAN *wait in* EDEN's *room. They stand apart, staring off in different directions, they note* EDEN's *chair, they look at each other.* ALAN *carries the flowers he will carry through much of the second act.)*

ADAM: Are you ready?

ALAN: I was about to ask you the same thing. I hope you're not going to disappoint her.

ADAM: I hope you're not.

ALAN: Is that any way to talk to a child?

ADAM: You're not a child. You said so yourself.

ALAN: What am I, then?

ADAM: Sometimes I think you must be some kind of gargoyle, the kind some crazy child psychologist might carve on a tomb; in short, a monster.

ALAN: A monster. Then that's why you wanted to send me to Monster Camp, to Monster School?

ADAM: That's it.

ALAN: Dad?

ADAM: What?

ALAN: Am I her monster? Has mom made me a...?

ADAM: That's enough about monsters. *(Approaching)* Alan, don't talk too much. Let her talk. She may not be used to much company. She's certainly not used to ours. Give her a chance. It may be difficult.

ALAN: And you.

ADAM: Me?

ALAN: Yes, you. No talk of "taking the pressure off," of "getting to know each other again."

ADAM: What's wrong with that?

ALAN: *(Walking away)* Oh, I don't know. There's just something wrong with the words...

ADAM: What's wrong with the words?

ALAN: Oh, I don't know... *(Suddenly facing him)* They're dead, dad. Dead. Shall I spell it for you? *(Slowly, with emphasis)* D—E—A—....

ADAM: Why, you little...! (ADAM, *violence in his hands, takes a step towards* ALAN.)

ALAN: Just one word before you lambaste me.

ADAM: Before I...?

ALAN: If it's not in your working vocabulary, look it up.

ADAM: *(Lowering his hand)* Is that your one word? "Lambaste."

ALAN: No. What I wanted to say is... *(Trying)* Dad, I've only got one mother, you know. I've only got one father and one childhood and... Maybe, for once, you could be a little bit out of the...

ADAM: *(Understandingly)* A little bit out of the what, Alan?

(Beat. Enter EDEN, *normal, healthy, beautiful, in a very professional-looking suit.* ADAM *sees her first.*)

ADAM: Eden...you're beautiful.

ALAN: *(Running to her)* Mom!

(Mother and child embrace fervently, ADAM *left out,* EDEN *finally holding flowers.*)

ADAM: Six weeks, and I forget how beautiful you are. I don't know why we didn't come up before. I just thought... *(Beat)* Dr Wright tells me they're having lobster today. I didn't even know you liked lob...

EDEN: *(Looking up from* ALAN, *but not letting go of him)* Hello, Adam,

ADAM: Hello, Eden.

(ADAM *takes an uncertain step towards her, not knowing what to do with his hands, but* EDEN's *self-possession stops him.*)

EDEN: We always have lobster on Saturday. Or quail. Fabulous desserts. Three wines. Dr Wright is justifiably proud of his cellar. *(Beat)* It's like this in all the nuthouses.

(As ALAN *and* ADAM *laugh uncertainly and* EDEN *takes a step away from her son*)

EDEN: No need to pity us. We eat like kings and queens. It's part of getting better. Unforgettable bourdeaux. Romantic whispers. Our eyes sparkling in the candlelight. We lean close; we talk, mostly, of visits, our visitors...

(Beat)

ADAM: *(Too quickly)* As I was saying, we certainly thought of visiting. I even called Dr Wright, and he....

EDEN: Tell me, what did Dr Wright say?

ADAM: He said a visit might just upset you, your staying there, here, then us, Alan and I, going away. He said, "Leave her to me; I'll take care of her."

EDEN: *(Smiling)* Did he?

ADAM: Yes, well. And did he? Did he make you better?

EDEN: I think perhaps he did. He sort of teased me out of it. You should see my ribs. *(Speaking as DR WRIGHT and elbowing the air)* "Come on, Eden, what is this crap you're handing me, what is this shit?"

ADAM: Pretty subtle. What a vocabulary the man has. If we'd known what a good time you were having...

ALAN: And the nights, mom?

EDEN: The nights were hell.

ALAN: If only I could sleep for you.

EDEN: *(Smiling)* Perhaps you did. I sure as hell didn't.

(Beat)

ADAM: I've been thinking of ways to take the pressure off, Eden, for us to get to know each other again.

(All look at each other.)

ADAM: I know I wasn't supposed to say that, but I couldn't think of anything else.

EDEN: Who told you not to say it?

(Both turn to look at ALAN.)

EDEN: Why shouldn't your father say that, Alan, except for the obvious reasons?

ALAN: That's just it. The obvious ones.

EDEN: If you're always correcting people, Alan, you won't have time to come up with anything of your own.

ALAN: *(Looking pointedly at her)* I see.

(EDEN and ALAN's eyes lock.)

EDEN: Do you?

ADAM: Yes, well, speaking of time, Dr Wright said twelve sharp. Yes, I think I hear the lobsters screaming. Our bibs are waiting. Eden. Alan.

(A gesture toward the dining room causes EDEN to step out in front, but ALAN hesitates.)

ALAN: Mom. Where's the...?

(EDEN *points in the direction of the bathroom.* ALAN *exits opposite as* ADAM *and* EDEN *leave in the direction of the dining room,* EDEN *somehow leaving the flowers on the chair. A horrendously loud toilet is heard. Enter* ALAN, *zipping his pants. Hurrying towards the dining room, he notes the flowers and pauses to caress the back of* EDEN's *chair. As if he is suddenly, totally aware of her time in it, her feelings that have somehow been left in the wood or the metal, his hand cannot release it. He looks wistfully in the direction of the diners, turns to run his hands over the back of the chair. He releases it, starts off, only to be overcome by an irresistible fatigue. He yawns. He sinks to the floor. Too tired to walk, he attempts to crawl towards the dining room, before curling into a ball near the chair and falling asleep as the light fades.)*

ALAN: Mom, I'm just going to put my head down for a minute. I'll be sleeping for you, if you must know, and you'll be awake, witty, sparkling. Dad will fall in love with you all over again. You'll fall in love with him. *(Falling asleep)* Dr Wright, mooning in the kitchen door, will have to admit he's lost you, lost you forever... Dr Wright will have to let you go.

END OF ACT ONE

ACT TWO

Apéritif

(Later that afternoon, the distant light of day somehow felt beyond the walls. ALAN lies curled on the floor by EDEN's chair. He whimpers, begins to run in his sleep.)

ALAN: ...Mom, Mom...

(EDEN appears elsewhere in the shadows, wearing the outfit in which she will leave Long Hauls after lunch. She is looking into a mirror, putting the finishing touches on her face. Throughout this scene, she speaks to ALAN without removing her gaze from the business at hand. Her voice is soft, at times almost dovelike.)

EDEN: ...Sh...Alan...it's all right...you mustn't run...you mustn't... *(With some reluctance to use the word)* ...sweat...in your sleep... *(With some irritation)* Alan, you're not dreaming?

(ALAN moans. EDEN's voice becomes that of the mother with the authority to end his nightmare.)

EDEN: What did I tell you about dreaming? You should be reading, reading and...

(ALAN moans; EDEN speaks with resignation.)

EDEN: Perhaps if you lie very still, the dream will get restless and fly off. *(Lipstick)* It will settle elsewhere, someone else will run and... *(As before)* ...and sweat...

ALAN: *(Still curled on the floor; concerned)* Someone else? *(Suddenly opening his eyes)* Mom? I thought you were gone. Is that you?

EDEN: *(Eye shadow)* Who else only has eyes for her only son?

ALAN: No one, Mom. Only you. I don't want you to run and sweat, Mom. I want you to....

EDEN: Go back to sleep, Alan. I'm sorry I woke you.

ALAN: Oh, you didn't. I was just lying here, thinking things through, getting things straight...

EDEN: *(Hair)* I could never do anything silently. *(Smiling)* I'll never catch the mouse on the wing.

ALAN: You must have that one wrong, Mom. The mouse isn't on the wing... *(Sitting up, chuckling)* ...unless he's batty...

EDEN: *(With high seriousness)* Don't bring me down to earth, Alan. Your father was always...

ALAN: He just didn't want you to drink and fly, mom.

EDEN: *(Standing, checking the overall impression)* I can assure you, Alan, I've never even contemplated drinking and...

ALAN: *(Standing, looking straight up, terrified)* Flying?? You're not...!

EDEN: I'm alive and well, Alan, with both feet on the ground and getting the hell out of here.

ALAN: *(Staggering around looking up)* But I see you! I know you're no angel, but why are you flying, Mom?

EDEN: *(Playing along with him, getting smoothly further from the mirror, never looking at him)* Surely, if Wendy could do it...

ALAN: *(Still looking up, feeling her dizzying overhead circle getting larger and larger)* Where...where are you off to, Mom?

EDEN: I'm sure I don't know. I hope I didn't disturb your nap. I...I must have a look in the broom closet, yes... *(With one final glance in the mirror)* If you'll excuse me...

ALAN: Mom, you're no witch. There's no need to look in the...

(Exit EDEN. Immediately a feather flutters from above. ALAN catches it and, with it, his confidence.)

ALAN: Mom's right. I think we'd better resolve this situation at ground level. Yes. *(Waving his magic feather magically)* And Pepto-Bismol: Here is Dr Wright. *(With a shrug, when DR WRIGHT fails to appear)* Of course I could play any one of them—and better than they play themselves. But someone has to be the banished boy, and therefore... *(Pocketing his feather over his heart, calling off)* Oh, Doctor! We need you to be yourself for a moment. Never mind that heart only a mother could break. *(Calling again)* Oh, Doc...! *(Suddenly leaving)* These doctor types, their days heavy with professional concerns...

(Exit ALAN.)

Scene One

(DR WRIGHT stands before the mirror in his office in a specimen of his considerable repertoire of boxer shorts, this time the ones with the great orange carrots and the even more impressive yellow bananas.)

DR WRIGHT: If the Court will permit a passing paragraph from our own, our dear, Dr Wright... I would only like to point out that, in one PhD's opinion or—as any fool can see—the boy's mother has improved substantially while, mysteriously, the boy's father has visibly deteriorated. *(To himself, wriggling)* Oh, Wright, you Expert Witness you. *(To the Court)* But to the point, the long... *(Looking down)* ...and the short, of it is that the boy might now be returned to Legs—pardon me, I mean, of course, to his mother—that permanent custody might be granted to a certain Delectable Morsel; excuse me, that Dish; never mind, the Court knows who I mean—while, on the other hand, that Dull Legal Type might now be held well out of my way—careful, Wright, careful—I mean held for observation, of course. Thanks, Judge, I'm glad you agree with me. And now let's get the lady out in the big world where we can put her to the test... Gosh, I hope she doesn't flunk, I hope she isn't just dragged back to Long Hauls kicking and screaming, shall we say, forever? *(With pain and longing)* Oh, Eden...Eden...! *(Leaving; casually)* Come now, you Sweet Thing... *(Half lowering his eyes)* ...where have you hidden your sweet...?

(Unable, even with grasping fingers, to name it, DR WRIGHT *exits.* ALAN *appears from the shadows, wearing his* DR WRIGHT *outfit: white jacket, head mirror with little hole, oversized stethoscope.)*

ALAN: *(Aside)* I hope he hasn't forgotten. Checked her out himself just minutes ago. Wouldn't trust *that* to a subordinate, no sir! Checked her out very carefully. *(Checking a giant heartbeat in the air)* Mom, Mom: Are you still with us? Of course. But... *(To the offstage* DR WRIGHT*)* ...the problem now, if you'll remember, Doctor... *(Rubbing thumb and fingertips together in the age-old sign of $$)* ...is that a bed is lying empty...

DR WRIGHT: *(In the shadows, thinking of it himself, rubbing fingers)* ...right, right...

Scene Two

*(*ADAM *stands in* EDEN's *old room, the sunny afternoon somehow irrelevant on this side of the wired window. He is taking off his suit jacket, his tie. A pale flowered hospital gown identical to* EDEN's *waits on the chair at his side.* DR WRIGHT *in his comme il faut hospital business suit plus white jacket faces him.)*

DR WRIGHT: Well, Adam, how does it feel?

ADAM: I don't think I'm required to answer that one, Dr Wright. I'm not going to be here that long.

DR WRIGHT: Of course not. Slam/bang: You're out.

ADAM: So why do I have to wear these...these flowers?

DR WRIGHT: Rules, Adam. Sharp objects, belts, must be taken from even our most temporary—and cooperative—of guests. It just seems simplest to slap them in gowns. You'll get used to it.

ADAM: Will I...? By the way... *(Having removed shirt and undershirt)* Who made these accusations, Dr Wright? I believe I have the right to confront my accuser.

DR WRIGHT: You certainly do, when it's courtroom time. For now I just have to protect my patients. Some of them are very sensitive.

ADAM: *I'm* very sensitive, Doctor, and one of my sensors is telling me you might, under certain circumstances, conceivably be willing to change your opinion...yet once more.

DR WRIGHT: Inconceivable, Adam. Once my Expert Testimony is given, I am unchangeable. Evidence means nothing.

ADAM: Perhaps there's something stronger than evidence.

DR WRIGHT: Really? Stronger than...? *(Dreamily remembering something; to himself)* I wonder what that might be. *(Recalling himself to the present with an appropriately impatient gesture)* Pants, Adam, pants.

ADAM: Do I have to...? *(Undoing his pants)* I mean: everything?

DR WRIGHT: I can tell you one thing right away. You can keep those pasty pale boxers on. Whatever induces an apparently normal male of the species to wear such plain, predictable, might I say pedestrian, boxers? You'll never have nurse crawling all over you in those. *(Flashing his boxers; he's already changed to the yellow ones with great green celery stalks.)* Just take a gander at these, young man. Knocks their eyes out, I can tell you. *(Closing his pants)* Now if you'll just fold your pants and hang them on the chair. Nurse will be in to tie your hands—I mean your gown, of course—behind you.

ADAM: *(In boxers, argyles and wingtips)* This is so unnecessary, I...

DR WRIGHT: God, what socks, Adam! Argyles! Was your dear wife right? Have you no imagination at all? I'd show you mine, but modesty forbids.

ADAM: I have a feeling, Dr Wright, you may find yourself explaining more than your socks when you're back in court.

DR WRIGHT: Really? Stand up there. Imagine yourself in court, Adam, the courtroom that awaits us all, and very nearly jay naked, as it were, because before the prosecution is through you're going to have to let it all hang out.

ADAM: We'll see who's going to have to let it all...

DR WRIGHT: *(Impatiently)* Gown, gown.

(As ADAM tries to find his way into the gown)

DR WRIGHT: I don't have to explain anything, Adam. You're the one who's going to have to do a little explaining. You told your wife you knew you weren't up to caring for your son, you "knew he was different," you "weren't raising little lawyers." We thought this meant nothing worse than Wheaties in the morning, nothing lousier than Lean Cuisine at night. We didn't know it would mean holding him, moaning... *(With pain and longing)* "Eden, Eden!" ...at bedtime, did we?

ADAM: Whatever makes you think I held Alan and moaned "Eden, Eden" at bedtime?

DR WRIGHT: I'll tell you. We had the boy wired, Adam. Yep. He was wearing a wire.

ADAM: Alan would never....

DR WRIGHT: We'll never know.

ADAM: What do you mean, "We'll never....?"

DR WRIGHT: He didn't know. We sewed it into his P Js, Adam. What do you think of that?

ADAM: You son of a....

DR WRIGHT: Court order, Adam. Like a wiretap. All part of the modern world so well understood by lawyers who have not fallen behind the times, like your lawyer, Lawless. What a boob! Yep, your wife's lawyer, Lockup, knew all about it. It was his idea. While the boy slept for his mother, I understand, yes, our men of science were busy sewing, sewing into the wee hours. And before you knew it a bunch of us—I was called in on a professional basis; my Expert Testimony proved indispensable—were sitting around listening to you moan "Eden...Eden...!" into the microphone. Amazing how charges backfire and boomerang, isn't it? First your wife was having a little trouble sleeping, then you were; first one of you was being held by the boy, then the other was holding him. What a mess! As if a great wind were whirling us all about, isn't it? Very very "as if." Believe me, it's best not to hold our children at all these days. Yes, that's the solution, and I assure you it took a clear mind to get that right....and to get the right person under observation.

ADAM: I'm sure it did.

DR WRIGHT: You were holding him, weren't you?

ADAM: He needed holding. I think we both did.

DR WRIGHT: Well, if you—either of you—would have preferred that Doll, that Pussycat, to do the holding, you shouldn't have got her sent off in the first place, Adam. You should have thought of that. You should have walked and talked as she wanted and never gone running after an Expert Witness to give Expert Testimony.

ADAM: You're no expert, Wright. What I don't understand is how you arrived at the highest bidder. What were you offered, Wright?

(As DR WRIGHT *slips away into dreamy memory)*

ADAM: Why didn't you get back to me to see if I could better it? I still might. Wright? Tell me, what could my wife possibly offer that I...? Dr Wright, are you listening?

DR WRIGHT: *(Coming out of it)* What's that? Right. Wright, here. Dr Wright. Are you talking to me? *(His professional self again)* I'm sorry, Adam. I'd tell you what I have in Postal Savings, but my Financial Advisor advises me against it. I'm sure you remember playing Post Office yourself, you lucky... But that was then and this is now. *(With a smile)* Here.

(Taking the gown from ADAM, holding it open)

DR WRIGHT: This is easier than you think. Just stick your arms out, young man, as if you were sleepwalking.

(With a larger smile as ADAM does so)

DR WRIGHT: As I said, nurse will be in to tie them behind you. Then I'll be back. Then nurse. Then I. Have a seat, Adam. Relax. Close your mind with lock and key. Whatever you do, don't imagine, don't even think about, what that Raving Beauty might be up to without you...

(ADAM stands wondering at the extreme length of his sleeves—they reach, perhaps, to his knees—as DR WRIGHT hurries off to be heard laughing in the distance and the light fades on ADAM. Before it's gone, however—in fact, immediately— DR WRIGHT looks in once more on his patient.)

DR WRIGHT: By the way, Adam. The nights here are unforgettable. Yes. Or so they tell me. Oh, and I wouldn't worry about time, Adam. You've only just arrived. You're still digesting a remarkable lunch, and in fact, a certain Lovely is only now leaving the grounds. I'd just hold onto my marbles if I were you, young man. Don't let anything upset you. We wouldn't want you here on a permanent basis; oh, no/no/no/no....

(Exit DR WRIGHT. Enter NURSE EDEN behind ADAM with a cup of stinking, steaming chicken soup; the cup, naturally, emblazoned with a chicken behind bars.)

NURSE EDEN: Nurse here. Everything under control, patient?

ADAM: *(Not recognizing her)* Well, I wouldn't exactly call it under...

NURSE EDEN: *(Raising her cup with the falsest of smiles)* A little nightcap does sometimes help.

ADAM: I'm not spending the night, nurse, just awaiting results. The jury's out. It seems I've been accused of....

NURSE EDEN: Nurse knows. Everyone on staff knows. *(As the painfulness of this begins to sink in, her eyes lead his to the window.)* Like the view from your window, patient? Previous patient just loved it.

ADAM: Well, I...

(As ADAM turns to his window with a sigh, NURSE EDEN sets her cup of chicken soup on the chair and steps up close behind him. She speaks intimately.)

NURSE EDEN: Doctor tells staff men shouldn't have to wait, men should get what they want right way.

ADAM: That's one philosophy I...

NURSE EDEN: *(Gently tying ADAM's sleeves behind him)* Slam/bang, Doctor says.

ADAM: Slam/bang... *(Becoming aware of his confined arms)* Nurse, what have you done??

NURSE EDEN: Sh, now. Chicken soup is what patient really wants, isn't it?

ADAM: Not really. *(Struggling to free his arms)* But why...??

(Having retrieved her cup of soup, EDEN administers a little to ADAM on this last question. ADAM, with a pained look, flinches away from it.)

NURSE EDEN: Too hot? Not to worry. Nurse will take care of patient. Deep freeze, here I come. *(Leaving with her cup of soup)* Nurse shall return.

(Exit NURSE EDEN. ADAM remains in a slowly dimming light, standing alone in his hospital gown, staring off, while a pool of light reveals ALAN, seated on his stool, his fingers resting on his laptop computer. He does not speak directly to his father, and ADAM does not hear him.)

ALAN: Honestly, Dad, I didn't know about the wire. Or the sleeves. Or the soup. Anyway, I think Dr Wright just wants to put Mom to the test, that's all, late one night, when no one is in a position to "take the pressure off" or insist on "getting to know her again." Dr Wright wonders if she's going to flunk out—*or is it in?* For now, I'd just look out the window if I were you. Believe me, Dad, time will pass... But *what if* it passes a *little* less rapidly than that first night in boarding school would have. That's what I wonder. *(Bending over his laptop, typing as the light fades first on ADAM, then on him)* "Nurse, what have you done?" cries Adam. "Blah-blah-blah and chicken soup," says Nurse as the light fades on Adam and rises on Eden waving bye-bye to Long Hauls. Eden: "Funny. I've forgotten which way the cars go..."

(Light fades on ALAN, rises on EDEN.)

Scene Three

(EDEN, dressed to kill, waits in front of the hospital, that same afternoon full of sunlight, of hope. She looks both ways for ALAN. A suitcase full to bursting stands at her side.)

EDEN: Funny. I've forgotten which way the cars go. Only six weeks out of this world and I might as well be from outer space. *(Turning in response to the disturbance on the unseen second story of the hospital behind her, she waves coquettishly.)* Hi, there, honey. Aren't you the lucky one? Got my old room.

My sheets, my pillow. You're not going to be lonely, are you? *(Calling up)* Don't worry, Adam, you're only there for observation, for tests. You'll be out in a day or two. Even earlier if you speak up for yourself in the infamous courtroom scene. But here comes Alan to meet me. He's a man now, as you can see if you press your face against the bars. He's taking your place, Adam, in a sense. *(With a gesture not meant to be seen by anyone else)* Bye, now.

(EDEN fiddles with her hair. Enter ALAN, carrying his flowers.)

EDEN: Well, where were you? We thought you were just taking a little pee.

ALAN: I meant to join you, honest, Mom, but I touched the back of your chair and I was out like a light.

EDEN: Alan, you mustn't say "out like a light."

ALAN: I know. Did you have a nice lunch, Mom? How were the lobsters?

EDEN: At the last minute the lobsters got away, Alan, at least mine did.

ALAN: He did! He got away? Lucky lobster. What did you have?

EDEN: Oh, nothing...chicken wings...chicken soup...chicken salad sandwich...

ALAN: That's a lot of chicken.

EDEN: There wasn't much chicken. It was all a kind of glue, a kind of paste, I suppose, holding things together that were never meant to be held together. But that's enough about chicken. Where's the bus?

ALAN: Where's Dad?

EDEN: Where's Dad? Is that all you've got to say to me after I spend six weeks in the loony bin? Think of what I...

ALAN: Where's my father? I came here with him and....

(There is a desperate banging on the second story. As ALAN looks up, EDEN embraces him, turning him away from the building.)

EDEN: Oh, don't look up there. Some of these people are just awful to look at. Skin. Hair. Faces just...

ALAN: ...just falling apart. I know. Dr Wright told me.

EDEN: Never mind what Dr Wright told you. Where's my kiss?

(ALAN kisses her perfunctorily.)

ALAN: I'm glad you're out, Mom. That place didn't suit you.

EDEN: I'm glad to be out, Alan. You'll never believe it, but Dr Wright told me I'd checked myself in, all I had to do was....

ALAN: Is that what you've done, Mom? Have you checked yourself out?

EDEN: That's it. I'm free as a bird. *(They look at each other.)* I hope it's all right to say that.

ALAN: Of course it is, but does that mean you're free of...that you're no longer interested in a finger or two?

EDEN: I beg your pardon?

ALAN: A dram, a jigger, a little gargle?

EDEN: Where did you learn those expressions, Alan?

ALAN: I'll give you a hint, mom: It wasn't in *Peter Pan*. As I was saying, does that mean you're free of the pig sweat, the sheepdip, the snake medicine, that you're no longer a sot?

(Beat)

EDEN: I don't know, Alan. We'll see when I'm sitting at my table and....

ALAN: Yes. That's what Dr Wright has in mind for you, isn't it: the big test?

EDEN: The big test. ...when I look over... *(Seeing it)* ...and see that lovely label, the musty rich red glowing behind it...

ALAN: Yes... *(Taking her arm)* Let's go home, Mom, and find out.

EDEN: Yes... *(Hesitating)* Wait. *(Trying to laugh)* You know, somehow I'm not ready to leave here.

ALAN: You're not. Why not?

EDEN: I don't know. It's almost as if I...as if I've left something—someone—behind.

ALAN: Dr Wright.

EDEN: *(Laughing outright)* No one would mind leaving Dr Wright behind.

ALAN: Then who...? Another patient? That hairy woman they keep strapped? The therapy dog?

EDEN: Very funny. If you'll just wait a moment, I'll go back to my room and check.

ALAN: So long, Mom. I hope you're not just checking yourself in again.

EDEN: *(Moving away, about to leave)* Don't be silly, Alan.

ALAN: You don't have a bottle up there, behind the bucket and the mop maybe? Is that where you've been holding your Cabernets up to the light, Mom, in the broom closet?

EDEN: Alan, I don't know how you can be so suspicious. *(The bus sounds begin to grow unnaturally loud.)* Oh, is that the bus now? *(Stopping midstage, looking up at the clinic windows, looking in the direction of the bus, looking back up, making her decision)* I guess they can just send me, well, whatever it is.

ALAN: Yes. Very good, Mom. I think that's the right decision. Home's the place for you. We'll set you down at your table and see what happens.

EDEN: Yes, you're right. *(Taking his arm)* Come on, Alan, we're going home...

ALAN: Yes... *(Hesitating)* Wait. *(Trying to laugh)* You know, somehow, you won't believe this, but I'm not ready to leave here.

EDEN: You're not. Why not?

ALAN: I don't know. It's as if *I*...as if *I've* left something—someone—behind.

(The bus sounds become a roar.)

EDEN: What nonsense! You've hardly been here an hour. Come on, Alan. The bus...

ALAN: Never mind the bus. You catch the bus. Here's a dollar.

EDEN: Thank you. And you?

ALAN: I'll catch the next one.

EDEN: But, Alan, what are you doing? What are you up to? You're only twelve, remember!

ALAN: That's right. What could I be up to at my age? You see, Mom... *(His flowers under his arm, holding the "globe" in both hands)* ...if there were only some way I could take this world, this life, in my hands...

EDEN: Alan, my bus.

ALAN: Go on, Mom. You'll miss it.

(EDEN starts rushing off.)

ALAN: Oh, Mom, here. I almost forget. These are for you.

(ALAN attempts to hand her the flowers, EDEN makes a grab at them, but rushes off, perhaps one way then the other, after her bus...in slow motion.)

EDEN: I'd better keep going. This is the only bus in the world for me, Alan; I'd better catch it.

ALAN: *(Holding up his flowers as he rushes after in slow motion)* But...Mom...Mom...

EDEN: Give them to me later, Alan, later...

(Stopping, ALAN watches her, his bouquet extended. A monstrous bus door is heard opening off. The bus drives off. ALAN waves wistfully, then discovers her suitcase.)

ALAN: Mom, your suitcase... *(Picking it up)* So long, Mom. Wait for me. Wait up. I'll be back before dark—if all goes well. *(As the light fades)* Oh-oh: Before we know it, it's night, late night. It may be even time for the infamous courtroom scene.

Scene Four

(ALAN *is gone. Night falls further.* ADAM, *on his chair, his arms bound behind him, softly feigns a scream. The lights blink on, off, then on brightly.*)

ADAM: *(A calm aside)* You know why I'm screaming, don't you? Because I can't tear my hair. That's all there is to it.

(*Suddenly* ADAM *screams a real scream of terror.* DR WRIGHT, *fresh from the shower, in the act of dressing for the evening, perhaps at this point in undershirt and scoring boxers—the white ones with dripping red hearts—in the shadows, cocks his ear at* ADAM's *scream and dances a little, perhaps humming to himself.*)

DR WRIGHT: ...guilt, guilt, guilt, guilt, guilt, guilt, guilt...

(*Suddenly in character,* JUDGE WRIGHT *is pacing, speaking into one or the other of the handy microphones concealed in his matching silver hairbrushes, both of which are connected to the Long Hauls public address system. His voice booms, harsh and penetrating. He remains unseen by* ADAM *throughout and does not look at him until indicated.*)

JUDGE WRIGHT: Wright here. The Honorable Judge Wright presiding. Will Counsel—if he is in his right mind—please address the court.

(ADAM *stands quickly, his arms still bound, his mouth half open.*)

JUDGE WRIGHT: If Counsel cannot open his mouth, I'll just have to issue a snap judgment and, against nature as it may be, give the child to its mother.

ADAM: Your Honor, my apologies to the Court. *(Looking down at his shoes)* My wingtips just wouldn't take the shine that means so much in this day and age.

(*As the amplified phrase "day and age" echoes through Long Hauls, a pained and dimly lit* EDEN *is seen riding her bus and raising her hands to cover her ears.*)

DR WRIGHT: If counsel cannot avoid the clichés so painful to the Beauty in the Case, I shall reach a decision myself strictly on merits...that is, alone with Beauty in Chambers... *(To* ADAM*)* Proceed.

ADAM: Counsel stands rebuked. My wingtips are a badge of honor, Your Honor. I wouldn't want the Court to think that I rise, or have ever risen, to defend the...the down-at-heel or, for lack of a better word, the, the.... What is that word?

JUDGE WRIGHT: I'm sure I don't know.

ADAM: Your Honor, I am a lawyer. That's L-A-W-Y-E-R. Your Honor will understand, therefore, that, unlike your average Expert Witness, who speaks for the Prosecution on Mondays and the Defense on Wednesdays, I am not about to be sold to the highest bidder. I am a man of principal...*and* interest, which is to say capital. In that regard, I would like to inform the Court that I have served as past president of Republicans Against Clean Air and Clean Water, Republicans Against the Trees and the Birds in the Trees, Republicans Against the Arts, Education, and Health Care...except, of course, for those who can afford them...Republicans Against Taxes in General and the...the Poor in Particular—that is the word I was looking for—may they shiver sick, wet, and cold! May they listen to their empty bellies!—Republicans Against the Minimum Wage, Safe Working Conditions and Legal Assistance, and, lest Your Honor get the impression that my causes, have been, shall we say, in the negative column, I will remind the Court that I was also Secretary *and Treasurer* of Republicans for the Legalization of White Collar Crime, not to mention chief lobbyist for the Comfy Bouncy Safety Net for Business—dot.gov., that among those rights we hold to be self-evident, if not indeed the only rights worth mentioning, are the Right to Make Money and the Right to Hold Onto It...and that's why, in conclusion, your Honor, we are against anything—anything!—for anybody who hasn't already got it.

JUDGE WRIGHT: *(Aside)* I think we may have this fellow in the right place after all—that is unless he's needed in Washington. *(To* ADAM*)* I must admit the Court is having a little trouble here. You mean *and therefore* the child should be taken from its mother?

ADAM: If the Court will allow me another moment—for we all know time is running out, that childhood, youth, yes, and even love, courtship, and marriage are often over before we know it—I would just like to add that, in American Law, Corporations are considered to have the same rights as individuals, that one of the most Sacred Rights of the Corporate Individual, indeed the holy of holies...

(As the amplified phrase "holy of holies" echoes through Long Hauls, a pained and dimly lit EDEN, *still riding her bus, once more raises her hands to cover her ears and, this time, there is an amplified sigh from her.* DR WRIGHT, *in the shadows, speaks into his microphone.)*

JUDGE WRIGHT: If the Beauty in the Case cannot restrain herself from sighing at the young man's clichés, the Beast—I mean, of course, the Court—shall have the Sergeant at Arms tape her lovely mouth, and if the Sergeant at Arms is nowhere to be found, the Beast—I mean, naturally, the Court—will do it with its Own Trembling Fingers. *(To* ADAM*)* The point, young man. The evidence—or lack thereof.

ADAM: If the Court will permit a little specificity...

JUDGE WRIGHT: *(With the most evil of smiles)* The Court will permit.

ADAM: I wish only to mention that among those rights considered to be self-evident is the Right of the Corporation to Happiness. There.

JUDGE WRIGHT: There? Where? I haven't understood a word you're...
You mean *and therefore* the child should be returned to its father?
The Court must admit it is, finally, unable to follow the....

ADAM: If Your Honor will forgive these American-as-apple-pie introductory
remarks—I am, in fact, merely warming up—I would like to point out that
my wife considers me incapable of intelligent speech *and therefore* unworthy
of custody of our son, but that's only because she has never observed my
performance in the courtroom. But, as the Court can now bear witness,
I am not as tongue-tied as she claims. Indeed, when push comes to shove...

*(As the amplified phrase "push comes to shove" echoes through Long Hauls,
a dimly lit EDEN, on her bus, rolls her eyes and signals thumbs down.)*

ADAM: ...I am as good a father as any and now...I stand before the
Court...accused....

JUDGE WRIGHT: *(Having seen EDEN's thumbs down)* If not condemned.
Yes, it appears to the Court you're guilty as hell, young man; that the
Beauty in the Case must therefore be the Victim of your dirty deeds,
if not an Old Girlfriend getting even. However. What does it matter?
The Condemned Man may now proceed.

ADAM: Thank you. Your Honor, I stand accused of several misdeeds, to wit:
of holding my son while moaning my wife's name; of offering, shall we say,
transportation to an Expert Witness in an earlier judgment in order to put
my wife away—already, His Honor can see the contradictions in the
Prosecution's case—and finally, and no doubt most heinous, abhorrent,
and inhuman of them all, of waiting for my wife in front of her house one
night only to observe her drive up around midnight with her—pardon the
phrase—health-care provider, only to witness a little final healing kiss-kiss
between my wife and...

JUDGE WRIGHT: Objection. Speculation. Why, such an event, even if it were
to occur, has not yet occurred. Chronology, Adam. Sequence. If the accused
had eyes to see, he would see that the health-care provider in question
is nowhere near the scene of the, ahem, "crime," and that, indeed...
(Looking at ADAM for the first time) ...the so-called witness in the case is
"up Shit Crick without a paddle," and unlikely to observe any such...

ADAM: ...between my wife and one who might well be somewhere in the
Court at this very moment, yes...

JUDGE WRIGHT: Young man, do I understand you rise against that Lovely
Thing, your wife...for the "possibly to occur at some point in the future
so-called crime" of showing her health-care provider a little heartfelt
gratitude?

ADAM: Your Honor, I... I request a change of venue. I do not believe that my
Client...that is me...can get a fair trial in this jurisdiction.

JUDGE WRIGHT: Sorry, young man. Truly sorry. A change of venue is the one request you cannot make. If the DefenDANT will please note the wire upon the window; if he will, indeed, take a closer look at his own, shall we say, wardrobe; if he will recall the recent dearth of the courtroom gestures he is so fond of making, he will see that he is no more permitted to check himself out of the, ahem, Courtroom, than he is to take sharp instruments or the all-too-handy belt into his padded cell.

ADAM: *(Noting the wired window, his gown, his tied hands; struggling to free himself)* My God! You mean this is your godforsaken clinic, Wright, this is all some miserable charade to keep me out of the way while the "possibly to occur at some point in the future so-called crime" occurs this very night?

JUDGE WRIGHT: Got it in one, my boy. What are you going to do about it?

(Beat)

ADAM: Your Honor. For some reason the Defense finds itself... *(Slowing, becoming inaudible)* ...incapable of speech...

JUDGE WRIGHT: And not a moment too soon. Now, if there is no further objection, the delightful, the irrepressible, scenes in question will proceed in the order in which they were always meant to.

(The scene fades and ALAN, the stuffed suitcase in one hand, a flashlight in the other, his bouquet under his arm, finds his way down creepy corridors.)

ALAN: Ladies and gentlemen, with the infamous courtroom scene at last behind us, Alan, alone, and still only twelve, is free to creep the creepy halls of Long Hauls, Dr Wright's very own for-profit sanitorium. Yes, and night, this night, has fallen further than he ever thought it would.

Scene Five

(Suddenly ALAN hears something, stops. Enter DR WRIGHT, still in undershirt and scoring boxers, slapping a little scent about his neck and feeling very pleased with himself.)

DR WRIGHT: What are you doing, Alan, wandering my beloved Long Hauls?

ALAN: I'm looking for my....

DR WRIGHT: *(Snatching the flashlight, shining it on ALAN)* A little boy should never look for his father, Alan. Who knows what his father might be up to? *(Suddenly facing him; pointing at the suitcase)* Quick/Alan/What's this?/What's this shit?

ALAN: I assume it's my mother's, the things she left...

DR WRIGHT: *(Holding it high)* Come now, Alan. Are these your mother's little moccasins, your mother's little bow and arrow?

(Dr Wright *holds the suitcase closer.* Alan *sees the mentioned items protruding, toys which would be more appropriate for a six year-old.*)

Dr Wright: Think again, Alan. Are you sure *you're* not going somewhere? Wasn't that *you* I saw waiting for a bus?

Alan: Yes...that is, my mother took the bus; at the last moment I...

Dr Wright: *(Aside)* Lord, the stories some of them expect me to believe. Quick, Alan./You know where you are?

Alan: No, I...

Dr Wright: Good. Just for practice then, we'll begin with the compulsory midsummer night's *nap*. You think that little shuteye you grabbed over lunch was a nap! My, my, what have we got here? This should make a happy camper out of almost anyone.

(Dr Wright *pulls on a loose end of material hanging from the suitcase and withdraws a flowered gown similar to* Eden's *and* Adam's. Alan, *after a brief hesitation, accepts it.* Dr Wright *tiptoes around in an exaggerated fashion while* Alan *exchanges his street clothes for the gown, and is soon wondering at the length of his sleeves.*)

Dr Wright: Find yourself a corner now, Alan, close your eyes. Smell the weenies going up in smoke, the marshmallows dropping in the flames. There's no need to go home, none at all.

(*Seeing* Alan *has found his way into the gown*)

Dr Wright: Good. Good. *(Suddenly pointing)* Look! Who is that nutcase in the distance? Looks just like you, my boy, only older.

(*As* Alan *looks off,* Dr Wright *ties his sleeves behind his back and begins to leave.*)

Dr Wright: Looking for his father, indeed. As if I'd have some hotshot lawyer wandering my beloved...

(Alan, *realizing his confinement, struggles until* Dr Wright *returns and places a deadly Long Hauls blanket from the suitcase over* Alan's *shoulders.*)

Dr Wright: Why, Alan, don't be afraid of a little *nap*; sometimes it's just when we're off into a little snooze, that our most *desirable* visitors come calling, when all the knockouts we have ever known line up at the door of consciousness begging to be admitted. They're just so full of heartache, of woe. You know why, of course.

Alan: *(Under the spell of the blanket)* ...Why...?

Dr Wright: Why, because, somehow, they never have time to get fully dressed. Yes, they're awfully sad about that. That's right, young man. And wondering why we—despite our most heroic efforts—never manage to save them... *(With deadly emphasis)* ...from the fate Fate has in store for them... But never mind that. Right now, Alan, close your eyes.

(Suddenly producing a feather, one very like the feather that fell from the sky earlier, and, as ALAN *closes his eyes, continuing hypnotically)*

DR WRIGHT: And Pepto-Bismol, as some of my nuts have been known to say, it's summer, endless summer; you're already engaged in a happy round of hide the...hide the...? What is that childish game? Ah yes, hide the bottle.

*(*ALAN *falls asleep on his feet.* DR WRIGHT *is once more aware of his own irresistibility, not to mention the evening before him.)*

DR WRIGHT: And now, if you don't mind...a few finishing touches to my toilette and I'll be... *(Puffing himself up)* ...yes, a great wind bowling over anyone the least unsteady on her feet. *(Leaving with the suitcase)* I'll just have nurse put this on the bus for you. Now where is that...? Nurse! Nurse! *(Exit* DR WRIGHT. *The door closes behind him automatically, with a clank. Headlights move across the ceiling, shadows dance on the walls. Someone is crying at a distance, someone else screaming, someone is moaning "Eden, Eden..." The glaring white lights blink on, then off, without reason.* ALAN *fades,* ADAM *is visible, his arms confined as before, staring out his wired window. Enter* NURSE EDEN. *As* ADAM *turns suddenly to face her, she deftly pours a little cold chicken soup into him.)*

NURSE EDEN: Good.

(As he shivers)

NURSE EDEN: Too cold? Not to worry. It works. Patient will sleep no matter *what* may possibly occur this very night.

ADAM: But I don't want to sleep. Wait. Haven't I heard that voice...?

(The light blinks.)

ADAM: Nurse! Nurse!

NURSE EDEN: *(Briefly stopping)* Patient will please keep his boxers on. Nurse will be back with catheter, enema, and drip—and nurse's assistant. Patient has met the hairy man, hasn't he? Somebody's got to strap patient down for that unforgettable first night...

(Exit NURSE EDEN *with a stunning smile over her shoulder as* ADAM *fades from sight.* ALAN, *visible again, in hospital gown, his arms still tied behind him, but without his Long Hauls blanket, wanders, calling softly in the darkness.)*

ALAN: ...Dad...? Are you here? Dr Wright's blanket put me to sleep, but I woke up looking for you. ...Mom...? Are you home yet? Did you remember to get off the bus? I hope you're not just riding around, raising a paper bag to your lips. Mom? Dad?

(The light blinks on and ALAN, *finding himself alone, speaks downstage.)*

ALAN: Ladies and gentlemen, there are nights when I wonder if it's possible to look for our fathers and make sure our mothers get home at the same time, nights I wish I had a little of that chicken soup Mom had to hold it all together...

(Enter NURSE EDEN *behind him with that cup of cold chicken soup.)*

NURSE EDEN: Doctor's drops could go in anything, of course—a fine Cabernet, for example—but chicken soup is what nurse has in hand.

*(*EDEN *forcibly administers the soup.* ALAN *gulps, coughs, loses much of it, but swallows some.)*

NURSE EDEN: Bad. Nurse will have to tell doctor anyway. Patient persisted in opposing his chicken soup to the end.

(Exit NURSE EDEN. ALAN *stands alone as the chicken soup enters his veins.)*

Scene Six

ALAN: That was god-awful, and I hope I'm not just being held out of somebody's way while the "possibly to occur at some point in the future so-called crime" occurs this very night, but, suddenly: Life does seem full of possibilities.

(As the chicken soup begins to affect him, ALAN *looks up, a strange happiness spreading through his veins; he addresses a spot where* EDEN *will soon appear.)*

ALAN: It doesn't have to be the way it's going to be, Mom, does it, when, on Dr Wright's advice, you come home?

(As the light rises to happy dreamlike levels)

ALAN: Ladies and gentlemen, my home, our home, the home of Adam and Eden... *(Suddenly moving freely, walking about)* Yes, ladies and gentlemen: Everything has worked out. Mom has come back to us, she doesn't drink anything wetter than hot chocolate; Dad reads the dictionary on his way home from work. He has yet to offend Mom's ear even once. I don't know why, but I think they're so happy because they've more or less forgotten about me. And I, ever since I discovered that, in fact, I'm something of a nincompoop, that I'm functionally illiterate—am having a hell of a time. Sh. Here she comes now. Let's give her a hand, please. It isn't easy for a modern woman to find happiness—especially at home—that's what my dad says, and he should know. *(Spotting his mother)* Bravo! Bravo! There's a mother for you.

(Enter EDEN, *wearing a nearly threadbare flowered house dress over black bra, panties, garter belt, stockings, and spikes and carrying a hot apple pie.)*

EDEN: *(Suddenly stopping)* Alan, you're not dreaming again?

ALAN: No, Mom, Scout's honor. Wide awake. Just had a nice cold cup of...

EDEN: Are you sure this isn't one of those *little snoozes* Dr Wright warned you about, when some of our most desirable visitors, all full of heartache and woe, forget to get properly dressed?

ALAN: How could that be, Mom? You look great!

(ALAN *continues his applause. Responding shyly to* ALAN's *cheers,* EDEN *puts a hand to her cheek.*)

EDEN: Alan, please, I'm blushing.

ALAN: Blushing? You haven't been boozing, have you, Mom, opening a bottle on the bus?

EDEN: Why don't be silly, Alan. I don't even know what the word means. Boozing! I've been baking. *(Feeling both cheeks)* It's bending into a hot oven that....

ALAN: Never mind. I like you best when you're blushing, mom. *(Warmly teasing)* Dad does too.

EDEN: *(Touching her hair)* Oh, Alan...! You'll turn me beet red. You shouldn't know about such things.

ALAN: I don't, mom. Not a Goddamn thing.

EDEN: Thank God for that. Here now. You know how you love a nice big slice of apple pie when you come home, when that smell is in the air.

ALAN: *(A pained, if ironic, look on his face)* Smell, Mom?

EDEN: You know, Alan: raked leaves, burning leaves, leaves thick as happiness. Our years together, Alan, present and precious: the smell of time passing.

ALAN: And to think that once upon a time I thought nothing would tear you from your book, your table, your fine stemmed glass. Certainly not the smell of time passing.

EDEN: How little you know me, Alan.

ALAN: Once upon a time I thought you'd never figure me out. I was... special, remember? You thought I was going to be one of a kind.

EDEN: I did! Oh go on, you're pulling my legs.

ALAN: Leg, Mom, leg. You're only supposed to pull one leg.

EDEN: Well, however many. Anyway, don't be silly—and don't worry. You're just an ordinary little boy. I've always known that. And I'm the girl next door; somebody's mom. In fact, yours. Now. What is that funny thing over your shoulders?

ALAN: This is my blanket, mom. I'm home, remember. They never did send me off to Boarding School.

EDEN: I'm so glad. Well, if we're home at last, you'd better find the table and sit down at it. *(Starting off in the direction of the kitchen)* I'm cutting you a big slice of...

(EDEN *stops in midstride as her inner debate rages, and* ALAN *speaks downstage unheard by her.*)

ALAN: That's right, Mom. Time for second thoughts. You don't really want to be down on your knees reaching way back there under the sink, back where you keep your embalming fluid, do you?

(EDEN *shakes her head, returning to a much-relieved* ALAN.)

EDEN: But what about Summer Camp, Alan? I seem to recall a touch of terror...

ALAN: More than a touch, Mom. The truth is, as harmless as Summer Camp may seem, I was scared shitless.

EDEN: You mean witless, don't you, Alan, witless? Nothing wrong with that. Our wits only get us in trouble. Yes, I seem to remember an incident or two. Well, well, water under the... No, I shouldn't say that. There's some reason I shouldn't say that. Anyway, life's a bowl of...of something...isn't it? How true! Never mind. There are no messes now, are there, Alan? You're a big boy. *(Becoming aware of a terrible thirst)* And I'm a big girl. *(Starting toward the kitchen, if not the kitchen sink)* It's a terribly dry day isn't it, Alan?

ALAN: No drier than usual. Oh, Mom? I think I hear Dad.

(EDEN *stops, her eyes widening in pleased anticipation.*)

ALAN: He's just left the Buick in the driveway and hopped over the picket fence; he's running up the garden path...

EDEN: *(Excited, preening with her free hand)* Is he? Oh, gosh! But I guess that's all right. I know he shouldn't be leading me up the garden path. That's a no-no, for some reason. *(Worried)* But why? Is it muddy? *(Looking down as if she is seeing her spikes for the first time)* Will I ruin my shoes?

ALAN: Never mind, mom. Who needs reasons? You know how Dad likes to see you baking. Just standing there with that apple pie. *(Lewdly)* MmmmMmmm. *(Innocently)* You'll melt his heart.

EDEN: *(Shy again)* Oh, Alan. But there's some reason you shouldn't say "melt his heart," isn't there? Do hearts melt anyway? *(Her eyes darkening)* I thought they just stopped one day, yes one day when we least expect it, we're just sitting at the table or walking across the room and...

ALAN: *(Gently)* Mom... The pie.

EDEN: *(Shyly, if slinkily, raising the pie overhead, posing, blushing, her eyes on the spot where she expects her husband to appear, as the happy light fades and she is lost from sight)* Oh, Alan...!

ALAN: *(His upbeat manner changing)* Ladies and gentlemen, I think the chicken soup may be wearing off. Yes, sooner or later even the driest of dreams has to end. Our mothers put their apple pies back in the oven, their black lace undies back in their hope chests. They stand before the sink wondering if there really is time to get down and reach behind the drain pipe before husband and son are both carried off by the years that carry us all. For let us not forget, as darkness falls a little further: it is the night mom really does come home; the night Dr Wright, in full sartorial splendor at last, really does go stepping. *(Softly)* Dr Wright...

Scene Seven

(ALAN, *wandering Long Hauls in his gown, his arms still bound behind him, calls out to stop* DR WRIGHT, *who passes dressed immaculately in tie and tails for a night on the town...*)

ALAN: Oh, Dr Wright...

DR WRIGHT: *(Stopping)* What? *(Brusquely)* Can't you see I'm on Clinic business? I haven't got time for just any nuthouse case. *(Recognizing him)* Oh, are you still here? How's your mother, son? Dry as a lake bed?

ALAN: Dr Wright, I...

DR WRIGHT: Shoot, son. I've always believed that honesty, even with those who can never get anything straight....

ALAN: I may be slow, Dr Wright, but....

DR WRIGHT: Indeed you wouldn't be the first candidate for Special Ed whose mother thought he was a genius.

ALAN: I may be slow—it's just getting through to me: But you've changed sides, haven't you, Doctor?

DR WRIGHT: Changed sides...? *(Patiently)* Alan: An Expert Witness never changes sides; the Better Business Bureau wouldn't allow it; the Chamber of Commerce would have conniptions—as we say in the profession. Something must be sacred, just as the relationship between a health-care provider and his broker must never be disturbed. *(Showing his bottle)* Now. Out of my way, son. Can't you see I'm on my way to administer a little test, however foregone the conclusion. Now why don't you just...

ALAN: *(In* DR WRIGHT'*s way)* Because I'm doing what I'm doing, Dr Wright. I'll never give up.

DR WRIGHT: Never is a long word, son, longer than a coffee break. First we give up on our fathers, then our mothers. *(Trying to get around* ALAN*)* Now, if you'll excuse me, on my way out this evening I'm barring a couple of windows...

ALAN: *(In his way)* Have you changed sides, Dr Wright? Is this a *real* test you're about to administer?

DR WRIGHT: Young man, a little respect must be reserved for our elders.

ALAN: Very little.

DR WRIGHT: *(Aside)* I trust my professional expertise is not being called upon. Ah well, when duty calls... *(Professionally, to* ALAN*)* As you say, very little indeed. *(Advancing upon him)* Because we have to leave room in the child for... Terror! *(Dragging* ALAN *about by the ear)* Can you guess where we wake up, when we wake up, before we're halfway into our compulsory midsummer night's *nap? (Breathing deep)* Ah, Lysol! *(Shaking him, dropping him to the floor)* Will the little boy who took the bus alone please step out! *(Calling out)* Coach! Tent Mother! Here he is, the little so-and-so. Mocked his father's few words, drove his mother round the bend *and* up the wall. Yep. Guilty on all counts. Guilty. But let us not rush to judgment. *(Moving toward* ALAN*)* I'm sure the boy can speak for himself.

(Helping ALAN *to his feet; with gentleness and understanding)*

DR WRIGHT: Alan: I don't suppose you feel a trifle, how shall we say...guilty?

ALAN: *(Losing his voice)* ...Yes, now that you mention it, I...

DR WRIGHT: Yes. *(Pointing at his face)* The proof is in that face on the point of falling apart—I've seen it before... Coach! Tent Mother! Now where are they? Can't pay these counselors enough! *(Leaving one way)* God knows what those two are up to! Under a tent flap somewhere, banging away in the bushes. Must be bow and arrow time, boy. *(Calling off)* Sebastian! We've got a little archer here, a bow man of the first water. I'd dump this idea of wandering Long Hauls all night, Alan. If you think of it, you really can't be two places at once: looking for your father *and* rushing home to your mother. Alan, are you getting enough sleep? Enough to eat? I feed my guests the very best chicken shit, you know. I'll just send nurse along with half a gallon. *(Easily getting past* ALAN*)* Now if you'll excuse me, on my way out, we're adding a couple of steel doors down the hall... *(Stopping to see that he has his scoring boxers on, the white ones with dripping red hearts)* Let's see now, I haven't forgotten my lucky scorers, have I? Ach, wunderbar! *(Placing his order)* Zwei kaffee, bitte... *(Sotto voce, while shaking a few drops of something into an invisible cup)* ...mit tropfen. *(Pocketing an empty—and invisible—vial.)* Not to mention... *(Feeling in another pocket)* Ah, yes. My voice scrambler. *(Another)* The keys to my Cadillac. *(Stopping to call back to* ALAN*)* On the other hand... *(Smiling)* Why *don't* you check on your mother, son? I don't see any harm in it. I'm sure she's home by now.

*(*DR WRIGHT *strides off, closing the offstage door, eclipsing the harsh slant of light behind him.* ALAN *looks up, moves toward the other "location,"* EDEN's *apartment.)*

ALAN: And so, ladies and gentlemen, one night it befell I took Dr Wright's advice and went home to my mother.

(As ALAN *goes home, however,* ADAM *appears, almost ghostlike, before him, drugged, his arms tied, his mouth open, the front of his hospital gown stained, his voice deeply distorted. Gowned, armless and frightened, they dance around each other.*)

ADAM: Ohhh...my...son... *(Noting* ALAN's *flowered gown and bound arms)* Have they got you too...?

ALAN: Dad... Dad, is that you?

ADAM: ...*What if*...they caught me, *what if*...they're keeping me in a cage...? ...won't you...let me out...Alan...?

ALAN: I don't think so, Dad, no. Not right away. Perhaps later. Oh, Dad, please don't think I've given up on you. I just have to check on Mom, Dad. I'll be back, believe me.

ADAM: *(Fading, his voice monstrous)* ...Believe you...? ...the truth is, Alan... I never believed in you...oh, I pretended, yes, but...

(ADAM's *gone.*)

ALAN: Dad, how could you say that—just when Mom's home and there's only me between her and...?

ADAM: *(Reappearing, normal if bound.)* Alan, I don't suppose you've seen a bubbler, a water fountain, in your wanderings; preferably one with a pedal?

ALAN: No, I don't think so.

ADAM: Thirsty as hell, somehow. Just have to keep looking, I...

(ADAM *leaves the way he came;* ALAN, *looking after him, fades.*)

Scene Eight

(EDEN *at her table; the book, the bottle, the glass; the bottle open, but untouched; the glass empty; the cork, the corkscrew lying on the table.* EDEN *wears a long diaphanous nightgown.* ALAN, *still wearing his flowered gown, his sleeves still tied behind him watches from a distance. When* ALAN *speaks, it is with some self-possession and confidence. Beat)*

EDEN: *(Without looking up from her book)* Is that you?

ALAN: Who else?

EDEN: Are you home?

ALAN: Where else...?

EDEN: Then you didn't find your father?

ALAN: He's well hidden.

EDEN: Beware of fathers who are well hidden, Alan. They...

(EDEN's *hand, almost by itself, reaches towards the bottle of wine.*)

ALAN: Mom...don't...

(*Without looking up from her book,* EDEN, *shaking her head, withdraws her hand. Beat. As before, her hand moves towards the bottle.*)

ALAN: Mom...please... I couldn't stand it if you began again. I know it was you in there, locked up, but, somehow, it's as if it had been me. I'm just not up to it again.

(*Beat.* EDEN, *still reading, withdraws her hand. Beat. Once more her hand moves towards the bottle.* ALAN *opens his mouth to beg once more but leaves the decision to her. When he hasn't spoken,* EDEN *looks up, her hand frozen near the bottle. Slowly she picks up the empty glass instead, looks into it, raises her eyes to his once more, then, holding the glass by its stem, taps it just hard enough on the table to break it.* EDEN *sits up, straightens, her eyes clearing.*)

EDEN: Was that all it took, Alan, to break the spell?

(ALAN *nods; they smile at each other.*)

EDEN: But what's this? How did you get all tangled up like some loony tunes? Come here.

(ALAN *approaches, stands with his back to her.*)

EDEN: How could this possibly have...?

(EDEN *unties* ALAN's *sleeves. He faces her. She rolls his sleeves up, freeing the hands, which she holds admiringly.*)

EDEN: These hands must never be constrained, Alan; I love these...

(EDEN *seems about to kiss his hands when the phone rings.* EDEN *does not move.* ALAN, *withdrawing his hands, answers it.*)

ALAN: Hello? (*Beat. Reluctantly*) I'll see. (*His hand over the mouthpiece*) Are you home?

(EDEN *nods reluctantly, once more taking up her book.*)

ALAN: Are you up to coming to the phone?

EDEN: (*Reading*) Am I...up to it?

ALAN: That was the question, I believe.

EDEN: Who's asking?

ALAN: Some man on a car phone, I think. His voice sounds scrambled.

(EDEN *looks up. Her eyes meet* ALAN's.)

EDEN: I'll take it in the bedroom.

ALAN: I'll listen in here.

(Beat. EDEN, without rising from the table, takes the phone. At various moments during the conversation, as ALAN stands against the wall holding his bouquet, EDEN unconsciously sniffs the cork of her opened bottle.)

EDEN: Yes? I thought it might be you. What did I tell you...? I know: This is this time. Do I want to stare temptation down? You think it might be therapeutic. *(Looks at her watch)* My schedule is pretty tight. I have a project... I'm not ready to talk about it; first, the research; then...who knows? A poem? What? You've discovered a lovely Viennese coffee house, with all the latest pastries, right here in the middle of our Godforsaken... *Wunderbar!* you say. Well... No more than an hour. *(She hangs up, addresses ALAN.)* What a phony conversation. If you hadn't heard him yourself, you'd have thought there was nobody there, wouldn't you? If you ever find yourself writing a play, Alan—ha-ha—I hope you'll write better dialogue than that. You have to give the impression there's really somebody there, though there never is, really. *(Showing the end of the telephone wire)* Those actors are all holding dead telephones, and alone as they'll ever be. What are you staring at? Have you never heard of a coffee break? You can wait up for me. *(Standing in her diaphanous gown, leaving to dress)* Now if you'll excuse me, Alan, I'm just going to slip into something a little less comfortable...

ALAN: ...your shroud....

EDEN: Pardon me?

ALAN: Your grave clothes. Mother, please...

EDEN: Alan, you have to allow your mother a little...

ALAN: A little what?

EDEN: A little space in which to try her wings, a little...

(Suddenly ALAN has his mother by the arms, shaking her violently, growling savagely and gnashing his teeth.)

ALAN: A little! You know what I'm worried about, Mom? It's a lot! A lot more than you can hold, a...!

(The shaking stops as suddenly as it began. For a moment they look at each other.)

ALAN: What are you anyway?

EDEN: I am myself, Alan. There's nothing you can do about it.

(Exit EDEN. ALAN stands looking down at the bottle, the glass, and the book. He raises the cork, sniffs it.)

ALAN: Ladies and gentlemen, my mother slips into something a little less comfortable. And I...? Maybe I never left that charming little enterprise, Dr Wright's very own for-profit sani....

(The light changes. Once more ALAN is confronted by his ghostly father, who merely looks at him in ghostly disbelief.)

ALAN: Really, Dad, Mom's at work on a new project, first she does the research, then; no, I think it's a kind of poem, an elegy really; she's taking a little coffee break, you see...

(ADAM, *looking at* ALAN, *shakes his head in despairing disapproval and disappointment.*)

ADAM: Dad, is there anything you'd like? A glass of water maybe. Dad?

(ADAM *fades.*)

Scene Nine

(DR WRIGHT *reappears, hurrying in the same direction as before and carrying a vintage* Chateau Neuf du Pape *under his arm. Once more* ALAN *steps in front of him.*)

DR WRIGHT: What? You again?

ALAN: Dr Wright. I thought you were long gone.

DR WRIGHT: If you must know, I forgot my *grand cru* and a couple of paper cups for later. But what about you? Can't manage to keep yourself out of the hall I'm charging down?

ALAN: I guess not. I...

DR WRIGHT: (*Advancing*) Ready for that first competition, Alan, the one that shows what our little so-and-sos are made of?

ALAN: Yes, Dr Wright. I may be a city boy, but: I'm ready.

DR WRIGHT: Very well, son. That's the spirit we like to see at Camp Squash.

ALAN: Camp *Squash*?

DR WRIGHT: Where did you think you were, son, playing on your mother's grave?

ALAN: My mother's alive and well, thank you, Dr Wright. I just...

DR WRIGHT: Well, of course she is. We can't imagine our dear Eden giving up, can we... (*Leaving*) ...her brain in a jar of grain alcohol, pickled?

ALAN: Unfortunately, I...

DR WRIGHT: (*Reappearing with the suitcase, once more dragging* ALAN *by the ear*) Why, here we are now. Archery 101. (*Pulling bow and arrow from the suitcase, placing them in* ALAN's *hands*) Where is that ne'er-do-well? (*Looking off*) Why do I always end up doing what my instructors are paid to do? Thank God I have a way with children. Just don't point that at me, you little son-of-a...! (*Moving, looking in the distant sky for the quarry*) Look up! Keep your eyes open.

(DR WRIGHT, *directs his attention at a circling target, off, but* ALAN *has no idea what to do with bow and arrow.*)

DR WRIGHT: No, no! *(Patiently evil)* Put the notch end of the arrow on the string. That's it. Pull the arrow smoothly over the top of your left hand, drawing it slowly back with your right. *(When he cannot)* What's wrong, you dimwit? Where are these instructors when you need them? *(Calling off)* Sebastian! Stop standing in front of the target and get over here!

(ALAN, *finally having a hold of it, attempts unsuccessfully to draw the bow, even turning red in the face, while* DR WRIGHT *watches, shaking his head.*)

DR WRIGHT: Come Alan, it doesn't take a Ulysses. Everyone can draw the bow at Camp Eden. Why, they don't even let you on the bus if you can't draw the bow. They did let you on the bus, didn't they?

ALAN: I don't know anymore. I feel so guilty, just like you said. I may have snuck on.

DR WRIGHT: Very likely, that is, if you can't draw the bow. *(Pointing somewhat higher, in a narrowing circle)* There! There she is! Shoot, you little...!

(ALAN *tries again but, unsuccessful at drawing the bow, droops, defeated.*)

DR WRIGHT: *(Shaking his head, calling out)* Coach! Tent Mother! Just look at him! Hiawatha here claims he hasn't slept a wink since he saw his mother circling like a bird in the moonlight. Lies awake, gawks at dancing shadows, cries out, "Mom, Mom!" and sometimes, "Dad!" What do you say, Tent Mother, have we got a place for him? Have we got a cot next to the showers, the stinking cans, the nightlight right in his eyes, the water running all night? *(To* ALAN, *suddenly looking straight up, his finger drawing a yet narrower circle)* There! See? There she is. Quick, little Indian, draw the bow...

(ALAN *does manage to draw the bow and shoots his arrow into the night sky. There is a wounded cry above, then feathers begin to flutter down around them.* DR WRIGHT, *very pleased, holds his hand out as if he is enjoying a snowfall.*)

DR WRIGHT: You know what these are, don't you, Alan? I don't need a PhD to tell you these are the feathers from your mother's wings.

ALAN: My mother's *wings*? What are you saying, Dr Wright? My mother's no angel, God knows, but she's alive and...

DR WRIGHT: Yes, of course she is, Alan. What's that you were saying: alive and what? *(More loudly)* Alive and *what*?? *(Straightening, every inch the clinician)* Yes, I think it would be better if you just stayed here awhile, Alan, here where everybody gets three good meals a day... Now, if you'll excuse me, I'll just have a word or two with my subordinates. *(Chuckling)* You dreamer. Camp Squash, indeed. Archery: what next? *(Leaving)* Coach! Coach! Tent Mother! Sebastian...!

(ALAN *curls up on the floor.* ADAM *appears in flowered gown, his hands still tied behind him;* ALAN *jumps up.*)

ALAN: Dad! Dad, is that you? I was looking...

ADAM: It's all right, Alan. Don't worry.

ALAN: Where are you off to?

ADAM: Just looking for the library, son. You know where the library is?

ALAN: No, I... What if Long Hauls doesn't have a library, Dad?

ADAM: I'll do my best, Alan, from memory.

ALAN: But why...what...?

ADAM: Antecedents, technicalities. I'm preparing my brief. I'll be out tomorrow. You can be sure of that. But what about you? I thought you were waiting for someone.

ALAN: I...that is, I...I'm looking for you too.

ADAM: One thing at a time, Alan. Go now. Go to your mother.

ALAN: *(Leaving)* Yes, Dad. *(Suddenly returning)* Hey, Dad! Did you see that nurse?

ADAM: What nurse?

ALAN: That one over there. What a looker, what a knockout!

(When ADAM turns to watch the unseen NURSE EDEN pass in the distance, ALAN dexterously unties ADAM's arms.)

ADAM: I don't see anyone. What are you...?

ALAN: Never mind. I guess I was mistaken. Here I go. Don't worry. Mom's going to be all right, Dad. I'm looking out for her.

ADAM: Well, of course you are, Alan. Of course you...

(Exit ALAN as ADAM watches him go, then discovers his freed hands. But the light fades on ADAM, and ALAN circles to the point where he can address the audience directly.)

ALAN: You see, ladies and gentlemen, it wasn't impossible after all to find our fathers while going home to our mothers. All I know is that even at the fanciest of displaced Viennese coffee houses, even the most imaginary of coffee breaks has to end. Well, doesn't it?

(ALAN fades from sight.)

Scene Ten

(EDEN's apartment. Late night. Someone rings the doorbell in the darkness, a long harsh ring. Footsteps fade off, down the unseen sidewalk. As he switches on a light in an unseen room opposite, ALAN appears in the slant of light still wearing his flowered gown and Long Hauls blanket, once more carrying his flowers. EDEN is

sunk in the open doorway opposite, dressed for a night on the town, unconscious, not entirely supine, her legs exposed; her knees dirty, scuffed as if she has fallen earlier. ALAN *stares at her, rubs his eyes, looks again.*)

ALAN: "Yesh, thank you, I ha' a wunerful time." (*Pulling up his flowered gown*) "My legs jus' keep shlipping out...I'm shorry."

(EDEN *raises her head to look at* ALAN.)

ALAN: I see a beautiful, well-dressed woman...so weak she's shlipping down in her own doorway, but her elegy's coming along nicely...

(EDEN *lets her head fall.* ALAN *turns away, sets his flowers on the table, but turns again, goes to her, picks her up under the arms and drags her in. Leaving her on the floor, he goes to close the door, after looking both ways into the street and listening to a car start and drive off.* EDEN, *awakened, bothered by the light from the hall, begins to crawl under the table.* ALAN *returning, sees her.*)

ALAN: I see her crawling underneath the table she's so fond of reading at. I see an early, a pathetic, death. (*Walking around the table she lies under*) That was the guy who's been calling, wasn't it? (EDEN *does not respond.* ALAN *leans over the table.*) You called him "friend," your voice dripping, even before you knew he drove a Cadillac. You said, "Listen, friend, this is just talk..." (*Drunkenly*) "...unerstan..?" (*Normally*) "...one word after another..." At least he waited to drive off until he saw you dragged in. Maybe he isn't as bad as you thought. Perhaps his language is equally impressive. Maybe, as Mr Barrie said of Captain Hook, "The man is not wholly evil: He has a thesaurus in his cabin." Is that where you were, Mom, in Captain Hook's cabin? Four hours home and you're hooked. On the other hand... I wonder what Captain Hook says when he has an irresistible urge to say "on the other hand." (*Doing Captain Hook*) "Oh, I can't use that tired old phrase; what'll my mother say?" On the other hand, Mom, I hope you weren't parked in the park like some teenybopper, or crawling up the Three Leaf Nature Trail like one of our ancestors. Mom??

(EDEN *attempts to crawl in the direction of her bedroom as* ALAN *walks alongside.*)

ALAN: Where do you think you're off to? It's a little late for bed, isn't it?

EDEN: (*Stopping in the crawl position, but not looking up, speaking with an effort*) ...I'm....

ALAN: You're sho shorry. Yesh, I believe I heard that. It's a little late to be shorry, isn't it, Mom?

EDEN: ...help me u...u...

ALAN: Up? Is that what you're saying, Mom? Up from where exactly? We haven't got time for evolution, have we?

(*Suddenly, almost violently,* ALAN *raises her to her feet, holds her up.*)

EDEN: (*Wavering*) ...I think...there was something in my drink...

ALAN: You think... Is that your poem, Mom? Is that the first line?

(When EDEN is clearly unable to speak or remain standing, he allows her to sink into her chair. Her head tilts back, her mouth hangs open. ALAN stands looking down into her mouth.)

ALAN: Well, well. Is that where the words come from? All the words you wanted me to learn? What was it you said to Dad anyway before all this happened, what words did you dredge up to send him packing? Do you even remember what you said...with one brow slightly higher than the other and your eyes on some spot on the floor? I should tear that pretty tongue out. I know someone who'd appreciate it. *(Bending closer)* Along with all those pretty teeth. Perhaps I'll be a dentist when I grow up. *(Holding her chin and the top of her head)* This crystal ball... *(Correcting himself)* ...this crystal goblet flush with some vintage forever older than I, holds all the secrets I never want to know... *(Bending slowly closer)* ...so softly curtained in its slippery crimson depths... *(Very softly)* What do you think, Mom? Are those the best of all possible words in the best of all possible orders? Are you sure I didn't pop out here, already talking a mile a minute?

(He is close enough to kiss her when EDEN snaps her mouth shut, stands, and lurches away. Staggering a few steps across the room before slipping to the floor, she is suddenly retching, her stomach empty. After a moment's hesitation, ALAN goes to her, kneels beside her, holds her shoulders and forehead until she is still.)

EDEN: ...Water...

ALAN: Water? Back into the depths?

(ALAN rises, is about to exit opposite. EDEN remains on knees and elbows, her head near the floor.)

EDEN: Alan.

(ALAN stops, looks back at her. EDEN's question is softly and sincerely asked, simply and honestly responded to by ALAN.)

EDEN: I haven't broken your heart, have I, Alan?

ALAN: It's too soon to tell.

(Exit ALAN. EDEN continues, unaware that he is gone.)

EDEN: ...I never wanted to break your heart, never... I tried, I tried so hard... I read, I rose before dawn to run...I wrote... *(Finding a closely typed, if much folded, piece of paper)* ...I have written the beginning...the beginning...

(Unable to unfold it, EDEN puts her head down on the floor and crumples awkwardly, the paper beneath her. ALAN returns, carefully carrying a glass of water; when he sees she is asleep, he stops at some distance from her.)

ALAN: Welcome home, Mom. Perhaps you'd prefer a little eye opener at this point. You know, it didn't have to be this way when you came home. *(His hand on the light)* It might have been stillness upon our faces, light after long darkness, after endless rain. You might have tried. (ALAN, *still holding the glass of water, switches off the light.*)

Entr'acte

(DR WRIGHT *stands alone in the darkness in tails, etc, immensely pleased with himself; only now his shirtfront is stained with wine, his tie askew, his collar open and smeared with lipstick.*)

DR WRIGHT: *(Wriggling)* Oh, Wright, you man, you. You man of many voices. You phone caller. You driver of cars in the night. You imaginer of Viennese coffee houses... *(Slyly)* ...you pharmacist, you carrier of tiny vials, you magician waving your hand over a steaming cup. And later... *(Scratching)* Oh, Wright...you crawler-up of Three Leaf Nature Trails in the dark. *(Aside)* I told her there was a view of civilization from the top that would leave her squirming; dazed, she believed me. And later, a *little* later... Oh, Wright, you leaver-off of lovely lushes in their own doorways. No, Your Honor, nothing—nothing!—would induce me to change my Expert Testimony, not even a half hour pawing in the park... *(As hysterical fingers remember handfuls)* ...my hands as busy as lawn mowers, as scythes...

(DR WRIGHT *is gone.* ALAN *stands where he stood before, his hand still on the light switch.* EDEN *is gone. The immense flashing red light of an ambulance outside the door plays across the walls.*)

ALAN: So much for my mother. So much for Dr Wright. My father... My father realized very quickly—much more quickly than someone I know—that he could check himself out. Yes, as soon as he found the sanitorium library, read up on precedents & etc, he decided to represent himself to the cleaning lady and, before you could say slam/bang, he was out, gone home, regretting much of his adult life and vowing never to remarry. In order to stay out, however, he had his lawyer, Lawless, on the phone before breakfast. For me, ladies and gentlemen, Summer Camp loomed larger than ever, yet, for a moment, this life held onto me...and I, I could not let it go.

(*The ambulance outside the door pulls away;* ALAN *listens, then:*)

ALAN: As you can guess, my mother has returned—though I cannot say the choice was hers entirely—to a whiteness whiter than white, which, however briefly, precedes a darkness darker than dark... And if those aren't the right words in the right order, Mom: too bad. They're the only ones I've got.

Scene Eleven

(EDEN *in a hospital bed, eyes closed, deathlike. The white light, the heavily screened window. Beat.* DR WRIGHT *entering as before in lipsticked collar, etc, bends over her.* EDEN *does not respond.*)

DR WRIGHT: You dreamboat. Your death throes would be passion enough for me. But I am sorry, Eden. We thought you'd checked yourself out and that was it. You were better, clear-headed, on the wagon. We just didn't know the wagon had a flashing red light, that the wagon was heading this way, as if caught in that great wind that puts everything, everyone, back where they belong. Very much as if. To tell the truth, Eden: Part of me is glad you've seen fit to return. Yes, to be perfectly frank... *(Fingering his lipsticked collar)* ...aside from the brief excursion on Clinic Business— I've been wandering the halls as if I—ha-ha—as if I were stark raving mad. *(Leaning close, whispering)* Eden, welcome home... *(Leaving, pausing)* Oh, by the way, Eden, I'll be right down the hall. If you want anything at all: Just scream.

(*Exit* DR WRIGHT. *The sun rises on* EDEN, *the upper half of her bed raised.* ALAN, *dressed in his street clothes as at the beginning, stands at the foot of the bed, flowers once more in his hand, a book under his arm. He is waiting for her to wake up. She stirs, she may open her eyes slightly without looking directly at him.* ALAN *raises the flowers, speaks softly.*)

ALAN: *(Tentatively)* ...Mom... You can't sleep all the time. The doctor said it was okay to wake you, to keep you awake. I knew the flowers would do it. ...Mom... *(No response)* Can I sit on the bed? *(No response. He sits on the bed at her side.)* Mom, women aren't supposed to have strokes. Dad says that's because they don't try to keep as much in their heads.

(EDEN *half opens her eyes but does not look at* ALAN.)

ALAN: You're not even going to tell me not to say that, are you? You'll just have to leave my words alone for a change.

(EDEN *closes her eyes.* ALAN *waits, then cannot wait any longer.*)

ALAN: And, to be perfectly frank—as someone would say—I miss your voice, Mom. Mom, I think I need it to go on. *(Earnestly)* Mom, maybe if you try real hard. Just decide: I am going to speak. I have something to say to my son, something he will want to remember, and I am going to say it. What do you think, Mom? Will you try?

(*A moment passes before* EDEN *opens her eyes. Then she does so, looks directly at* ALAN, *and tries. Her mouth opens, her eyes strain, she begins to sweat, but the only sound she is capable of making is a kind of gasping croak. It is a horrible sound, and* EDEN *sustains it longer than would seem necessary, until* ALAN *gently places his fingers on her lips and she closes her mouth. He wipes the perspiration from her forehead with the same hand. She closes her eyes.)*

ALAN: ...thank you... That's enough for now. We'll try again later. *(He puts his head down on her chest, still holding the flowers.)* I can hear your heart, Mom. There's nothing wrong with it. It's not going to just stop one day, when we least expect it. And even if you were never to say anything else to me, perhaps you've said enough.

(He looks up. They both smile, though EDEN's *eyes remain closed.)*

ALAN: I just want you to know I'm going to do it, whatever it is, and... Mom? *(Deliberately, his voice older than it has been)* Eden.

(EDEN opens her eyes.)

ALAN: Eden, would you like me to read to you? I brought your book, it was on the table. *(He places the flowers beside her on the bed, takes out the acting edition of "Peter Pan," stands and, moving freely, reads stage directions and does the voices with panache.)*
HOOK. Boat ahoy!
SMEE. *(Relieved)* It is the captain.
(HOOK is swimming—(Aside: Don't ask me how!)—and they help him to scale the rock. He is in a gloomy mood.)
STARKEY. Captain, is all well?
SMEE. He sighs.
STARKEY. He sighs again.
SMEE. *(Counting)* And yet a third time he sighs. *(With foreboding)* What's up, Captain?
HOOK. The game is up. These boys have found a mother!
STARKEY. Oh, evil day!
SMEE. What is a mother?
WENDY. *(Horrified)* He doesn't know!
(Seeing that there is no response from her.) And to think, Mom, I remember when you couldn't sleep at all. Shall I go on?

(EDEN seems to nod.)

ALAN: HOOK. Dost not know, Smee? A mother is— *(He finds it more difficult to explain than he had expected and looks about him for an illustration. He finds one in a great bird which drifts past in a nest as large as the roomiest basin.)* There is a lesson in mothers for you! The nest must have fallen into the water, but would the bird desert her eggs? *(PETER, who is now more or less off his head, makes the sound of a bird answering in the negative. The nest is borne out of sight.)*

(ALAN, having waved that nest out of sight with a grand smoothing gesture, stands carefully, backs away, speaking softly.)

ALAN: I'll be just outside, Mom. If you want anything...just make a sound....any sound at all... *(ALAN, book in hand, picking up her flowers, begins to tiptoe out.)*

ALAN: I'll just put these in water...

(*Though* EDEN *doesn't open her eyes, her voice stops him.*)

EDEN: ...Alan...

ALAN: Yes, Mom?

EDEN: Go to your father.

(*Beat*)

ALAN: Yes, Mom.

(ALAN *steps quietly out,* DR WRIGHT *carefully in. He's made an attempt to clean himself up, but doesn't look much better. He whisks a pocket mirror from his breast pocket, polishes it, inspects himself.*)

DR WRIGHT: Bit of a mess, Wright. Let's be honest. No one could love you. No one. But... Duty calls. Can't stand in the hall forever, not even the longest hall of all.

(*Unexpectedly, he holds the mirror to* EDEN's *face, looks at it, shrugs, begins to leave but, suddenly, with a cry of despair as great as* ADAM's *earlier scream, throws himself sobbing across her stomach.* EDEN's *hand moves slowly onto his head, his shoulders. After a moment,* DR WRIGHT *pulls himself together, stands. Turning, he finds that* ALAN *has reappeared to witness that which has just occurred but when* DR WRIGHT *speaks, it is as if nothing has happened and, indeed,* EDEN *and the clinic room fade from view.*)

Chaser

(DR WRIGHT's *office, the lighting as in the original visit.* ALAN *holds his book, his bouquet.*)

DR WRIGHT: Well, Alan, that was that. What do you think?

(ALAN *opens his mouth, but nothing comes out.*)

DR WRIGHT: True, very true. Your mother could not have said it better. The sky fell. That's the way it goes. You lose your mother. I lost mine. Our mothers lost their mothers. No, we don't save our moms, Alan; we never do. If it's any consolation: mine wasn't the looker yours was. I know you won't believe it, but mine looked like hell: hair, skin, eyes like.... Ever think you might lose your marbles, Alan? Well, it happens. Best to be prepared. Are you prepared?

(*As before,* ALAN *opens his mouth.* DR WRIGHT *speaks manfully.*)

DR WRIGHT: Yes, Alan; we have it from the horse's mouth there, all right: This is the end. Just to wrap things up though, I think I ought to tell you: Your father's used up so much in legal fees—it should happen to every lawyer—he's not sending you to Boarding School; no, nor Summer Camp either. And—surprise—I'm giving up on this business. Too easy. Cures to the left, cures to the right: Into the valley of death rode the six hundred. Besides, I'm tired of time. Pass, pass, pass. *(Confidingly)* I'm going to give space a chance. Yes, I've decided to become a sculptor, a stone cutter if you will. Don't ask how I'm going to pay for it without my cash cow, my beloved Long Hauls. I've sold my Cadillac. Even if I have to hang my head occasionally—when I drop in at Presbyterian—that'll keep me going. I have a tremendous work in mind. Monumental. A kind of memorial, a tribute. To the departed. Any comments, suggestions, anything at all you want to say, before we... *(Beat)* This is it, then. *(Holding out his hand)* Goodbye, young man. Life awaits. So long, Alan. Say hello to the future for me. May you hold your own children close, may their laughter fill your days. *(Barely opening the oversize door)* Goodbye. Goodbye. Just leave me wondering how it all began. How it ended.

(They shake hands. DR WRIGHT *holds open the oversize door.* ALAN, *about to step through, changes his mind, speaking with mature confidence and gesturing the way.)*

ALAN: After you, Dr Wright.

DR WRIGHT: What's that? That's right. Wright here. Dr Wright. *(Hesitating for fear of being jammed in the doorway, then stepping quickly through, sticking his head back; aside.)* Almost had me that time. *(He exits.)*

ALAN: Ladies and gentlemen... *(He hesitates, perhaps wondering what to say; then, presenting it with an almost grand gesture.)* An empty stage.

(He hesitates, then steps forward with his bouquet and lays it carefully on the ground. He steps back and stands, holding his book in both hands, looking down as the light fades.)

END OF PLAY

HOLD ME

CHARACTERS & SETTING

ROB, *early twenties. Short, thickly built, physically strong, thick glasses; though he has achieved the manners of the middle class, he sometimes has an inherited tendency to physically intimidate.*

DARREN, *a year younger than* ROB, *but a large man, large hands, born to the middle class.*

LARRY, *thirty. Medium height, wiry, troubled, speaks with difficulty; working class, he has a job as a surveyor for the city.*

LEWIS, *near forty.* LARRY's *elder brother, somewhat stiff, reserved, works for the state; though a bureaucrat, an intelligent, well-read man, supportive of friends and family.*

RICK, ROB's *father. Late fifties. One leg shorter than the other, wears a built-up shoe, short, thickly built, the same as* ROB, *also wears thick glasses. A tendency to aggressiveness at times, to intimidation.*

DREW, DARREN's *father. Sixty. Wheelchair bound, a college professor, quietly supportive of his son. A colleague and friend of the art teacher who assumes the alias.*

"BRANDY", *an assumed name. Thirties. Like* DARREN, *born to the middle-class, an art teacher eventually slumming as a bar dancer & etc; eventually also, she listens to every man's voice carefully, asking the suspect to hold her as she was held those times against her will. "*BRANDY*"'s transformation is so successful that those who know the art teacher do not recognize her.*

Urban settings, which are night scenes, are suggested by angled beams of cold light; sylvan settings, which are day scenes, are more gently suggested; indoor lighting designs, day or night, generally obviate the need for heavy props. Scenes of violence may be stylized, choreographed, slowed.

ACT ONE

Scene One

(Setting: St Paul, MN, an outdoor scene from the days of realist theater magic; lovely sunlight, giant, overhanging trees, ivy-covered brick walls of the college library, perspective, a horizon, and a carpet of thick grass—walls and lawn, possibly all, suggested with a fragment or two. One long, not-too-hot afternoon, the two friends recline somewhat languidly, at a distance from each other, each with an open book, reading; in a moment DARREN will stand, still at a distance, to make the overlarge gestures expected of declamatory speech. They are dressed appropriately for the summer, a few bottles of Coke and a couple of paper cups lie at their feet. If a word is in any way worthy of their attention, they emphasize it.)

DARREN: *(Standing, striking a pose, book in hand, declaiming to an imagined audience in our direction)* And so, gentlemen, we go our separate ways, I to die, you to live, who can say which is the *better*?

ROB: *(Closing his book, very casually)* I think I can. It's better to eat a hot dog...or a hamburger.

DARREN: *(Closing his)* Agreed. It's better to eat a napkin with mustard, to chomp down a paper cup with relish.

ROB: Agreed. It's better to have sex, even with a napkin.

DARREN: Agreed. Even without relish. The truth is, friend Rob, even if I become, *par example*...now that the liberal arts are behind us...

ROB: Far, far behind us, friend Darren.

(ROB slowly tears his book in half. DARREN is genuinely pained by this, but conceals it.)

DARREN: Yes, as I was going to say, before I was so...so *malignantly*, so *malevolently* I might add, interrupted...even if I become, *par example*, a genetic engineer of the first water, or, on the other hand, a sculptor, let us say, of the third rank, yes, and, though I've never studied either, the truth is I don't know how good I might be at...at creating women.

ROB: Better leave it to old You Know Who.

DARREN: What if, in the second case, that of the unborn worker in stone, they, his women, are sketchy, skin-deep: busts—or butts—without brains. Rob—I don't think I know women very well. I've never been inside one, except of course my mother.

ROB: We have been such good young men, haven't we, friend Darren?

DARREN: Maybe a little too good. But I sincerely hope that being inside will clear everything up. You go in, you have a look around. *Et voilà!* No more mysteries.

ROB: What if she talks?

DARREN: Talks? Oh, you mean at the moment? I hadn't thought of that. How distracting.

ROB: Or screams.

DARREN: *(Shaking his head)* No, I don't think I....

ROB: *(Standing)* Not to change the subject too much, old man, but, speaking of opportunities, these very blades which now bear our weight shall soon support...the graduation picnic!

DARREN: The graduation picnic! Can you believe it? And to think we were very nearly bored there for a moment.

ROB: Unthinkable. Picture it. *(Strutting the grounds of the approaching picnic)* And among the untouchables may well be Anna Whoozawhatsamova, your favorite sociologist and mine, her paper plate laden to the point of collapse, her Marxism clearly evident behind the only glasses in St Paul thicker than mine....

DARREN: ...not to mention that rebellious bosom, those monumental mammaries, circa 1917, adding to her already overburdened plate and dipped so innocently, so *ahistorically* one might add, deep in the mayonnaise of our malaise...

ROB: The mayonnaise of our malaise: I like that.

DARREN: *(Urgently, to a point in space)* Anna: I would ask you to explain, yet once more, this, uh....struggle...you're always...

ROB: The class struggle.

DARREN: Thank you.... This...uh, class struggle you're always mentioning, which is not the struggle of the graduating class with its natural urges, but which I cannot, nevertheless, seem to grasp...but, anticipating my question, your left eye fixing me through your left lens, your right eye drifting out over your right in the spirit of inquiry, you respond... *(In a thick Russian accent, yet lovingly)* "Boys, boys, do not mock those who work, for whom each day is toil..."

ROB: *(Spotting a woman in the distance, with enthusiasm)* Say, but who's that walking with such deliberation, that's no Anna.

DARREN: That's one of the art teachers, I think. Teaches one-dimensional art, or something like that.

ROB: One-dimensional art.

DARREN: I hardly know her.

ROB: But you do know her.

DARREN: To nod at.

ROB: Oh, baby. What's her name?

DARREN: Dunno.

ROB: *(Watching gaga as she passes from view)* Gone.

DARREN: Gone.

ROB: *(With subtle thrusts)* Oh. Oh. If I had a hold of her, I'd make her keep it all on: glasses, briefcase, those professional woman's shoes...

DARREN: Oh. Oh. And that trench coat, friend, don't forget the trench coat.

ROB: No. No.

(They dance a bacchanalian, with raised arms and active pelvises ["oh,oh,oh,oh"] as the light fades to black.)

Scene Two

(The ART TEACHER *in trench coat, her well-shaped body not revealed, and dark glasses, not the ones she will wear as* BRANDY, *stands before* DREW *in his office, which is suggested by the warm sunlight angled from a high window.* DREW *is in his wheelchair, reading a book and is not aware of her until she takes a deep breath before speaking.)*

ART TEACHER: Drew.

DREW: *(Pleased)* Hello, beautiful.

ART TEACHER: You can have the beauty. I've had a rather unpleasant experience.

DREW: More unpleasant than usual?

ART TEACHER: I'm not kidding.

DREW: No. I can see you're not. I'm sorry. It's just that I know how it goes, this teaching business. What, or who, is it this time?

ART TEACHER: I have no idea.

(They look at each other a moment. She removes her glasses, revealing a bruised face. He exhales audibly.)

DREW: That happened here, beneath the ivy-covered walls?

ART TEACHER: Here, where the women are full of bull and the men are cowed.

DREW: And you don't know who?

ART TEACHER: I have no idea. It was at night. I was tripped, I fell, he fell on top of me.

DREW: Were you...?

ART TEACHER: Not really. I fell on my face. *(Her hand rising to her face)*

DREW: This was....

ART TEACHER: Two nights ago.

DREW: And what do the police think? Have there been similar...?

ART TEACHER: I haven't told them.

(Beat)

DREW: Well, I think now's the time. While it's fresh...

ART TEACHER: Fresh. I'm not going to the police, Drew. I'm going to keep this thing to myself.

DREW: But... He's still out there.

ART TEACHER: I don't want what follows...I don't need it. Besides, I think he was more a child than a man. I was only hurt when I fell; it might have been accidental. All he did was hold me down, caress my hair. Then he just sat on me, in the dark. I think I felt his tears. If it hadn't happened the way it did, I might have held him.

DREW: But it did happen the way it did. No, I take that back. It didn't *happen*. It wasn't the rain or the wind or a falling tree. Someone waited for you, followed you, tripped you, sat on you. A man did that to you. It didn't just happen.

ART TEACHER: I'm not going to the police, Drew.

DREW: All right. You're not going to the police. What are you going to do?

(Beat)

ART TEACHER: Nothing. Keep my eyes open... *(Replacing her dark glasses)* ...when they open. Avoid the shadows. Otherwise, lead a normal life.

DREW: Why are you telling me?

ART TEACHER: I don't know.

(Suddenly she sits on her heels beside DREW, puts her head against his chest. He holds her with one hand.)

DREW: Oh, my friend...

ART TEACHER: *(Sitting back to look at him)* Will you keep it...as you might say...under your hat?

(Beat)

DREW: Whatever you wish.

ART TEACHER: And no...looking for him yourself...in your wheelchair.

DREW: No. No looking for him myself.

ART TEACHER: *(Rising)* Thank you. *(Replacing her glasses)* And now...I've got a class.

(Exit the ART TEACHER, DREW watching her go.)

Scene Three

(Return to ROB and DARREN by the ivy-covered walls, suddenly ending their bacchanalian)

ROB: And poof: the lightning strikes, the rains approach, Anna's gone. The picnic's over. Younger, shapelier women run in mock terror as two listless, languid, lethargic...

DARREN: ...not to say phlegmatic...

ROB: ...former undergraduates stand in a field of blowing paper. Where now? they ask. What now?

DARREN: What if, friend Rob, this time of innocence were some brief prelude, if we could...

ROB: ...transform ourselves, see how the other half...does it.

DARREN: That's it.

ROB: What if...we could go anywhere we liked? Anywhere. Not just the graduation picnic but—to seasons unknown, past and passing, where unlived lives lurk. Crime, petty and...and otherwise. The roll of the dice. Love, love for sale, and...and total, irremediable loss. In short: the roads we hardly know we've taken until we're halfway to the end. What if: all we needed to drive off down one or the other was a... *(Snatching them up)* ...a paper cup or two. What do you say, Dr Jekyll?

DARREN: *(Filling ROB's foaming cup)* Whatever you say, Mr Hyde.

ROB: *(Filling DARREN's foaming cup)* And then perhaps this moment of privileged dialogue beneath the trees will fade. We'll break windows, do time. Our degrees will be in death, our nightly prayers—dear God!— that we might just return to things as they were, to an unmemorable afternoon leading to a more or less forgettable picnic.

DARREN: Agreed. More or less.

(They drain their cups.)

ROB: Agreed.

DARREN: And now. The other side of the tracks! Where is it, by the way?

ROB: Not far, just over my shoulder, back where I came from. But wait. This is a democracy, isn't it, more or less?

DARREN: It is, indeed, more or less.

ROB: Shall we put it to the vote?

DARREN: We shall. To the other side of the tracks, then. To crime, petty and...and otherwise. To breaking and entering!

ROB: To entering and breaking!

DARREN: Whatever that is.

ROB: That's, uhhh, forcible entry, which is to say penetration followed by...uh, well, whatever follows it.

DARREN: Fair enough. One digit says we go, two say we go quickly.

(As they prepare to whip their hands out from behind their backs on the count of three)

ROB: Agreed. One...two... Three!

(Their hands come out, two digits on each. Starting off)

ROB: That's it. We're off.

DARREN: *(Hesitating)* By the way, friend, what does follow forcible entry?

ROB: *(Momentarily stopped)* I don't know, friend. A scream?

(They look at each other, DARREN troubled, ROB not, as the light begins to fade. In the half light the ART TEACHER passes, her manner cautious, nervous, occasionally taking a look around her. The sounds of her own shoes and the sound of following footsteps rise and fall, hurry and slow in no relation to her own steps, though, shaking her head, she recognizes this as symptomatic of her own anxiety. As the light fades to black, the distant sound of a breaking window is heard.)

Scene Four

(A colorless dusk, the daylight angled off the water. On the footbridge over the Mississippi, the edge of which parallels the stage. DREW and RICK, DREW's clothing decidedly middle class, RICK's working class. DREW enters right, in his wheelchair, in no hurry; a few seconds later RICK enters left on his built-up shoe, moving with some determination. They do not stop or linger until they see each other.)

DREW: *(Stopping)* You're Rob's father.

RICK: *(Stopping, taking him in)* You're Darren's.

DREW: *(His manner friendly)* Well, now that we've got that cleared up....

RICK: I understand your son thinks he's a little too good for the rest of us, for my son in particular.

DREW: Oh? I understand yours is a little lost, in spite of his intellect, prone to petty crime, to run-ins with the police, to taking our limited time...

RICK: You're right. I'd like to straighten him out. He doesn't listen to me.

DREW: Sons don't, not really, not till after.

RICK: After? Oh, you mean to our voices. In memoriam. We ought to drown 'em like puppies while we're still here.

DREW: No...

RICK: Why not?

(RICK *looks over the railing at the Mississippi passing underneath;* DREW *joins him.*)

DREW: *(Recognizing the impossibility of an answer)* Why not? Why? *(Looking underneath the railing)* Why is the water black?

RICK: Why are you in that chair?

DREW: I should think that would be obvious. Why are you wearing that built-up shoe?

RICK: One leg's shorter than the other. Likewise.

DREW: Likewise obvious?

RICK: That's right. It seems some fathers have got more in common than some sons.

DREW: Oh? What's that?

RICK: Impediments. Obstacles. The way not cleared.

DREW: *(Offering his hand)* I'm Drew.

RICK: *(Shaking it)* Rick.

DREW: You know what they call this place, Rick?

RICK: You tell me.

DREW: The dead poet's bridge.

RICK: Why is that?

DREW: Too long a story. I suppose because for people of imagination sometimes there's nowhere else to go.

RICK: Preposterous. Ludicrous. There's always somewhere.

DREW: One hopes. It seems, judging from your language, you're a bit of a scholar, Rick, like your son.

RICK: I'm a night watchman. On my way to work.

DREW: Oh? I didn't know. Don't let me hold you.

RICK: I can be a little late. Nobody there but me.

DREW: I'm, uh, I'm sorry. I didn't mean...

RICK: Nothing to be sorry for. That's the way things are. You?

DREW: I...teach.

RICK: Teach what?

DREW: Advertising.

RICK: Like that?

DREW: Like what?

RICK: In the chair?

DREW: It's not my picture they put on the billboards.

RICK: It's not mine. *(Beat)* You've got your excuse.

DREW: For what?

RICK: Not keeping your son in line.

DREW: Is that all it takes, Rick, a swift kick?

RICK: I'm not any better at kicking than you are. My son got hit in the head once. Knocked his brain loose, I think.

DREW: I wish it were so simple.

RICK: You think your son is complex and mine is....?

DREW: I don't think anything like that. You've been to see Rob?

RICK: Of course.

DREW: Any problem with bail?

RICK: You offering me money?

DREW: We wouldn't want Rob in the hoosegow, Darren on the streets... just for the way their fathers' pockets were lined or not lined, just for the way the dice fell.

(RICK *looks at* DREW, *who continues looking down at the black water.*)

RICK: Just for the way things are. I accept.

DREW: Thank you.

RICK: Why thank me?

DREW: I'm glad to be able to do something. Otherwise I'm as helpless as....

RICK: ...as an adman in a wheelchair.

DREW: Well...

RICK: ...as a night watchman with a son so bright he found college so dull he wondered if petty crime might liven it up.

DREW: ...as any father would be whose son is throwing it away.

RICK: At least yours has got something to throw away.

DREW: Yours has too. He has intelligence, language. They're friends, those guys, they're equals. They're in this together. Uh, Rick... Your son: he hasn't tried anything that wasn't petty, has he?

RICK: What do you mean?

DREW: I mean he... He's not malevolent, is he?

RICK: Malevolent?

DREW: Malevolent, malignant, malicious. Violent.

RICK: He never has been.

DREW: Good. Good. *(Rolling back from the edge)* Well, speaking of ways, I was going one way...

RICK: *(Not moving)* And I was going the other.

DREW: My lawyer will deal with this. *(Offering his hand)* I'm glad we've met, Rick.

RICK: *(Not taking the hand, still looking into the river)* You know what's going to happen, don't you, when they get out? They'll just get into more trouble. Worse. Why not leave them where they are?

DREW: Why not give them the chance to take it, well, wherever they take it?

RICK: *(Stabbing a finger at the water)* They're going to take it right down there.

DREW: *(Rolling off)* That remains to be seen. So long, Rick.

(RICK *doesn't answer. Exit* DREW *in his original direction.*)

RICK: *(Not moving, still looking into the water, not intending to be heard by* DREW*)* So long, Drew. Limited time, you say...? *(Looking at his watch, hurrying off in his original direction)* Malevolent, malignant, malicious... *(Shaking it out of his head)* Violent?

(Light fades. In the half light the ART TEACHER *passes again, still careful, only less so. She is not hearing footsteps in her mind. She exits as the light fades to black.)*

Scene Five

(The holding cell. DARREN *and* ROB *in their own clothes. A toilet without a seat, light and shadow from a heavily screened window.* LARRY *stands downstage, smoking.)*

ROB: Well, this is different.

DARREN: Doing time is going to be.

ROB: Maybe, if we were in another country, we could send out for...for a woman.

DARREN: A couple of white Anglo-Saxon undergraduates might not know what to do with a white Anglo-Saxon woman.

ROB: Might not. *(Beat)* Too bad we don't smoke.

(They look at LARRY, *who does not respond.)*

DARREN: What'll we get: a year to eighteen months?

ROB: I think your father is going to get you out.

DARREN: Won't yours?

ROB: He hasn't got the money. Your father's lawyer's going to pin it on me. I'm a bad influence. I'm older than you. I've risen above my station. I'm stupid. Exhibit A: I break into houses. What did I hope to find: an old television set, a toaster worth twelve to eighteen?

DARREN: I wonder if...if we get out...it won't all happen again. I'll go back to a life of crime. The excitement of one break-in after another as the night grows young...

ROB: *(Moving downstage 'til he is parallel to* LARRY, *who continues facing downstage)* Yes. I advance silently to the window, my only baggage the tools of the trade. I listen. I look for the beam of a flashlight, dogs. I check for wires. I make sure I'm not overlooked, that no cars are passing in that playful night. No longer stupid enough to break in, I silently cut my ring of glass... *(Doing so)* I reach in...

DARREN: You know, Rob, there's something about breaking and entering that's like penetrating a virgin.

ROB: Oh? What's that?

DARREN: You wonder what's inside.

ROB: Do you? *(To* LARRY*)* What about you, friend? What are you in for? *(Beat)* Too terrible to tell?

LARRY: *(Speaking with difficulty)* Sometimes I p-play cards, s-sometimes I drink.

ROB: *(Looking him over)* Beer?

LARRY: How'd you guess?

ROB: Native intelligence: You can see how far that's got me. Why? For pleasure?

LARRY: I drink... *(With hesitancy)* ...because I lose.

ROB: Ah, you're a loser. You must be the guy who loses the girl too.

*(*LARRY *looks at him; he looks at* LARRY.*)*

ROB: What do you do when you're not drinking or losing?

LARRY: I s-survey for the city. I build roads.

ROB: *(Moving)* Hm. Now let me see if I've got it right. The night is young when you get off. You lose your money because something's missing in that surveyor's life, then you drink to forget your losses. You're stumbling in front of cars, sinking down against a building. Then you're in here being asked what you do, why you do it. Then you're at work, surveying the prospect, building roads. Then you're back losing your money, swilling hops, stumbling in front of cars; back sinking down against the building.

DARREN: Rob...

ROB: Stay out of this.

LARRY: *(To* ROB*)* I'd listen to my f-friend, if I were you.

ROB: *(To* LARRY*)* But I'm curious: What's it all about? What's going on in that working-class brain, what's going to happen to you? Someday...

LARRY: S-someday you and I will meet....

ROB: Yes! Over a hot crap game some cold night, or maybe you'll just stumble over me, this white Anglo-Saxon Protestant who just got tired of it all one day, was bored to death by his last break-in, lying there with his bag of tricks, his intelligence evident in the little ring of glass he holds, in front of a building he just couldn't get up the energy to enter. What will you do then?

LARRY: *(Confronting him, speaking more readily and with resolution)* I'll just lay you out, where you are, Rob, legs straight, arms at your sides. In the morning I'll build a road over you.

(DARREN *&* ROB *laugh appreciatively.*)

DARREN: Not bad for a working man. *(To* LARRY*)* Got your cards?

(LARRY *nods.*)

DARREN: Why not teach us a thing or two? How to win gracefully, for example. What have we got to lose?

LARRY: More than I have. *(He takes his cards out, does a midair shuffle.)* You s-sure?

(They nod. A door clangs in the distance.)

ROB: Get ready, Darren. It's your father's lawyer. Don't worry about me. I've got a new friend. When I get out I'll be ready for new experiences, like winning.

DARREN: Ready for that white Anglo-Saxon woman.

LARRY: *(To* DARREN, *pocketing his cards as footsteps approach)* Maybe your father's lawyer... *(With hesitation)* ...'ll get us all out.

DARREN: Maybe. Then you'll owe me one, won't you?

LARRY: I guess I will.

DARREN: What's your name?

LARRY: Larry.

DARREN: Larry...

(Light fades. In the half light the ART TEACHER *crosses. Free of the sense that she is being followed, she is no longer on her guard.)*

Scene Six

(Late night a few nights later. Between the buildings. A summer's night, a card game spread on the asphalt. LEWIS *enters right, looking for his brother,* LARRY. LEWIS *is almost formally, if colorlessly dressed. It's obvious he's not a businessman. His walk is stiff, his manner wary. A second later,* DREW *rolls on left, looking for his son. The sight of the game stops them. They circle it before they speak.)*

LEWIS: Been here long?

DREW: No longer than you.

LEWIS: You haven't seen a young fellow in jeans?

DREW: Just about a hundred and fifty of them. Who are you looking for?

LEWIS: My brother. I'm looking for my brother. What are you doing here? Are you a player?

DREW: Do I look like a player? I'm looking for my son. And, in general, keeping my eyes open.

(They move slowly in their original directions, DREW, *of course, in his chair;* LEWIS, *stiffly and warily.)*

DREW: What's your brother like? He's not...violent, is he?

LEWIS: Larry violent? It would certainly be a surprise to me. Your son?

DREW: Darren? That would be a surprise.

(They both look right, hearing, seeing RICK. *Enter* RICK *opposite* DREW *on his built-up shoe.)*

RICK: Drew.

DREW: Rick.

RICK: You haven't seen Rob, have you?

DREW: You haven't seen Darren?

*(*RICK *rolls his eyes.)*

DREW: You were right. That's what we get for getting them out. We could have visited them where they were, kept track of them, given them advice...

RICK: Who's this fellow?

DREW: I don't know. Just met him.

RICK: *(To* LEWIS*)* You. You a cardsharp, a low roller...a cop? Don't tell me. By day you sit in an office, third desk on the left, one hand full of pencils, the other of paper clips.

LEWIS: *(Stiffly smiling)* What makes you think that?

RICK: You're sallow, pallid, pasty, pale. You're dusty. Certain lights would show you covered with pencil shavings, your hands the shape of the forms you fill out, the blanks you fill in. You're either a cop or a....

DREW: Rick...

RICK: Stay out of this.

LEWIS: *(Stiffly laughing)* I do work for the state, but it's got nothing to do with police work, unless you consider...

RICK: By night you play, you seek the excitement of the alleys. You corrupt young men.

DREW: *(To* RICK*)* That's a bit much.

RICK: I told you to stay out of this.

DREW: You can tell me anything you like. That doesn't mean I'll do it.

LEWIS: *(To* RICK*)* I think you might have it wrong. I don't play. The name's Lewis. You're both looking for your sons, I take it. I'm looking for my brother, my younger brother.

RICK: Does he play?

LEWIS: I guess he does. He's no gambler. He's just a little lost now, seems to enjoy losing money.

RICK: Yours? His own?

LEWIS: *(He nods.)* That's the way it is. He earns it.

RICK: Then it's his business, isn't it?

LEWIS: I try to look out for him. You only get so many brothers.

RICK: You only get so many sons. I don't know what's wrong with mine. Oh, I mind. It's not the money. It's the waste, it's the danger.

DREW: I know what you mean.

LEWIS: I do too.

RICK: Well, it seems they were just here. Or somebody was. Look at the hot cards, the smoking pavement. Well, what'll we do? Stake out the place? I have to get to work.

DREW: *(Looking at his watch)* Why don't we just go our respective ways and leave them to work it out?

LEWIS: Because I'm worried.

RICK: I am too. There are pros in this game, but if they hurt my son, I'll kill them.

DREW: I know how you feel. But it's probably irrelevant.

RICK: Don't tell me I'm irrelevant.

DREW: No, I'll let you find that out for yourself. Listen. Since we didn't drown them when they were puppies, let's not push them now from a little breaking and entering to a little gambling to anything worse.

RICK: Like...?

(A second passes in which all look at each other.)

DREW: I don't even like to think about that. I'm going home. I've looked. There isn't anything more I can do. So long, Lewis. Nice meeting you.

LEWIS: So long, Drew.

DREW: *(Leaving, nodding)* Rick.

RICK: Drew.

(Exit DREW right)

RICK: *(Confronting LEWIS)* Well, where are they?

LEWIS: I don't know any more than you.

RICK: I think you do. I don't believe this brother business. *(Advancing with his hand in his pocket)* You tell me where my son is.

LEWIS: Rick... This makes no sense.

RICK: It does to me.

(As RICK withdraws an automatic from his pocket, LEWIS smoothly—and in stylized, perhaps prolonged motion—kicks it from his hand. The gun skids out of reach.)

LEWIS: Surprise. I guess I'm tougher than I look. Didn't even drop my paper clips. Or my pencils.

(RICK moves toward the gun.)

LEWIS: Don't make me hurt you.

(RICK has stopped.)

LEWIS: I don't want to hurt you.

RICK: Who do you want to hurt? Who have you hurt?

LEWIS: Maybe no one, ever, but you're right about some things. Except for my brother, I live alone, as, I guess, you do. I go to work in the morning. As you say, I wrestle with forms. I man the telephone. At night I don't gamble on the sidewalk. I put on my sweats, I practice kicking guns out of people's hands. I've never really done it till tonight.

RICK: You did it pretty well.

LEWIS: Yes, I surprised myself. *(Picking up the gun, pocketing it)* Come on. Your friend is really looking that way, he's not going home. We'll look this. They're around somewhere, maybe not together, but we might stumble on one or the other, Drew's son or your son or my brother, someone making a fool of himself.

RICK: What's your brother's name?

LEWIS: Larry. Your son's again?

RICK: Rob.

LEWIS: Rob and Larry and... And Drew's son?

RICK: Darren.

LEWIS: Rob and Larry and Darren...and the list goes on.

RICK: What list?

LEWIS: The list of those throwing it away. I guess we don't know youth is gone till it's gone.

(Moving left, though RICK doesn't move)

LEWIS: Not coming?

RICK: Not with you.

LEWIS: *(Leaving)* Suit yourself.

RICK: Lewis.

LEWIS: What?

RICK: Can I have my gun?

LEWIS: I think you're better off without it. We'll meet again. I'll return it then...without the bullets.

(Exit LEWIS. RICK stands a moment, suddenly, violently, kicks the game, perhaps in retarded motion, a kind of a dance on one bad leg, scattering the cards. He hurries off to work as the light fades.)

Scene Seven

(DREW's office. DREW, his forehead in his hand, the ART TEACHER facing him)

ART TEACHER: Drew.

DREW: Oh, hi, beautiful. I thought I was all alone.

ART TEACHER: Drew. It happened again.

DREW: And this time...?

ART TEACHER: No. Nothing. Not even tripped, just...restrained, just held by the wrists, talked to. I've been getting careless.

DREW: And then: He touches your hair, he cries?

ART TEACHER: No.

DREW: What happened this time?

ART TEACHER: Nothing. He was just in a good mood, that's all. Laughing, friendly, but holding my wrists...until he felt he didn't have to.

DREW: And then.

ART TEACHER: Then, when I could go, only I didn't and just stood there, then he said goodbye.

DREW: Did you get a good look at him?

ART TEACHER: He chooses a place where it's dark, where what light there is is always behind him.

DREW: What are you going to do about this? Next time...

ART TEACHER: *(Interrupting)* I think that was the end of it. I don't know, Drew. Don't push me.

DREW: *(Seizing her wrist)* Would I be more convincing if I restrained you...

(As she attempts to withdraw her hand.)

DREW: ...if I held you? *(Suddenly releasing her)* I'm sorry. I take that back.

ART TEACHER: *(Holding her wrist)* Men think they can take everything back, don't they? *(Their eyes lock, then she changes.)* Forget that. My turn to be sorry. Drew, I did do something. I stood there. I didn't run. As I said, I think it's over. If it isn't, I'll find a solution of my own. I'll think of something.

DREW: What?

ART TEACHER: *(After a moment, changing the subject)* How's your son? How's Darren? Is his foolishness behind him?

DREW: *(Raising his hands without an answer)* I...

(The light fades. In the half light, the ART TEACHER is again crossing in the night. Suddenly a blackened figure appears in front of her, she turns, attempts to run, finds herself facing another blackened figure, turns and is knocked down from behind. One figure holds her wrists as she lies face down and the other approaches from behind, draws her skirt up her legs. Suddenly car lights play across the scene, the dark figures have second thoughts as a car is heard stopping and a horn—loud, close—is held down. The figures run, the car door is heard opening, followed by other mechanical sounds. The ART TEACHER sits up, a moment later DREW barely rolls on, barely visible in the shadows. She stands, aware of him, one hand to her

face as they look at each other from a distance. She discovers blood on her hand, and her voice at first is broken.)

ART TEACHER: You said you wouldn't....

DREW: I didn't. I wasn't. I happened to be here. It was chance.

ART TEACHER: *(Her self-possession returning)* Well. Thank you, chance. *(As she turns to go)*

DREW: What now?

(Since she neither turns nor answers, more gently)

DREW: What are you thinking?

ART TEACHER: *(Not turning back)* I'm thinking, in a good mystery, the hunted becomes the hunter. Or the huntress.

DREW: Don't be absurd. Leave it to...

ART TEACHER: *(Facing him)* I'm not leaving anything to anyone, Drew. I can handle this.

DREW: But what...?

ART TEACHER: You'll see. *(Leaving)* Then maybe again, you won't.

(Exit the ART TEACHER. DREW *makes a sudden, violent gesture with the blanket that usually covers his knees. The light fades to black.)*

Scene Eight

(A suggestion of a downtown bar: the bar, the playing lights of an offstage jukebox. LEWIS, *the bartender, shirtsleeves, polishes glasses. Enter* LARRY, *sits at the bar without recognizing* LEWIS. *Beat)*

LEWIS: What'll it be, fella: Hamm's?

*(*LARRY *just looks at the bar.)*

LEWIS: Couple minutes our gal'll be along.

*(*LARRY *as before)*

LEWIS: Gotta drink something, you don't get anything for nothing. Not in this life. Hamm's?

LARRY: Hamm's.

*(*LEWIS *sets the bottle on the bar, drums his fingers till the money is shoved across.* LARRY, *watching the money go, recognizes* LEWIS.*)*

LARRY: Well, well. My brother Lewis. I didn't know you were a bartender.

LEWIS: *(Coolly polishing)* I get around.

LARRY: *(Coolly)* What do you do: run ahead of me, slip down the alley, duck behind the bar, hang up your coat, pick up a glass, get to polishing just in time to say "What'll it be, fella, Hamm's?"

LEWIS: That's about it.

LARRY: You still have to hang onto that day job.

LEWIS: I do.

LARRY: Is it worth it: setting 'em up for who knows who before I come along, making up drinks so you can find your kid brother, get him home?

LEWIS: It's worth it.

LARRY: *(Turning on his stool, his back to the bar)* What if some fella asks for... a sidecar? You grab a likely glass, pour from a couple of likely bottles, set it down...and then what: wait for him to throw it in your face?

LEWIS: They drink what I set before them.

LARRY: *(Shrugging, turning back to the bar)* Why not? *(Raising his Hamm's)* I'm easy, I guess.

LEWIS: You're no problem. In that regard.

LARRY: *(His Hamm's still in the air)* My last.

LEWIS: Good. Lose it all?

LARRY: Don't I always? Seems like every day's the same. The sun comes up, I work; the sun goes down, I find the game; I lose, I have my beer or two or three; you find me—or the police do.

LEWIS: That's about it.

LARRY: How long can you keep it up?

LEWIS: As long as you, brother, longer.

LARRY: What: Did somebody promise somebody he'd never lose sight of me?

LEWIS: *(Indicating himself)* Somebody wouldn't lose sight of you, even if he hadn't promised somebody.

LARRY: Somebody's dead.

LEWIS: May she rest in peace.

LARRY: Amen. Yes, I'll be quiet about it, I won't disturb her anymore than I have to. Well, here I am, brother, take a good look, this is me: my youth, my health, my....

(The ART TEACHER, *her face bruised, blood spots in her eyes, comes strutting out along the bar as* BRANDY, *in black tights, scanty sequins, spikes. She exhibits a sensuality we wouldn't have known was there in her original incarnation. Cat's-eye dark glasses with rhinestones cover her eyes at first. She wears a short platinum wig.)*

LARRY: Say, what's this?

LEWIS: Our gal. Told you she'd be along. Name's Brandy. *(Introducing them)* Larry, Brandy. Brandy, my brother Larry.

(LARRY *half rises*, BRANDY *glances at him, removing her glasses. This is the point at which her bruised face is revealed.*)

LARRY: What happened to her?

LEWIS: Fell off the bar one night, I hear, listening to the customers. Doesn't do it anymore. I didn't work here then.

(BRANDY, *smiling at both, winking, replacing her glasses, dances her way to the heavy curtain at the end of the bar, does a subtle and sentient bump and grind with it, dances back past* LARRY, *who calls softly to her, his voice soft, her name nearly garbled.*)

LARRY: ...Bra-a-ndy...?

(BRANDY, *stopped by something in his voice, dancing more slowly as the music fades to silence, raises her fingers to her chest interrogatively as* LARRY, *nodding, speaking shyly, is hardly able to look at her.*)

LARRY: ...yes...you...a g-girl like you...what are you doing here...d-dancing for strangers...tell me... *(Again nearly garbling her name)* ...Bra-a-ndy...

(BRANDY *still moving slowly, rhythmically, in the silence, innocent hands raised, indicates she doesn't know why she's here.* LARRY *looks at* LEWIS. BRANDY *dances to the far end of the bar. Suddenly she hears the sound of her own shoes at night moving in time with her footsteps and at times independently of them as she begins to walk as she did that night, so that she holds her ears, staggers or clings to the curtain as the sound of the footsteps fade.*)

LEWIS: *(Calling to her)* You okay?

(BRANDY *nods, returns to her slinking rhythmic bartop walk.*)

LEWIS: Sorry, old man. Brandy just showed up one day they say, looking for work. Didn't seem like this was her kind of work, but as you see, she's okay. Now she dances...and watches the clientele, don't know why, that is, when she's not bumping and grinding the curtain. Brandy doesn't talk now, not to anyone, though sometimes she listens, head cocked, as if she were listening to something inside at the same time.

LARRY: She wouldn't listen to me.

LEWIS: Why not?

LARRY: You know, brother. I can't make anything clear, even to myself. If I could talk...

LEWIS: *(Shrugging)* Try her. What have you got to lose?

LARRY: *(Turning out an empty pocket)* True.

(*Half rising as* BRANDY *dances closer, talking somewhat better than before*)

LARRY: Brandy...if that's your real name, I want to ask you something, but I don't know what it is. Tell me: Do I want to wait for you in the alley, to follow you home... *(With hesitation)* ...like a dog. Tell me: What do I want?

(BRANDY, *smiling, raises open hands without an answer, begins to dance slowly off along the bar.*)

LARRY: *(Very softly)* Tell me. *(No answer)* Please. Then I'll talk, Brandy. You can listen.

BRANDY: *(Over her shoulder)* Maybe you want to stop losing, Larry. Maybe you want to win something—or someone—for a change.

LARRY: *(Half rising)* How did you know? How did you know that?

(BRANDY *raises her open hands without an answer, exits, still dancing.*)

LEWIS: That's funny, she never spoke before. I didn't know she could. And a whole sentence, or two. You must have made an impression.

LARRY: *(Sitting back)* Lewis. She heard me. She saw me. Nobody sees me. You haven't been telling her about me?

LEWIS: You know I wouldn't, kid.

LARRY: Then how...? Listen. You know her. You know me. What do I do now?

LEWIS: *(Shrugging)* Send roses to the stage door.

LARRY: Seriously. *(Looking down the bar)* Lewis, it's just you and me. Do I go back there? Will she come out in a minute, sit on my lap, put her tongue in my ear? Will we hold hands and talk? Will she want a taxi?

LEWIS: You want me to ask her?

LARRY: Yes.

LEWIS: *(Starting off, stopping)* Ask her what?

LARRY: All of the above. Just ask. Let her know. You know what I....

LEWIS: You'll watch the bar?

LARRY: Sure.

(*Exit* LEWIS. LARRY, *searching his other pockets, comes up with nothing, shakes his head at himself.*)

LARRY: L-loser, loser. *(Her words, heard again, without mockery)* "M-maybe you want to stop losing, Larry. M-maybe you want to win something or someone for a change."

(LARRY *disposes of his Hamm's, heads around behind the bar, picks up a glass, polishes. Enter* DARREN *and* ROB.)

LARRY: What'll it be, fellas, Hamm's?

DARREN: What? Do we look like we swing a pick all day?

ROB: Like we stick a shovel in the ground, ride an air hammer, eat dust. My turn. What'll it be, Darren?

DARREN: Imagine the wine in this hole. Maybe I will have a beer. What the hell. So what if I have to pee. There are worse fates.

LARRY: *(Quietly)* Yes, there are.

ROB: What? What? Did you say something? That's all we need is a smart-ass bartender. Say, look at this fella. Doesn't he look familiar?

DARREN: Sure does. Larry? Is that you? I thought you built roads. How'd you get out? Did my father...?

LARRY: They just kept me overnight. I haven't been in m-much trouble.

ROB: That doesn't mean you can't get in it.

LARRY: *(Facing* ROB*)* Some trouble might be worth getting in.

DARREN: *(Defusing it, in a thick Russian accent to* ROB*)* "Boys, boys do not mock those who work, for whom each day is toil..." *(Sitting. To* LARRY*)* So you're a bartender now?

LARRY: *(Returning to his glasses)* Just s-standing in for my brother.

ROB: Say, are there any White Anglo-Saxon women round here? You know what I mean.

LARRY: I know what you mean. N-no, nobody like that here.

DARREN: *(Suddenly standing)* No? No? Look at this. What do you think of this, Rob?

ROB: By God, you're right, Darren. Heel marks, heel marks on the bar. You haven't got a bar dancer here, have you?

LARRY: Nah. This is her night off.

DARREN: I'll bet it is.

ROB: We want to give her a night on. Don't we, Darren?

DARREN: That's about it. But where are our beers?

ROB: And, say, Larry, you got your cards? You were going to show me the way to certain riches.

LARRY: I don't play here. Can't get my brother in... *(With hesitation)* ...in Dutch. *(Taking out a slip of paper, scratching an address on it)* But here's a place I play, it's a kind of a ruin, but once you're inside they've got everything you want.

ROB: Everything?

LARRY: Everything.

DARREN: Is that a guarantee?

LARRY: Yes.

ROB: *(Standing)* If it isn't...

LARRY: It's p-perfectly safe there.

ROB: *(Facing* LARRY*)* P-perfectly safe.

DARREN: *(Taking* ROB's *elbow, steering him away from confrontation)* What do you say, Rob: Do we give him five bucks?

ROB: Sure. What the hell. *(To* LARRY*)* You want five bucks?

LARRY: S-sure.

ROB: *(Handing it over, leaving)* This had better not be....

DARREN: *(Leaving)* ...a snipe hunt, a merry chase, a labor of Sisyphus.

ROB: 'Cause if it is...

DARREN: ...we'll be back, is what my friend Rob wants to say, for another Hamm's, that first one was so good. Isn't that it, Rob?

(ROB *nods.* LARRY *nods. Exit* ROB *and* DARREN. *Enter* LEWIS. LARRY *walks out from behind the bar, straightening himself up for* BRANDY.)

LARRY: Lewis, you can't lend me a little till Friday? I've got a fiver, but she... What? What is it?

LEWIS: Sorry, fella, she's gone.

LARRY: Gone! But where?

LEWIS: Just... *(Raising his hands somewhat as* BRANDY *did)* ...gone.

(LEWIS *returns to his polishing,* LARRY *sits.*)

LARRY: Gone.

LEWIS: *(Handing another bottle across the bar)* This one's on me. If it's any consolation, kid, she said a few words before she left.

LARRY: What'd she say?

LEWIS: She wanted to know who you are, what sort of work you did.

LARRY: And you told her?

LEWIS: I told her you worked for the city, built roads, that you were working up on Summit Avenue now.

LARRY: That's good. That's something. Unless she thinks what a dumb guy, working on the road, what a loser....

LEWIS: Oh, I don't think she was thinking that.

LARRY: Oh? Why?

LEWIS: I asked her why she spoke to you when she usually hasn't got a word for a customer, if there was something special about you....

LARRY: *(Shaking his head)* Something special about me.

LEWIS: She said sure there is...

LARRY: Oh?

LEWIS: Yeah, and I said what.... *(Drawing it out)* ...and she said....

LARRY: Come on, Lewis, what'd she say?

LEWIS: Not much. Sorry for building it up. She just said his voice, something about his voice, meaning your voice...

LARRY: My voice...?

LEWIS: Yeah. About the way you speak.

LARRY: The way I... *(Urging him)* And...? And then?

LEWIS: And then we just looked at each other.

(Light fades.)

Scene Nine

(Nighttime alley: a world of garish neon spills, offstage sirens, etc. DARREN *and* ROB *on their way.* BRANDY's *theme is heard buzzing from her Walkman as she appears in the shadows in wig and cat's-eye glasses;* ROB *and* DARREN *do not recognize the* ART TEACHER.*)*

BRANDY: Hey, fellas.

ROB: Hey, look at this. *(Approaching)* How you doin', sweetie?

BRANDY: I'm fine, big fella.

ROB: Big...? I always thought I was a little guy.

BRANDY: You're big enough for me.

ROB: Yeah? What about my friend Darren? Are you big enough for him?

BRANDY: *(A beat as she looks at* DARREN*)* Sure. I'm big enough for the whole world. You looking for a place?

DARREN: Yeah. The bartender told us....

BRANDY: What'd he tell you?

DARREN: *(Showing her the address)* He said....

BRANDY: Yeah, that's the place, but that's not here. It's by the river. It's just a ruin. You know the way?

ROB: It must be this way.

DARREN: Must be. *(To* BRANDY*)* Is it?

BRANDY: Sure. This way, that way. That's where the game is. I play too. Trouble is I always lose.

ROB: What happens when you lose?

BRANDY: I take it off.

ROB: You...? *(To* DARREN*)* Say, that sounds pretty good, doesn't it?

DARREN: Just about right.

BRANDY: You wanna know the way?

DARREN: Sure we do. You going to show us?

BRANDY: Maybe.

ROB: Why only maybe?

BRANDY: You have to do something for me first.

DARREN: What's that?

BRANDY: Hold me.

ROB: *(Reaching for her)* Sure, I can do that.

BRANDY: *(Stepping back)* Wait. Just the wrists.

(She holds her wrists out to DARREN.*)*

BRANDY: Go on.

(When DARREN *hesitates, she turns to* ROB.*)*

BRANDY: What about you?

*(*ROB *hesitates, takes her wrists.)*

BRANDY: Harder. *(She shakes her head, turns back to* DARREN, *holding her wrists out.)* Well?

DARREN: No thank you.

BRANDY: "No thank you." And I know why. You guys are weak, aren't you, both of you? What do you do: go to school? You know what work is?

DARREN: Maybe not. I've often thought...

ROB: *(To* BRANDY, *reaching)* Give me another chance. I've worked.

BRANDY: *(Moving off)* You had your chance.

DARREN: Wait. You going to show us the way...?

BRANDY: *(With gentle sarcasm)* If you're looking for the public library, go to the end of the alley and turn left.

(Exit BRANDY *left.* DARREN *and* ROB *stand looking after her.)*

DARREN: Goddamn.

ROB: Goddamn.

DARREN: What do you think, friend Rob: Are we not as tough as we think?

ROB: I wouldn't want to think that, friend Darren. You didn't want to crush her hands in those big paws, did you?

DARREN: How'd you guess?

ROB: I wouldn't mind hurting her, just a little. *(Starting right)* Come on, let's find that hole.

DARREN: *(Looking left)* She wasn't much help, was she?

ROB: Not much.

DARREN: *(Still looking after BRANDY)* I think she's got something on her mind.

ROB: *(Leaving right)* Yeah? So have I, friend, so have I.

(Exit ROB. After a second's hesitation, DARREN follows him as the light fades.)

Scene Ten

(The next day, one of those sylvan scenes: lovely warm daylight, summer trees overhang the road. LARRY surveys. Enter BRANDY, not in her dancing outfit, not wigged, but still in character, dressed more like an off-duty dancer in tight pants, tight blouse, with two heavy, stuffed suitcases.)

BRANDY: So here you are, this is what you do.

LARRY: *(Pleasantly surprised)* Well! Yes, this is what I do. Hello.

BRANDY: Hello.

LARRY: Is your name really Brandy?

BRANDY: Let's assume Brandy is assumed.

(Beat)

LARRY: What's your real name?

(Beat)

BRANDY: Brandy will have to do. You're talking better today.

LARRY: I talk better outside.

BRANDY: Oh?

LARRY: *(Looking in his scope)* You know, we build these roads with only a quarter-inch variation in a quarter mile. How many things are done like that?

BRANDY: Not many.

LARRY: *(Standing aside)* Have a look in here.

(As she does so)

LARRY: Do you see the bend in Summit Avenue, the old mansions, the University Club, the landscape falling away, the trees, the river?

BRANDY: *(Shuddering)* I see a bridge.

LARRY: A bridge?

BRANDY: A bridge I don't like, a kind of foot bridge.

LARRY: Like it or not, there's no bridge that way. Look again.

BRANDY: *(Looking)* Oh, oh. That's a young man I know, parked in his clunker. He's not alone. Oh, no. It's not Anna Whatshername, our only surviving Marxist!

LARRY: Our what?

BRANDY: She seems to be holding him against her chest. He... *(No longer looking)* Oh, I don't think I want to watch that.

LARRY: You're seeing things. Look again.

BRANDY: No.

LARRY: Look.

BRANDY: *(Looking)* I see...a night scene, a woman walking, going home from work. Wait. There's a man. He's...going the same way. *(Looking at LARRY)* Ever think of that, Larry, following someone from shadow to shadow until you can tell she's listening with the back of her neck?

LARRY: *(After almost looking in the scope himself)* You're making things up.

BRANDY: Am I?

LARRY: Yes. You've got i-imagination. I like a woman with imagination.

BRANDY: You do? Do you like me?

LARRY: Yes. *(Beat)* Where are you going with your suitcases, Brandy?

BRANDY: I don't know. Down the street.

LARRY: Maybe you'd like to learn how the other half lives.

BRANDY: Maybe. You build roads. You build one I could travel?

(LARRY shrugs.)

BRANDY: You build roads all by yourself, you haven't got a friend that helps you?

LARRY: Well, I have a little help, but at this stage, there aren't too many of us, though if you look down that way you'll see a fellow holding a stick.

BRANDY: I'm not going to look in that thing again. What I meant was, what do you do when you're not building roads? Did you ever think a woman might come walking into your life with two suitcases?

LARRY: No. You haven't quit dancing, have you?

BRANDY: No, but aren't you going to ask me: What have you got in those two suitcases, Brandy?

LARRY: No.

BRANDY: *(Raising one)* Well, there's my parrot, my goldfish—that's the plural: goldfishes, unless one has eaten the other by now.

LARRY: *(Half smiling)* Are you crazy?

BRANDY: What do you think? *(Continuing)* There's my phonograph, my sweaters, my underwear—oh, and a little sachet to make them all smell sweet.

LARRY: It seems you're ready for anything.

BRANDY: It does, doesn't it? *(Holding out her wrists)* Hold.

LARRY: Hold?

BRANDY: Hold my wrists. *(He does so.)* Ow!

LARRY: I'm sorry. I guess I don't know my own strength.

BRANDY: I guess not. Well: Are you going to take me with you?

LARRY: Where?

BRANDY: Home. To meet your mother.

LARRY: My mother's dead. I live with my brother. He works for the state when he's not tending bar, he's in an office all day. I work for the city. I'm out all day. At night I'm out too. I find card games on the sidewalk. I lose everything I made during the day. Then I drink. I don't eat regularly. I haven't got a girl. I wish I could settle down. I wish I had a home to come home to, but I haven't.

BRANDY: Oh, I didn't tell you. *(Raising the other suitcase)* I've got sheets and blankets and pillows and an ironing board and dishes and knives and forks and spoons and toilet paper and paper towels and orange juice and bacon and eggs.

LARRY: *(Laughing this time)* You are crazy, aren't you?

BRANDY: *(Also laughing)* Only half. I hope my character isn't too one-dimensional for you.

LARRY: *(Puzzled)* No...

BRANDY: You see: I'm my own creation. I think everybody ought to be, don't you?

LARRY: I suppose.

BRANDY: Do you like a good breakfast, Larry?

LARRY: I love a good breakfast.

BRANDY: Okay, then. Let's go.

LARRY: Wait. I've been down this road before. Isn't there someone else? Tell me.

(BRANDY *hangs her head.*)

LARRY: Well?

BRANDY: Well, there may be someone, a man younger than I am. What do you think of that? Is that all right?

LARRY: I guess so.

BRANDY: He doesn't even know my name, but I know a thing or two about him. He's just finished college. His father teaches advertising. He's always had everything. But what he wants is to go a little this way, a little that, to see what it would be like if this happened or that. He's dabbling. You understand?

LARRY: I guess so.

BRANDY: You don't have that luxury, do you?

LARRY: No.

BRANDY: Lately, with his friend, he's gotten into trouble.

LARRY: What kind of trouble?

BRANDY: Ridiculous trouble. Breaking into houses. Getting caught. Spending the night in jail and...

LARRY: I see. And what if this younger man comes to you?

BRANDY: Unlikely, but... I'll have to be honest with you, Larry. That young man has only to knock on the door and I'll go with him. I'll walk right off with a dripping dish in one hand and a wet dishtowel in the other. I won't come back. Unless he decides he'd rather park his clunker for a history lesson with Anna Whoozawhatsamova.

(*Beat*)

LARRY: That seems a very sad story, Brandy, sad for the man who shares those dishes, sad for you.

BRANDY: There are sadder. But yes, I suppose it is. Even if years had passed, Larry, if we'd had children and they were there in the kitchen behind me, throwing food at each other, I'd leave with my young man. At least I think I would. In my imagination I would. But nothing like that will ever... He hardly knows me to see me. We nod at each other. Well, there, I've told you. Do you still want me?

LARRY: Yes.

BRANDY: Okay, then.

(LARRY *takes one of her suitcases, and they start off. Seeing what trouble she's having, he takes the second bag, which is also weightless to him.*)

BRANDY: Thank you. But, what about your magic scope?

LARRY: Oh, my partner'll keep an eye on it. Nothing to worry about. This way, Brandy.

BRANDY: Of course. This way, my working man. This way to the bacon and eggs, this way to the hot, buttered toast... *(Stopping)* But wait. What about your brother, what about Lewis? Won't he...?

LARRY: Lewis won't mind.

BRANDY: Still, I'd feel better. You'd better call from a pay phone.

LARRY: *(As they go)* I will, Brandy. I'll do just that. I'll call him at his office.

(Exit BRANDY & LARRY.)

Scene Eleven

(LEWIS & LARRY's. LEWIS still in his bureaucrat's black suit, enters left crosses, exits right. Beat. Enter BRANDY left, she stands still, taking the place in. Enter LARRY behind her, her two suitcases in hand. She faces him, he looks at her hopefully.)

BRANDY: I can't live here.

LARRY: *(Still holding her suitcases)* W-why not?

BRANDY: *(Taking another look)* It's...dingy. *(Breathing the air)* Dusty. I can't breathe.

LARRY: B-Brandy, two men living together... *(Trying another tack)* It's my brother's dust. It'll go away.

BRANDY: *(Shrugging)* When he does? I'm sorry. I didn't think it'd be like this, I think I'm leaving.

LARRY: *(Still with those suitcases)* But w-where will you go? What'll you do?

BRANDY: I don't know. Dance.

LARRY: You weren't meant for that.

BRANDY: Maybe I'll paint pictures.

LARRY: Are there...are there jobs for p-people who p-paint pictures?

BRANDY: I don't know. I'll have to look.

LARRY: So you're... *(With hesitation)* ...dabbling too?

BRANDY: Let's just say I'm looking for something. Or someone.

LARRY: Well, 'til you find it, you can stay here. The dust won't bother you, you'll be out all day. *(Smiling)* Looking for work.

BRANDY: *(Hanging her head)* I'm sorry, Larry. I was raised to shiny things, to things that sparkle.

LARRY: But you l-left that.

BRANDY: True. It wasn't the life I wanted. Oh...I had to go slumming for a while, I had to see how the other half lived. Still... *(Looking up)* ...even the ceiling sparkled...

LARRY: I can do that. *(Putting down the suitcases)* I can spackle, plaster, paint. I can make the ceiling sparkle.

BRANDY: I need light.

LARRY: I'll give you light. What kind of light? Daylight? Here, I'll knock out this wall, I'll put in a window, floor to ceiling. I can do it.

BRANDY: I'm sure you can. But when? Don't you have to work?

LARRY: Of course I work. Everybody has to work. I'll do it at night. Instead of laying out the cards, I'll be here, knocking down the walls, putting in the windows.

BRANDY: What about the landlord? I'm sorry, Larry, I don't mean to be difficult. You don't own the place, do you?

LARRY: Of course not. The landlord? He'll own the improvements. What'll he care? "Four rooms, light and b-b-bright."

(Beat)

BRANDY: *(Hanging her head again)* I'm sorry, Larry.

(They face each other. LARRY picks up the bags. They move left, stop, sniffing the air. Enter LEWIS right, an apron over his black suit. They face him.)

LARRY: Brandy, you know my brother Lewis.

LEWIS: Larry, thank you for your call. Brandy, welcome. Wait, before I forget... *(Smiling)* ...Greek olives, stuffed celery...and then: chicken cacciatore, whipped potatoes, string beans with almonds, a bottle of Chianti—maybe that's wrong, the wrong wine I mean—a little cheese, French vanilla ice cream, black coffee... I just didn't have time to get the menu printed.

(BRANDY covers her eyes with one hand, suppresses her laugh.)

LEWIS: What did I say?

LARRY: Nothing. Go back in the kitchen. Can't you do something about this dust?

LEWIS: What dust?

LARRY: The dust in the air, damn it. Don't you ever take that Goddamn suit off? It's on that, it must be on that.

LEWIS: *(Looking at his sleeves)* What...?

LARRY: The dust, Lewis, the Goddamn dust!

(Suddenly BRANDY *crosses to place her head against* LEWIS's *chest. Half holding her,* LEWIS *looks helplessly at* LARRY. BRANDY *mumbles what* LEWIS *bends to hear.)*

LARRY: *(Helpless, still holding the suitcases)* What did she say?

LEWIS: She said she'll stay.

LARRY: She'll stay?

*(*LEWIS *and* LARRY *look at each other as the light fades. In the darkness* LARRY *appears downstage, fumbling with his cigarette, then* BRANDY, *a sheet wrapped about her. He steps closer, drawing compulsively on his cigarette, staring at the outline of her body.)*

BRANDY: Be careful.

LARRY: Of c-course I'll be careful.

BRANDY: *(Laughing)* Oh, I don't mean that. I mean: You're very excited, aren't you?

LARRY: Y-yes.

BRANDY: I mean be careful. I don't want to break your heart, Larry.

LARRY: G-go ahead. Break it.

BRANDY: You don't mean that.

LARRY: I do.

BRANDY: Okay. *(Half lowering the sheet)* You'll remember it was your idea.

LARRY: *(Lowering his cigarette, advancing as the light fades to black)* I'll r-remember.

Scene Twelve

(Later the same night. Moonlight. A sound only she can hear. BRANDY *raises her head, listens, sits up drawing the sheet about her. Now the sound of a window rising left causes her to sit still. A moment later* DARREN *enters, a bag in hand. They speak very softly. At first she gasps, he jumps and faces her. Recognizing him, she laughs.)*

BRANDY: What's this? Still dabbling?

DARREN: No more than you.

BRANDY: Are you trying to make me die laughing? *(When he doesn't answer)* Darren.

DARREN: So, Ms Art Teacher, you know my name? You're wondering how this happened, aren't you, what I'm doing here? Chance. Pure chance. I'm just breaking into the houses on this block tonight.

(He laughs, she almost does.)

DARREN: No, the truth is I've been watching you, all year, passing in the distance, going around the corner. I've felt...I felt...you...you were watching me too. Was I right?

(BRANDY *looks away.*)

DARREN: Recently I met someone reminded me of you; she gave me directions to the library. What's your name anyway?

BRANDY: B-brandy.

DARREN: B-brandy?

BRANDY: This is ridiculous. How did you find me?

DARREN: I'm not going to bother you with that.

BRANDY: Bother me. I don't like mysteries.

DARREN: Well...

BRANDY: Yes.

DARREN: I was sitting in my car, my clunker.

BRANDY: Uh-huh.

DARREN: I looked up.

BRANDY: From what?

DARREN: I don't know. I had my head down anyway. I looked up.

BRANDY: Go on.

DARREN: I saw you, your two suitcases, some fellow, some surveyor, carrying them.

BRANDY: Why didn't you offer us a ride?

DARREN: There was something I had to do first.

BRANDY: I see.

DARREN: When I'd done that, I came back, I drove down the block. Some other fellow was loading the equipment. I asked him where his buddy was.

BRANDY: And his buddy gave you this address?

(Beat)

DARREN: I gave him a couple of dollars.

(Beat)

BRANDY: Go away, Darren.

DARREN: Not without you.

BRANDY: You have no right. We've never even spoken. I...I'll call my new friends and have your neck broken.

DARREN: No, you won't. You're having too much fun.

BRANDY: *(Standing with the sheet wrapped about her)* I'll have you built into a road, I'll...

(DARREN, looking her over, holds his arms open. Beat)

BRANDY: What about my things?

DARREN: *(His arms still open)* We'll come back for them later.

(She steps into his arms. He kisses her deeply, slipping the sheet half down her.)

BRANDY: Darren, no...

DARREN: I want to know.

BRANDY: Know what?

DARREN: Whatever it is I'll know when I'm inside you. I'm so young, Brandy.

BRANDY: *(Half laughing)* Don't I know it? You won't know anything, you'll be in the dark. Darren...

DARREN: I'm in the dark now.

BRANDY: *(As he walks her back toward the couch)* Darren, this isn't going to last, not if you start it like... I...I like you. Wait, wait.

DARREN: I can't wait. *(Lowering her onto the couch)*

(The light fades to black.)

Scene Thirteen

(LEWIS & LARRY's. The next morning. Light rises on BRANDY asleep on the couch, her clothes on a chair. LARRY, dressed for work, stands left, puzzling. BRANDY awakes with a start, looks around her, sees LARRY almost with fear.)

LARRY: It's all right. It's me. I have to go to work. *(Beat)* The d-door was open. Did you open the door?

BRANDY: ...No...

LARRY: *(More lightly)* Do you walk in your sleep?

BRANDY: ...No...

LARRY: That's good. I wouldn't want you to walk out of my life as suddenly as you walked into it. You won't d-disappear, will you?

(BRANDY shakes her head.)

LARRY: You'll be here when I get back?

(BRANDY nods, LARRY turns to go.)

BRANDY: Larry? *(He stops.)* Do you have to go right now?

LARRY: If I want breakfast I do. It's the ninety-nine–cent special gets me through the day.

BRANDY: I'll make breakfast for you.

LARRY: You will?

BRANDY: You haven't forgotten: I have bacon and eggs in my suitcase, hot buttered toast...?

LARRY: *(Smiling)* I haven't forgotten.

BRANDY: Does Lewis like bacon and...?

LARRY: He'll eat anything on the way to work.

BRANDY: *(Drawing the sheet about her)* Turn your back.

LARRY: Why?

BRANDY: Turn your back.

(He does so, she rises.)

BRANDY: How much time have you got?

LARRY: I can be late.

BRANDY: *(Securing the sheet about her)* Do you work for the city or does the city work for you?

LARRY: The-the...

BRANDY: Stop talking like that. Your heart isn't already broken, is it?

LARRY: N-no. Not yet.

BRANDY: I don't like men with broken hearts. They belong to the mothers who broke them.

LARRY: Can I turn?

BRANDY: Okay.

(He turns. They look at each other.)

BRANDY: I'm going to the kitchen. You smoke your cigarette. I'll be fast.

LARRY: *(Watching her walk)* You're so... *(With hesitation)* ...beautiful.

(BRANDY *looks back, exits smiling.* LARRY *lights a cigarette. Enter* LEWIS *in his black suit. He nearly sleepwalks out the door.)*

LARRY: Wait a minute, big brother. She's making breakfast.

LEWIS: *(Pausing)* I don't usually...

LARRY: I know. But it's bacon and eggs. She asked if you like bacon and eggs.

LEWIS: I don't know what I eat in the morning.

LARRY: That's what I told her.

LEWIS: Let me out, Larry. She's your girl.

LARRY: She's ours. She only stayed when she saw you in your apron.

LEWIS: Open the door, brother.

(LARRY, *resigned, opens the door to sunlight and to* DARREN.)

LARRY: You.

DARREN: You. You're the surveyor. And the bartender.

LEWIS: Bartender? I thought I...

DARREN: *(To* LARRY*)* I'm still wondering why they let you out.

LARRY: *(Shrugging)* They could always send me back if I did something stupid.

DARREN: But something tells me you won't. Is...uh...is Brandy ready?

LARRY: Ready for what?

DARREN: To go. I...

LARRY: Brandy's making breakfast.

DARREN: Making breakfast?

LARRY: That's what I said, but suddenly I'm not very hungry.

(Enter BRANDY *still in the sheet, a frying pan in her hand.)*

BRANDY: Larry, do you like...?

(All look at each other.)

LEWIS: This is too much for me. I'm not even awake.

BRANDY: Larry, Lewis...this is Darren.

LARRY: We've met. *(To* LEWIS*)* This fella thinks Brandy's his girlfriend.

LEWIS: I thought she was ours.

DARREN: Ours? What's going on here? Brandy, I was getting the clunker, I parked about a mile away. I got lost. Larry, I don't know what Brandy told you about me but... *(Suddenly laughing)* ...but it's all true. I'm a rat. Or an idiot. Or overfond, shall we say, obsessed. Yes, that's it. Obsessed. I'm obsessed with my art teacher.

LARRY: *(With hesitation)* ...art teacher?

DARREN: Yes. I don't think I know who I am or what I'm doing. *(To* LARRY*)* Do you?

LARRY: What do you mean?

LEWIS: He means, I suppose, one man's as lost as another, we don't know where we're going, what we're doing...

BRANDY: I know I'm making breakfast. I know Larry and Lewis have to go to work. Darren's a man of leisure, but maybe he'll join us.

DARREN: *(To* BRANDY*)* This is a dream. I didn't think you'd ever make breakfast for me.

BRANDY: This is the first and very possibly the last time.

LARRY: Well, that's good news. Maybe I'll...

BRANDY: Maybe you'll skip the ninety-nine–cent special after all. How do you like your eggs, Larry? Over easy?

LARRY: Over easy.

BRANDY: Lewis?

LEWIS: Over easy.

BRANDY: Darren?

DARREN: Sunny side up please, not more than a couple of minutes. Whole wheat toast, hold the butter. That is if you haven't got a Danish.

(Exit BRANDY *as* LEWIS *and* LARRY *look at* DARREN. LARRY *offers him a cigarette, which* DARREN *refuses as the light fades.)*

Scene Fourteen

(That night. Light rises on BRANDY. *She's stuffing one of her suitcases, obviously intent on leaving, wearing her Walkman, and moving rhythmically to her dance music, the buzz of which is audible.* LEWIS, *home from work in his dusty suit, carrying his briefcase, enters behind her, unheard. He watches her a moment. On the one hand, she's dancing; on the other, she's leaving. He steps up behind her, places his fingertips almost reverently between her shoulders. In a rapid and totally unsuccessful response to her surprise,* BRANDY *attempts to elbow him in the stomach and hit him in the face. Both motions are parried easily, reflexively, by* LEWIS *who, dropping his briefcase, has left her on her back, legs apart, looking up at him.* LEWIS *blinks, looks away.)*

LEWIS: I'm sorry. That was instinctive. I didn't mean to...

BRANDY: No. *(Having landed heavily, rolling onto her side, shaking her head)* It was my fault. For a moment I thought...

(Beat)

LEWIS: *(Still not looking at her, his head almost bowed)* You thought...?

BRANDY: *(Gathering herself)* Never mind. *(Standing)* Nothing. Funny how the body remembers, even when you begin to forget. *(Tearing off her Walkman)* I hate these things. *(She dashes it to the floor.)*

LEWIS: *(Turning to face her)* You shouldn't do that.

BRANDY: *(Crushing it with her heel)* Why shouldn't I?

LEWIS: It's a thing, harmless.

BRANDY: It made me vulnerable. *(Picking it up)* Well, it still works. *(She looks at him.)* How did you do that?

LEWIS: What?

BRANDY: Dump me.

LEWIS: It's second nature by now, two nights a week I...

BRANDY: You've got a black belt?

LEWIS: Nothing so fancy. I'm average.

BRANDY: In all things, uh?

LEWIS: I guess so.

BRANDY: I didn't mean that. Of course, I don't really know. *(Gently)* I never will.

LEWIS: No.

BRANDY: You have quite a body.

LEWIS: Average.

(They laugh.)

BRANDY: Then how...?

LEWIS: Come here.

BRANDY: *(After a moment's hesitation, cautiously)* Yes...

LEWIS: This is how... Anybody can.

(He walks her softly through her dumping.)

BRANDY: I see. How simple.

LEWIS: Yes, using the assailant's own energy. Now do it to me.

BRANDY: But your suit.

LEWIS: Nothing that happens to this suit in this life or the next could possibly matter.

(She laughs. He walks her through the action with small talk, allowing her to assume the offensive role.)

LEWIS: Not bad, but not exactly. Here. Once more, come at me. Slowly. In slow motion, do exactly what you did before. Here, we'll stand in exactly the same place. Now.

(Slowly he dumps her, though this time, knowing what to expect, she attempts to trip him up and does, in fact, bring him to his knees over her just as LARRY looks in the door. Unaware of him, LEWIS and BRANDY laugh together. LARRY linger a second, unbelieving, almost enters, then leaves, unseen and unheard.)

BRANDY: What's that? In your briefcase?

LEWIS: *(Removing* RICK's *gun)* Oh, that. *(Working the action)* It's empty. You'll never believe me. I was intending to give this back to a man whose son seems to wander the streets like Larry, just waiting for bad luck.

BRANDY: What's his name, the son's?

LEWIS: His name? Oh, Rob, I think.

BRANDY: Rob. A friend of Darren's.

LEWIS: Yes. Yes, I think so. Rick's son. Rick and Drew sort of know each other. Drew is Darren's father.

BRANDY: I know. And you're Larry's brother.

LEWIS: Yes. It's simple, really. We're just talking about a couple of young men a couple of fathers and a brother are trying to prevent from doing anything worse.

BRANDY: Anything worse than what? What did they do?

LEWIS: I don't know if I should tell you.

BRANDY: Tell me.

LEWIS: Not much. Well, you know Larry gambles. Rob and Darren were breaking into houses, for a lark. But no more.

BRANDY: Rob... I think I may have met him once. Yes. His hands are like yours, only different, and his voice. I'm trying to remember his voice. What's his voice like?

LEWIS: I never met him, Brandy.

BRANDY: You can put your gun away now. You'll teach me?

LEWIS: What?

BRANDY: To dump people.

LEWIS: If you like.

BRANDY: I'll pay you.

LEWIS: That won't be necessary.

(Beat)

BRANDY: Let me up now.

LEWIS: *(Beginning to rise)* Of course.

BRANDY: No. Wait. Hold me.

LEWIS: What?

BRANDY: Hold my wrists. *(After a moment)* That's right. Harder. Really hard. *(After trying unsuccessfully to free herself)* All right. You can let go.

LEWIS: *(Doing so, rising)* What was that all about?

BRANDY: *(Rising)* Nothing. It wasn't you...

LEWIS: It wasn't me...

BRANDY: Holding my wrists.

(They face each other, his attention goes to her open suitcase.)

LEWIS: But you're leaving.

BRANDY: I was. I didn't go with Darren. And then I found I couldn't stay. I was laughing too much.

(Beat)

LEWIS: At us?

(They look at each other a moment.)

BRANDY: I'm sorry. I'm not laughing now. And I'm not going now, not until I can do what you can do.

LEWIS: It's for defense, Brandy. Like the man's gun. It's not to be misused.

BRANDY: I was misused, Lewis. Teach me to misuse.

LEWIS: I...

(LEWIS hesitates as the light fades. In the half light, LEWIS and BRANDY, barefoot, dance a slow dance of stylized kicks and body blows. She is quickly learning, trying to do as he does as LEWIS fades. BRANDY, alone, dances sharp, deft kicks and punches with an invisible assailant who obviously suffers each blow since the following blow assumes he is in the position resulting from an effective preceding kick or punch. DREW rolls on. Suddenly BRANDY does a kick at DREW's head, which she stops short, laughing, her leg in the air.)

DREW: *(Gently taking her foot)* This isn't you.

BRANDY: Who is it? *(Lowering her foot, continuing her dance of vengeance)* How am I doing, Drew?

DREW: It's what you're doing that bothers me.

BRANDY: Don't be bothered, Drew.

DREW: *(Shaking his head)* You'll break my heart.

BRANDY: Hearts are meant to be broken. *(Proudly)* I can break knees, backs, necks...

DREW: But you won't.

BRANDY: *(Leaving on the balls of her feet)* Who knows?

(Exit BRANDY.)

DREW: *(Looking after her as the light fades to black)* I thought I did.

END OF ACT ONE

ACT TWO

Scene One

(ROB *and* DARREN *in that sylvan setting of the first scene of the first act. However, the season has changed. It's late fall, dark, leafless, with the occasional sound of wind.* ROB *and* DARREN *have also changed. Dressed for the weather, they stand a moment, shuddering, drinking steaming coffee from paper cups. Suddenly* DARREN *steps back to declaim.)*

DARREN: And so, gentlemen, we go our separate ways, I to die...

ROB: Forget it, old man. We're not the guys we used to be.

DARREN: We're still standing around under the trees.

ROB: But the graduation picnic is a dim memory. We're not standing around because we're bored.

DARREN: I'm standing around because I lost the girl. You're standing around because you're too smart to break into another house, and neither of us is smart enough to find a job.

ROB: That's about it. *(Holding up his cup of coffee)* Well, where'll it be, Dr Jekyll? We've seen the other side of the tracks.

DARREN: It's seen us. Perhaps there's something on this side, Mr Hyde.

ROB: Perhaps. Say...ever notice that old house on the river, by the bridge? It must have been a mansion once. Now it belongs on the other side of the tracks, it just isn't. It looks abandoned by day, but I have a feeling there's a little action there after dark. And, in fact...

DARREN: Yes...

ROB: The address is the one our friend Larry gave us that night we never made it there.

DARREN: Is that so? What are they into? Controlled substances? Girls?

ROB: I think so, but they're only there for the stuff. I doubt if there's furniture in that place. Mattresses, rats, stand-up comedies in the stairwell.

DARREN: Sounds irresistible, Mr Hyde. No, I've never noticed it. What nonsense have you got in mind?

ROB: *(Pacing, sipping)* Well. We park your clunker in the shadows. We watch. After enough suckers have gone in and come out, each leaving a little handful of moolah, we go in as if we were looking for the easy dream, only we come out with what the others left behind.

DARREN: *(Laughing)* Say, this is big time. You mean: Hit the girls.

ROB: *(Laughing)* It shouldn't be necessary to hit 'em, or even hold 'em down. We'll just grab that wad of greenbacks, the one they keep in the top of their stockings, and run out the door.

DARREN: *(Laughing)* Sounds easy. But do they deal in sufficient sums to make it worth the grab?

ROB: You got a better idea?

DARREN: We could go to Chicago, look for work.

ROB: Wouldn't that go better with a few bucks in our pockets? *(The clincher)* Since you're not accepting any help from your old man.

(Beat)

DARREN: Oh, okay. What the hell. To the house by the river, to a really bright scheme.

ROB: *(As each puts a hand behind his back)* One digit says we go, two say we go quickly.

DARREN: Fair enough.

ROB: One, two...

DARREN & ROB: Three!

(Blackout as their hands come out)

Scene Two

(RICK and DREW meet on the bridge dressed for the cold: DREW in a businessman's topcoat, hat, etc, RICK in a red wool plaid coat, etc.)

DREW: Rick.

RICK: Drew.

DREW: Got your gun back?

RICK: No. Not yet. Maybe I'm better off without it.

DREW: Maybe so. Heard anything yourself?

RICK: No. Rob surfaced for a while, but he seems to have gone back underground. Darren has too. There's a girl.

DREW: Yes.

RICK: Brandy. Heard of her?

DREW: Perhaps not by that name.

RICK: Seems she's taken up with the younger brother of that fellow we met over the game.

DREW: Lewis.

RICK: Yes. Larry. Larry's the younger brother. Brandy's moved in with him, but Lewis is teaching her to kick.

DREW: Then "Brandy" won't have anything to worry about.

RICK: It's someone else ought to worry. She's looking for someone.

DREW: Who?

RICK: The guy, or guys, that got her.

DREW: That couldn't be Rob or Darren.

RICK: No. But what if she thinks it is? What if she makes a mistake? She might, you know. What then?

DREW: I thought you were the one who understood vendettas, vigilantes, revenge...

RICK: I am.

DREW: Then?

RICK: She's not going to hurt anyone, even by mistake, not if I get to her first.

DREW: Rick.

RICK: What?

DREW: You're just full of mistakes yourself.

RICK: I always have been. It's too late to change now.

DREW: It may be. Rick. Don't hurt someone who's been hurt. That's not the way to stop anything.

RICK: What is?

DREW: I don't know.

RICK: I didn't think you did. *(Leaving)* When you do, look me up. I'll listen. You're not the bad guy. I am. I have to be in character, don't I?

(Exit RICK. DREW, *worried, looks after him.)*

Scene Three

(Nighttime alley: a world of garish neon spills, offstage sirens. BRANDY, *wigged, wearing her cat's-eye glasses, etc, leaning against a wall. Her own theme barely audible on her Walkman.* RICK *hobbles by, spots her, approaches.)*

BRANDY: Hi, fella. Lonely?

RICK: Is it that obvious?

BRANDY: Yep.

RICK: How can you tell? Is it the way I walk?

BRANDY: You call that a walk?

RICK: What would you call it?

BRANDY: That's a pretty nasty limp.

RICK: You sound pretty nasty yourself.

BRANDY: Maybe I like a man with a nasty limp.

RICK: Maybe I like a nasty girl. I never really thought about it. How much?

BRANDY: For what?

RICK: Information.

BRANDY: Information? What are you looking for?

RICK: My son.

BRANDY: Your son? Well, every woman didn't say no to you.

RICK: I guess not.

(BRANDY *signals $$$ with thumb and fingertips.* RICK *pays.*)

BRANDY: What's his name?

RICK: Rob.

BRANDY: Rob... Never heard of him. He look like you?

RICK: I guess so.

BRANDY: Right down to the limp?

RICK: No. I guess he was lucky there. Have you seen him?

BRANDY: I don't think so. Well, is that it?

(RICK *nods,* BRANDY *looks over his head.*)

BRANDY: Better move along, mister. You cramp my style; I wouldn't want people to get the idea I...

RICK: *(Moving along, turning back)* By the way, what's your name?

BRANDY: Sherry. My friends call me Sherry. If you belong to a limper's club or something like that, send some of your friends along.

RICK: Sherry, huh? You're pretty bright for a....

BRANDY: For a what?

RICK: *(Shrugs)* You sure it's not Brandy?

BRANDY: You think I don't know my own name?

RICK: Hmm. Well. Thanks.

BRANDY: For what? Anyway, you're welcome. Come back when you want some more information.

(He hesitates, looking at her.)

BRANDY: What are you looking at? You're always on the point of falling over, aren't you? What is it: You want to lean up against me? Okay, okay. Round the corner, though. Not here.

(He hesitates, she glances around, takes his hand, leads him off. They exit, reappear in a darker alley.)

BRANDY: Okay. Here we are, honey. This is it. This is where you tell the truth.

(Suddenly she twists RICK's hand, bending him double, his arm straight out behind him. She holds him with one hand, effortlessly.)

RICK: Ow, ow, ow! Damn...

BRANDY: *(Applying pressure)* Damn me?

RICK: Damn me for a fool. I should stay home.

BRANDY: Yes, people like you should stay home. Listen. I haven't got time to waste. Why are you looking for Rob? What did he do?

(Beat. She applies pressure.)

RICK: Ow! All right, all right. Just let me go.

(She hesitates, releases him, stands back, ready without effort.)

RICK: Not much of anything, that's the problem. I'm afraid something's going to happen to him.

BRANDY: What?

RICK: He's going to get hurt.

BRANDY: Who did he hurt?

RICK: Nobody.

BRANDY: Who's going to hurt him?

RICK: Somebody. It's a case of mistaken identity. There's a woman looking for the man that done her wrong.

BRANDY: Is there? Only one? Sounds like Frankie and Johnny.

RICK: Yes. Well. I told you. May I go?

BRANDY: Of course. It's a free country.

(He starts off at a great pace.)

BRANDY: Where are you going so fast?

RICK: To get my gun...or one just like it.

BRANDY: Then you're going to shoot me?

RICK: No. I'm going to shoot her.

BRANDY: The woman looking for the man?

RICK: That's her. *(Leaving)* If I find her...

BRANDY: Bang! Bang!

(*Exit* RICK. *Calling after him*)

BRANDY: Good luck!

(BRANDY *going back to her corner, disappears, reappears, turns her Walkman up, adjusts her dark glasses, dances to a music the buzz and beat of which are audible as car lights pass, night sounds of the city are heard.* DREW *rolls on.*)

BRANDY: Hi, good lookin'.

DREW: You mean me?

BRANDY: *(With a nod)* Whatcha got cookin'?

DREW: Not much.

BRANDY: Don't tell me: You're looking for your son.

DREW: Maybe.

BRANDY: Some gal took pity on you too.

DREW: Me too?

BRANDY: You and all the others, bud. Is this son of yours rolling around like you?

DREW: No.

BRANDY: What's his name?

DREW: Darren.

BRANDY: *("Trying" to remember)* Darren, huh? Darren...

(DREW *pays her.*)

BRANDY: No, I don't know no Darren. What'd you name him Darren for? Just to make life difficult. You sure it's Darren?

DREW: I think so. Who are you?

BRANDY: Who wants to know?

DREW: I do.

BRANDY: Why?

DREW: If you're Brandy, I think somebody may be looking for you.

BRANDY: Oh, yeah? Who? Not a man with a limp?

DREW: You certainly know a lot. You know why he's looking for you?

BRANDY: Suppose you tell me.

DREW: He's heard you're looking for someone. He's afraid you might make a mistake, break his son's neck instead of...

BRANDY: Instead of...? *(No answer)* Yes...?

DREW: Instead of the neck of the guy that held you down.

BRANDY: How do you know so much?

DREW: A lot gets around.

BRANDY: It certainly does. You know Lewis? Is Lewis a friend of yours?

DREW: Maybe.

BRANDY: I guess he isn't a friend of mine, not if he's warning guys.

DREW: He doesn't want you making a mistake, that's all. You'd be worse off then, "Brandy," than you are now.

BRANDY: I'm not going to make a mistake, Drew.

DREW: Drew? You know my name?

BRANDY: A lot gets around. Now, if you've got the information you require....you're crimping my style...not all my regulars are in the Special Olympics... What're you looking at? What do you want? You want your blankets rearranged? Okay. Round the corner though, not here.

(She looks around, rolls a protesting DREW into her alley.)

DREW: Wait. No.

(They disappear, reappear in the half light of a darker alley.)

DREW: *(Grabbing his wheels)* That's enough. I don't like being pushed.

BRANDY: Would you rather be held down?

DREW: No.

BRANDY: *(Suddenly, effortlessly, holding him immobilized by the back of the neck)* Then here's something you won't like.

DREW: *(His head forced forward, quietly)* That hurts, Brandy.

BRANDY: It's only so you don't move. I don't want to hurt you.

DREW: That's something. Why are you doing this?

BRANDY: I want to know what your son's told you, what he's confessed.

DREW: He doesn't confess to me, and I don't speak when forced.

BRANDY: *(Applying more pressure, without results)* No? You want more? Do I have to break your neck? *(Releasing him)* Okay. You win. I'm not going to break your neck.

DREW: *(Rubbing his)* I didn't think you would.

BRANDY: Why not?

DREW: *(Turning his chair to face her)* It isn't in you, Brandy. Not really. Those folks only get themselves in the end.

BRANDY: What folks?

DREW: Those with sweet revenge in their veins, with the wrath of God in their eyes.

BRANDY: This isn't the end, not that end. Meanwhile...

DREW: Meanwhile, as I seem to be advising everyone these days, I advise you to go home.

BRANDY: Such a wise man, Darren's father. Why didn't some of it rub off on your son?

DREW: I had a feeling you knew him. You like him, don't you? Well, he's hard not to like. I like him. You're a bit older than he is.

BRANDY: So?

DREW: So I think you might be good for him. You're just what he needs now.

BRANDY: You're opposites, aren't you?

DREW: I don't think so. There's just forty years' difference.

BRANDY: A late son. The last son.

DREW: The only son. The only child. *(Turning his chair)* So long, "Brandy." I'm glad we met.

(Exit DREW. BRANDY speaks after him, quietly and unheard.)

BRANDY: I am too.

(BRANDY disappears opposite, DREW reappears in a darker, less garish, less raucous corner of the night world; he stops, looks around, rubs his neck.)

DREW: *(Knowing he's alone)* I think you turned my head, Brandy. I'm too old to be prowling. Where the hell am I?

(DARREN appears in the shadows behind him, stops in surprise.)

DARREN: What the hell are you doing here?

DREW: *(Turning his chair, pleased)* Darren! Well, I'm not looking for you, I'm not following you around.

DARREN: I know that. Who are you following?

DREW: Rob's father. Rick.

DARREN: Why?

DREW: He's got it in his head Brandy is going to break his son's neck, Rob's.

DARREN: Is she?

DREW: Only if he's the one who held her down.

DARREN: He isn't.

DREW: How do you know?

DARREN: I just know.

DREW: I know you didn't.

DARREN: How do you know that?

DREW: I just know.

DARREN: You just know. I suppose I'm lucky to have a father sitting alone somewhere who knows me that well.

DREW: It's possible.

DARREN: But we don't appreciate those things until we're much, much older, till our fathers are gone, in fact. *(Affecting a sculptor's stance)* Maybe someday I'll cast you in bronze.

DREW: *(Rolling his wheels a little in opposite directions and striking a pose; ending the pose)* I don't think I'd want to see me in front of the library.

(They both chuckle.)

DARREN: I wasn't thinking of the whole ensemble.

DREW: That's good.

DARREN: Want to go home?

DREW: I think that is what I want. I got turned around here.

DARREN: *(Hesitating)* Mind if I push?

(Beat)

DREW: I don't mind.

(DARREN *rolls* DREW *off.* BRANDY *dances as before to her own Walkman music as the garish lights, the raucous sounds return. Enter* LEWIS *in his sweats, a towel around his neck. His movements are so quiet without being obviously catlike,* BRANDY *doesn't hear him at first.)*

LEWIS: Hello, Brandy.

BRANDY: What makes you think it's Brandy?

LEWIS: I just know.

BRANDY: *(Removing her glasses)* You know too much. What're you doin' here? Back from your kicking lesson?

LEWIS: That's about it.

BRANDY: Got any more to teach me?

LEWIS: You know everything I do.

BRANDY: *(Looking around, then)* Shall we practice?

(Waving a distracting hand, she delivers a quick kick to his kneecap, but stops it just in time. LEWIS *does not defend himself.)*

LEWIS: Very good. I wish you weren't here though.

BRANDY: Quit wishing.

LEWIS: You're going to try one of those when someone is coming up behind you. You're just going to get hurt again. Is that going to do you any good?

(BRANDY *shrugs.*)

LEWIS: Come home, Brandy.

BRANDY: Where's home? With you?

LEWIS: With me, with Larry. He misses you.

BRANDY: So?

LEWIS: Come. It's as much of a home as any of us have. I'm going shopping now. Tomorrow night we're having...

BRANDY: When I want the menu, I'll ask the waiter. You go home, Lewis, if it's so important to you. I've got something else cooking.

LEWIS: When you need me, I'll be there.

BRANDY: Uh-huh.

(*Beat. Exit* LEWIS. BRANDY *replaces her glasses, struts. Suddenly, a blackened figure appears in front of her. She stops but is attacked by a blacked-out figure from behind. She whirls to deliver her blow to the kneecap but only sets him hopping in pain. When* BRANDY *whirls to face the first figure, she finds him gone. She returns to face the other, who is leaving.*)

BRANDY: Wait. (*He hesitates.*) Don't go.

MAN: (*His voice muffled*) Why?

BRANDY: You wouldn't have had to.... (*Approaching slowly*) Really.

(*He hesitates. She doubles him with a blow to the midriff and is about to follow it with something worse when* LARRY *enters behind her.*)

LARRY: Brandy!

BRANDY: (*Gasping from exertion*) What? Are you following me?

LARRY: M-maybe I am, but killing him won't do you any good.

BRANDY: Are you sure?

LARRY: I'm sure. Leave him. He won't bother anyone else for a while.

BRANDY: I don't want him bothering anyone else ever. (*Watching her assailant stumble off*) That isn't him, is it?

LARRY: I don't know.

BRANDY: (*Suddenly sagging*) Oh, God, I'm tired.

LARRY: (*Suddenly very unsure of himself*) W-won't you c-come home?

BRANDY: Home. Where's that?

(When LARRY can't speak)

BRANDY: Why?

LARRY: B-because I don't want you on the street.

BRANDY: Why not?

(Again LARRY opens his mouth and nothing comes out.)

BRANDY: Larry...

LARRY: W-what?

BRANDY: Go away. I have something to do. *(He hesitates, then turns to go.)* Oh, and Larry.... *(He stops.)* Don't follow me.

(LARRY shakes his head once, exits. The light fades.)

Scene Four

(The ruined house by the river, blackened walls, broken glass on the floor; it is empty except for an old straight-backed chair and a hanging wire. Enter DARREN and ROB, flashlights.)

DARREN: *(Walking on the broken glass)* Looks like you were wrong, friend. Not a crackhead, not a stained mattress.

ROB: Not a T V set, not a toaster. Well, you were right, I was wrong.

DARREN: Let's go.

ROB: Where?

DARREN: Chi-town. We'll be there by dawn. My clunker'll die at Randolph and State, we'll be at the Trib Building when the want-ads hit the street. Interviews that noon, celebrations that night. Work on Monday, first paycheck on Friday.

ROB: Sounds good.

(They start left, hear something, stand still. The unmistakable sound of someone walking on broken glass rises from below; it is a scary, uneven walk. ROB, the chair in hand, silently takes his place behind the door, which soon opens. Enter RICK, his hand in his pocket. He and DARREN stare at each other as ROB raises the chair.)

RICK: All right, young man. Where's my son?

DARREN: Right behind you.

(RICK steps back quickly against the wall, drawing his gun. He and ROB, chair still raised, face each other. Suddenly both laugh.)

RICK: *(Pocketing his gun)* Damn you, Rob. I might have shot you.

ROB: And I might have broken your skull. What are you doing here?

RICK: I might ask you the same question.

ROB: You followed us, didn't you?

RICK: Maybe.

ROB: Why?

RICK: To keep you out of trouble. Remember: You hung your head, you expressed regret, you said you were through with breaking and entering.

DARREN: This isn't breaking and entering.

RICK: You stay out of this. I'm talking to my son.

ROB: He's right. The place was wide open.

RICK: What're you here for: to smoke a cigarette, tell dirty stories?

DARREN: It's not a dirty story, it might be a long one.

RICK: I thought I told you to stay out of this.

ROB: We had a strategy. It didn't work.

RICK: You want to tell me about it?

ROB: It's too stupid. It was a game really.

RICK: Can anyone play?

DARREN: It's not that kind of game. (RICK *glares at him.*) You've got to stop following us, Rob's father. It's making us paranoid.

RICK: I'll show you paranoid.

(RICK *advances more quickly than might be thought possible, but* ROB *grabs him from behind. As they struggle...*)

ROB: Dad, Dad... What are we going to do with you?

DARREN: Well, we could...

ROB: *(Still struggling)* We could what?

DARREN: Leave him in that chair for a while.

ROB: *(Struggling)* You mean: tie him up?

DARREN: If necessary.

RICK: *(Trying to free himself; to* DARREN*)* You damn rich kid, I'll....

ROB: Dad...

(ROB, *restraining him, actually seats* RICK *in the chair.* DARREN *quickly pulls the wire hanging from the ceiling, hands it to* ROB, *then holds* RICK *as* ROB *deftly ties him to the chair, hand and foot.*)

DARREN: What: Were you a cowboy in another life?

ROB: Knots 101. I forget what I needed it for. *(Standing back, looking at his handiwork, immediately regretful)* Darren. I can't do this.

RICK: You already have.

ROB: *(To* RICK*)* Well, maybe I ought to with you following us around all the time. What's that supposed to be: love? *(Making the decision)* I'm going to leave you here, Dad, because I can just remember being left somewhere once upon a time.

RICK: That wasn't my fault.

ROB: Who's was it?

RICK: It wasn't anybody's.

ROB: Tell that to a ten year-old. You know I'm still standing in the window watching you hobble away as if the house was on fire.

RICK: I'm...sorry.

ROB: I'm sorry for this, but I'm going to let it be my little revenge. Maybe after this... Never mind after this. This is one night. You know how long you were gone?

RICK: I'm making up for that.

ROB: By never losing sight of me?

RICK: By never losing sight of you.

ROB: Well, you're losing sight of me now for a while. So long.

RICK: Just tell me where you'll be. I'll leave you alone.

ROB: You'll leave me alone anyway. But it's Chicago. I'll send you a postcard.

(ROB *starts left,* DARREN *shrugs, follows, closing the door. Exit both, followed by the sound of their descent, a pause, the sound of the clunker starting in the distance.)*

RICK: *(Quietly)* I hope you've got my address...son.

(RICK *begins to struggle to untie himself. He seems to be succeeding when once more, the sound of someone walking on glass rises from the stairwell. This is a very different sound.* RICK *sits still, listening to it. The door opens. Enter* BRANDY, *in her street outfit and rhinestone glasses.* RICK's *chair is facing away from her. Beat. She walks around in front of him.)*

BRANDY: Well, if it isn't limpers. What is this: the clubhouse?

RICK: Not who you were looking for?

BRANDY: How do you know who I'm looking for? I thought you were looking for someone.

RICK: I am. I figured it out: *You're* the one looking for the man that held you down. You're going to break his neck.

BRANDY: You're looking for me so I don't find your son before you do.

RICK: Well. We're quits. Because I win. I found him and he's gone.

BRANDY: Gone where?

RICK: Just gone.

(Beat)

BRANDY: Did he hold me down?

RICK: I don't think so.

BRANDY: Why not?

RICK: He's not like that. He hasn't got it in him.

BRANDY: He's got this in him. He tied you up, didn't he?

RICK: Another guy was pushing him.

BRANDY: Maybe another guy pushed him to do something else. Listen: It almost happened again. I was looking for one man, another man found me.

RICK: You must be getting used to it.

BRANDY: *(Advancing on him)* Listen, you old...

(RICK *draws his gun.*)

RICK: Surprise.

BRANDY: *(Stopped)* I guess so. Want to see me kick it out of your hand?

RICK: Want to see me shoot it?

BRANDY: Didn't someone take that gun away from you? I seem to remember... Did he give it back?

RICK: This is another one, just like the first, bought for the sole purpose of keeping my son out of trouble.

BRANDY: Did it work?

RICK: It's working now.

BRANDY: You're going to shoot me?

RICK: You're going to keep me company for a while.

BRANDY: *(Moving sinuously toward him)* Oh, well, why didn't you say so, limpers...?

RICK: *(Cocking his automatic)* Hold it right there. (BRANDY *stops, then starts moving slowly toward the door.* RICK, *still tied by the feet, forces his chair to face her.*)

RICK: Don't you...

BRANDY: *(Stopping, her back to him)* You going to shoot me in the back?

RICK: Back, front, it's all the same.

BRANDY: *(Swinging her hips as she starts again toward the door)* That's how much you know.

RICK: *(Aiming at her)* Brandy...!

BRANDY: Go on, old man: Shoot.

(RICK, *holds the wrist of his gun hand, aims at her back, then at her leg, his hand trembling. She pauses at the door, her back to him.*)

BRANDY: Well?

RICK: *(Lowering the gun)* I...can't. Another surprise.

BRANDY: You haven't got it in you.

RICK: I guess not.

(*A car door slams outside.* RICK *and* BRANDY *look at each other.*)

BRANDY: It seems there might be worse evils than you or me.

RICK: It's possible.

BRANDY: *(Laughing softly)* So we'll both die here.

RICK: *(Smiling)* It's possible...but not necessary. Untie me.

(BRANDY *hesitates, then moves to untie* RICK's *feet. They talk quietly, more than half listening to street sounds.*)

BRANDY: Shall I tell you something?

RICK: Tell me.

BRANDY: I'm thinking it might have been someone put up to it by someone I know, someone in the shadows, laughing. Tell me it couldn't have been Darren.

RICK: He's got money.

BRANDY: What's that got to do with it?

RICK: He's got money, he's bored. He can pay for what he wants.

BRANDY: But he's not like that. *(Rising, standing back from him)* You and Rob have something in common, though I don't know what it is.

RICK: Maybe you have it too. *(Seeing he's untied, standing)* Thank you.

BRANDY: Don't mention it. Are we on the same side now?

RICK: We appear to be.

(*Another street sound causes them to listen.* DREW, *off, calls.*)

DREW: Rick! Rick, I know you're in there. I can't make it up those stairs. Come on out. The boys are gone.

(RICK *smiles, shakes his head to himself.*)

RICK: It's almost like having a friend.

BRANDY: Is that anything like having a son who ties you up?

RICK: Or a boyfriend who might be the man you're after?

BRANDY: Where'd you hear that?

RICK: In your voice. When you said his name. Darren. *(Limping toward the door, stopping, looking back at the chair, the wire)* I didn't like that. I guess there is something worse than limping.

BRANDY: I've always thought there might be.

RICK: *(Facing her)* I'm sorry for what happened to you. If I could have prevented it, I would. I still don't think Rob...

BRANDY: We'll see.

RICK: Does that mean we're on different sides again?

BRANDY: I have to be on my own side now.

RICK: Why?

BRANDY: Because I don't know who else is.

RICK: You don't know nothin'. You've got a whole team. Lewis and Larry and Drew and....

(DREW, off, calls RICK.)

RICK: Brandy, the boys are long gone. This is no place for you.

BRANDY: You've been following, I've been following, it seems your friend, my "boyfriend's" father, has been following...and I'll tell you something, Rick: I'm being followed too. Maybe somebody who was hired in the first place but then decided he liked it so much he'd do it for nothing. *(Sitting in the chair)* I think I'm just going to sit here awhile.

(Beat. RICK limps over to her, places the gun in her lap, leaves. BRANDY looks down at it, smiles, listens to RICK's descent, to the sounds of RICK and DREW getting in a car, to the sounds of the house, to the sound of another car, another car door. BRANDY familiarizes herself with the gun, sees there are bullets in the clip, that the safety is off. She listens to the footsteps on the stair. She raises the gun toward the door. Enter DARREN. BRANDY laughs, with a kind of hysteria, but without lowering the gun.)

BRANDY: Your story, please sir.

DARREN: I've been wondering if you were all right.

BRANDY: And so you came back.

(DARREN nods.)

BRANDY: From where?

DARREN: We, Rob and I, we were on our way to Chicago to look for work.

BRANDY: How did you know I was here?

DARREN: I knew you were following us.

BRANDY: So why didn't you just wait for me?

DARREN: You already dumped me once, remember? Why didn't you take off after us when we left?

BRANDY: I knew your friend's father was up here. I saw him arrive, I wondered what was going on, why you left him.

DARREN: You did. Well. Where is he?

BRANDY: *(Lowering the gun)* Gone. With your father. And why didn't Rob come back—to his father?

DARREN: He was teaching him a lesson, but he had second thoughts. He's outside, in the clunker. We agreed I'd come up and let his father go. He didn't want a scene. *(Moving earnestly toward her)* Brandy, that's why I'm here, to untie an old man, not to waylay you.

BRANDY: *(The gun raised)* Hold it!

(He stops. She stands.)

BRANDY: We don't need your friend for this scene. You thought it would be interesting to...to degrade someone while you watched, or without her even knowing it was someone she knew, didn't you?

DARREN: Come now...

BRANDY: I know: You're not like that. Perhaps you were just wondering what it would be like if you were like that. And so you hired someone... for a demonstration.

DARREN: I never...

BRANDY: *(The gun still raised)* Were you ever made to stand in the corner, that is, when you were more of a little boy than you are now?

DARREN: I think, maybe...

BRANDY: Don't talk. Face the corner.

(He hesitates, does.)

BRANDY: This is how I should have dealt with you in the first place. Put your hands on the wall.

(He does.)

BRANDY: Higher!

(He does.)

BRANDY: And to think you came to me then, after, as a friend, as a lover. I'm so mad, so hurt. I'm thinking how to hurt you as much as.... Tell me, Darren, what should I do? Where should I stick this gun? Would that give you some idea...?

DARREN: Only the idea that you're crazier than I thought.

(BRANDY fires into the wall over his left hand. DARREN flinches, but doesn't turn.)

BRANDY: Won't you say that again, Darren?

DARREN: Only the idea that you're crazier than I....

(BRANDY *fires into the wall over his right hand.*)

BRANDY: Are those the hands, Darren, the hands that held me? Would you like to hold me again?

DARREN: No.

(BRANDY *steps closer, carefully shoots* DARREN *in one hand, then stands ready for him to turn around. Not turning, his hands still raised, he slips somewhat down the wall, one hand leaving a trail of blood.*)

DARREN: I knew I'd give the wrong answer eventually.

BRANDY: Is that what it was, Darren, the wrong answer?

DARREN: *(Not turning)* That's what it was.

(*There are sounds in the street.* BRANDY *quickly steps closer again, steadies the gun, shoots him in the other hand, steps back ready. This time* DARREN *wheels to approach her. He walks slowly toward her, both hands cradled against his body.*)

BRANDY: *(Backing)* Don't come any closer. I don't want to kill you.

DARREN: So there are limits.

BRANDY: Hold it. Hold it right there.

DARREN: *(Moving toward the chair)* I just want to sit down... Brandy, I never.... What a laugh!

BRANDY: What a laugh? Part of the same laugh, Darren?

(DARREN *sits suddenly.* BRANDY *is holding the gun to his head when the door swings open.* DARREN *and* BRANDY *both face it. Enter* ROB.)

ROB: *(Taking the scene in)* God. I thought my father... *(To* DARREN*)* You're hurt!

DARREN: Just my hands.

ROB: Why...? What...?

DARREN: You'd better ask Brandy.

ROB: Brandy... You look familiar—except for the gun.

BRANDY: The gun is all it takes. You put Darren up to petty crime, didn't you? Did you put him up to something else?

ROB: To what?

BRANDY: To following somebody one night, to throwing her down, holding her...

DARREN: Oh, Brandy...

BRANDY: *(Still to* ROB*)* Or did he put you...?

ROB: *(Approaching)* No. You've got the wrong guy.

BRANDY: *(Raising her gun)* Which one of you is the right guy?

ROB: Neither. Give me the gun, Brandy.

(ROB *is approaching her with his hand out as* LARRY *enters, laughs, stands looking at all of them. As they stare at him, he produces his cards, does a spectacular midair shuffle.*)

LARRY: *(To* DARREN*)* I th-thought you boys were looking for a little action.

DARREN: I think we've had enough.

LARRY: Does that g-go for you too, Rob?

ROB: For the moment.

LARRY: *(Pocketing his cards, laughing)* Too bad. This was your chance to lose your shirts. *(With a deadly step toward* ROB*)* You're perfectly s-safe here, you know. *(Suddenly stopping, indirectly to* BRANDY*)* I thought, I was beginning to think, I thought for a while... I can't talk. *(Directly to her)* I thought you were mine.

BRANDY: I'm not anyone's, Larry, or I'm everyone's. I told you to go away; I told you not to follow me. I told you not to get your heart broken. I told you if...if someone came to me...

LARRY: But that night... He was gone, you were still there. I saw Lewis almost on top of you. You were laughing, both of you. Then, the next day, it s-seemed, it seemed you were mine again. And s-so it went.

BRANDY: Lewis was teaching me. You know that.

LARRY: You were making him happy when I wasn't there.

BRANDY: No. Maybe keeping him from unhappy, but not...

LARRY: Well. W-whatever. Now we're all unhappy. Aren't we? Well, aren't we? Are you unhappy, Rob?

ROB: I'm unhappy.

LARRY: *(To* DARREN *who is doubled over his hands)* What happened to you? *(To* BRANDY*)* What's the gun for?

BRANDY: It's for shooting Darren. *(Returning to herself, her concern revealing itself; to* ROB*)* Maybe you ought to get your friend to a doctor.

(ROB *nods,* DARREN *shakes his head. To* LARRY)

BRANDY: It's Rob's father's gun.

LARRY: How did you get it? I thought Lewis...

BRANDY: That's too long a story.

LARRY: *(Stepping toward* ROB*)* Maybe Rob would like to tell it.

ROB: Rob doesn't know it. *(Concerned)* Come on, Darren. Let's get you out of here.

DARREN: No! Not 'til I know what's going on. Brandy thinks I...I threw her down, and...

ROB: Brandy, the worst thing I ever did was to tie my father up. Less than an hour later, I'm ashamed. Darren's much more sensitive than I. Do you know why his hands are so strong?

BRANDY: You tell me.

ROB: He sculpts, that's what he does when he can, when he has time, that's what he wants. I know him. You don't. That's why he wouldn't hold your wrists that time. He's too strong. He wouldn't want to hurt you. Do you think he'd use those hands....?

BRANDY: I don't suppose Darren can speak for himself.

DARREN: Sculptor or not yet, Brandy, I'm not a piece of clay. No one ever pushed me to do anything I didn't really want to. I've wanted you to want me; really, that's the whole pleasure of it, isn't it, for anyone, her wanting him, not him tearing it from her...?

BRANDY: Yes, that is the pleasure of it.

DARREN: Maybe there was bodily harm...in this body, or at least the potential for....

ROB: Breaking and entering, entering and breaking.

DARREN: Yes. *(To* BRANDY*)* But that was before I...before we....

(He's silent, looking down.)

BRANDY: Can I believe you?

DARREN: You might as well.

BRANDY: If I can, if you're telling the truth, then of course I... *(Changing)* Oh, Darren, if I'm wrong I'm so....

DARREN: Don't even try to get it out. *(Standing, his hands tucked under his arms.)* Apologies accepted. *(Walking toward the door)* Goodbye, Brandy.

BRANDY: Darren...

ROB: *(His hand on* DARREN's *back)* Come on. You've lost some blood.

(Exit DARREN *&* ROB. BRANDY *stands looking at the doorway,* LARRY *comes up to her, gently removes the gun, pockets it. Together they listen to car doors, to the clunker being driven rapidly away.* BRANDY *goes to the window, looks down into the street.* LARRY *comes up behind her, embraces her. She allows the embrace until she feels its constraint. When she attempts to free herself,* LARRY *easily controlling her, pushes her to the floor, face down.)*

BRANDY: Larry, it was you.

LARRY: *(Caressing her hair with his free hand)* W-was it, Brandy? No, it wasn't. Not then. It is now.

BRANDY: Why now, Larry?

LARRY: I don't know who...who hurt you, but you...in your search, I guess...I didn't know you were just searching...I was a s-suspect, wasn't I, and...and... you hurt me. And I...I... *(Caressing her back)* You don't know what it's been... having you every night while you learned to kick, then...nothing...you're gone and...I...I can't even say it...I...I walk around...ready for you...my body ready for your body, as anyone can see who looks...all day. There. I said it.

BRANDY: I'm sorry, Larry.

LARRY: Too late for sorry. I...I can't stop now. I love you.

BRANDY: This isn't love, Larry. Let me turn...

LARRY: I th-think it might be f-fair to hold you down. I th-think maybe this is what you have coming.

BRANDY: Maybe. Maybe not.

LARRY: Yes, a h-hurt for a hurt. Isn't that what they...? *(Suddenly releasing her, still sitting on the backs of her legs)* I can't do this.

BRANDY: It isn't in you.

LARRY: No.

(Enter LEWIS silently. He shakes his head, moves silently behind LARRY, kicks him easily, suddenly, not killingly, in the small of the back. It is a controlled, restrained kick, but LARRY grunts in pain, half turns, lies unable to turn.)

LARRY: Who...who...?

BRANDY: *(Rising with difficulty)* I think you know who.

(BRANDY and LEWIS look at each other from as great a distance as it is possible to arrange and down at LARRY, who continues to writhe.)

LEWIS: I'm sorry, brother. If that's the kind of trouble you had in mind for yourself, I should have gotten to you much sooner.

BRANDY: It wasn't him, Lewis.

LEWIS: Are you sure?

BRANDY: I'm sure. I remember the hands now, the laugh, the smell. My body remembers. It wasn't Larry. Or Darren. Or Rob. Or any combination thereof.

LEWIS: Then who...?

BRANDY: *(Moving)* No one I know. Not even you, though I wondered for a while. God, I've been crazy. *(Looking down into the street)* It was someone out there, someone who doesn't deserve to live, but I'm not going to find him. I've looked long enough. Maybe it doesn't matter who it was. To me. It was done. To me. It happened. To me. But it's over. I'm not going to live the rest of my life with...with it in my arms. I'm just going back to...to one day after another, to my life. So, Lewis, Larry, you've been my friends, I've cared for you, both. *(Leaving)* But I'm going back.

LEWIS: Goodbye, Brandy.

LARRY: *(On the floor still, able to turn now)* ...Bra-a-ndy...

BRANDY: No. I'm sorry, but that's all, Larry. I'm sorry.

(Exit BRANDY. For a moment the brothers listen to BRANDY's descending footsteps on the stairs, then LEWIS goes to help LARRY to rise as the light fades to dark.)

Scene Five

(That sylvan scene. The library, the ivy-covered walls, another spring. ROB and DARREN, in summer clothes, DARREN with both hands partly bandaged. They stand at some distance from each other, having just rendezvoused. DARREN wears comfortable casual clothes, ROB is dressed for more formal work.)

ROB: Quite the boxer with those wrappings, old man. *(With a gesture at hand exercises)* How's the therapy?

DARREN: To be perfectly honest, I find it a little repetitive.

ROB: Oh, no. You're not bored again. Remember what happened the last time.

DARREN: I seem to remember...something... What are you up to—in that outfit?

ROB: You wouldn't believe me if I told you I was selling encyclopedias.

DARREN: No.

ROB: Then I won't tell you. Darren, there's no work for us. Our educations were a waste. What's a philosopher to do these days?

DARREN: Grin and bear it: That's all the philosophy you need. No, there's nothing, except room for...further studies...

ROB: Further studies... Speaking of "further studies," seen "Brandy" lately?

DARREN: I haven't seen her at all. Have you?

ROB: No. Not even on the street. I hope she's not going down, down, down...

DARREN: Somehow, I don't think so. "Brandy's" gone for good. A certain someone—her creator—has returned to herself. I see her from time to time, more grown up than we, doing something only she can do...

ROB: ...putting something of her own together...perhaps teaching it to others...

DARREN: *(Nodding)* That's it. Teaching others. The art of.... *(Gazing into the distance)* Ah, but isn't that Anna Whoozawhatsamova, your favorite sociologist and mine, her Marxism clearly evident behind the only glasses in St Paul thicker than yours...

ROB: *(Gazing in the same direction)* I believe that may well be her. That rebellious bosom, circa 1917, is a giveaway. Ah, well, there she goes. *(Anna Whoozawhatsamova passes unseen.)* By the way, whatever happened to the mayonnaise of our malaise...

DARREN: The mayonnaise of our malaise... I think it may have turned.

ROB: Turned. I hope that isn't sour grapes.

DARREN: Oh-oh. *(As Anna reappears)* There she goes the other way. *(Calling into the distance)* Anna! Oh, Anna: Won't you explain this, uh....class struggle...you led us to believe...was rampant and pervasive?

ROB: Gone. I don't think she heard you, old man.

DARREN: Ah, no, but forever, in my mind, our dear Anna will be forever anticipating my question, her left eye fixing me through her left lens, her right eye drifting out over her right in the spirit of inquiry...

ROB & DARREN: *(Ensemble. In a thick Russian accent)* "Boys, boys do not mock those who work, for whom each day is toil..."

(They laugh.)

DARREN: If only there were an Anna.

ROB: But there is, my friend. That was her. There she went. We both saw her.

DARREN: No, no, my friend. *(Looking at his hands, the movement coming back into his fingers)* I could never create a woman. Only old You Know Who...

ROB: You created her. And, believe me, as those fingers well know, Anna Whoozawhatsamova will never be happy with less than three dimensions.

DARREN: Nor should we, my friend, nor should we.

ROB: By the way, speaking of three dimensions, look at this paragon. *(Producing a small, beautifully bound book)* Recognize it?

DARREN: Well, it's about the same size... It's not your Plato, the one you tore limb from limb?

ROB: The very one. *(Handing it over)* Bound it myself.

DARREN: *(Examining it)* Well, I'll be damned... I didn't think you could...

ROB: There's one thing won't fall apart in this world.

DARREN: *(Fluttering the pages underneath his thumb)* Nor will we, my friend, nor will we.

(First ROB laughs, then DARREN. They begin to leave together upstage.)

DARREN: *(Stopping suddenly, looking back at the ivy-covered walls and all that)* But wouldn't it be interesting if those unlived lives, the roads not taken, and those who travelled down them with us, just kept on going, kept right on going, after we'd let go of them?

ROB: It would indeed. Especially the women. Or the woman. Muse on that one for a while.

DARREN: Indeed. Ruminate and conjecture.

ROB: *(Savoring the last word, as he moves his hand across the space they leave behind them)* Surmise....

(Exit ROB & DARREN together upstage. The ART TEACHER enters right, briefcase, trench coat, her sensuality once more muted. DREW enters left. They face each other. DREW shakes his head, turns, rolls off.)

ART TEACHER: Drew... *(Alone, not speaking to be heard by him)* Drew... I'm sorry about Darren, in more ways than you know, but he's going to be okay, he's going to be all right. And...I take it all back.

(She laughs at herself, shakes her head, walks on through suggestions of a changing landscape as the day declines toward twilight. She is wandering, somewhat aimlessly, through another spring, into another summer, when the light loses its color precipitously and she finds herself on the dead poet's bridge.)

ART TEACHER: Aha. The bridge I didn't like, the one that wasn't there. But, of course it wasn't there, it's here, right here.

(She looks around her and, moving to the edge of the stage, down at the water as the day darkens further.)

ART TEACHER: Why is the water so black? *(Spotting LARRY in the shadows, moving toward him)* Larry.

LARRY: Who are you?

ART TEACHER: I was "Brandy."

LARRY: Not anymore?

ART TEACHER: Not any more.

LARRY: You're not following me?

ART TEACHER: I don't think so. And you... You're off work, on the way home?

(He nods.)

ART TEACHER: No cards? No beer?

LARRY: No cards, no beer.

ART TEACHER: What are you doing here?

LARRY: Looking at the water.

ART TEACHER: Just looking?

LARRY: You think I'm going to throw myself into it?

ART TEACHER: I hope not. *(Beat)* May I look with you for a while?

LARRY: For a while. *(Beat)* And then you'll tell me your name.

ART TEACHER: And then I'll tell you my name.

(She stands beside him. Together they look down into the water as the light fades to black.)

END OF PLAY

HELEN'S PLAY

CHARACTERS

THOMAS, *late fifties, somewhat taller than* HAL, *every inch the elder brother, a playwright, rich, talented, semifamous, a bachelor.*

HAL, *forties, his younger brother, father of one, an aspiring screenwriter, temporarily out of the other work that pays the bills.*

HELEN, *early thirties, an aspiring and talented actress, wife of* HAL, *sister-in-law of* THOMAS, *mother of* TOM.

TOM, *thirteen, only child* of HAL *and* HELEN.

EFFI, *thirteen, very adult, accustomed to wealth and class.*

JACKSON & HÉLÈNE, *the Pflaum-Smythes, a wealthy couple, parents of* EFFI.

Various renditions of "Bless 'em All" are sometimes heard on the radio, eventually progressing to vocalized ones. The vampire tale, *Mrs. Amworth*, is by E F Benson, 1867-1940.

ACT ONE

Scene One

(Chicago, 1940. THOMAS's *luxury apartment on the near North Side. A doorway, right, leads to the bedrooms; another, right center, leads to the kitchen. There is a high window covered with rich, heavy, floor-length drapes, possibly maroon, up right. An elevator, left center, opens directly into the apartment; lighting is subtle, modern; the furnishings dark, understated, masculine; a substantial library lines the back wall; a couple of modern prints are tastefully hung and individually lighted. A radio console stands against the back wall.)*

(A winter's evening. Wind and the occasional sound of Lake Michigan's winter waves building the ice formations are heard before the light rises. Among other choices, a crystal decanter of cognac stands on the drinks cart; a silver coffee pot on the table, empty cups. HAL, THOMAS, *and* HELEN, *returned from the opening night of one of* THOMAS's *plays, and all in evening dress, are seated at a folding table constructed of beautiful old dark wood polished to a deep glow.* HAL *and* THOMAS *smoke fine cigars,* HELEN *a cigarette. At open: The three, almost simultaneously, are sipping from their snifters. They listen to the wind off the lake.* TOM *is asleep in the next room.)*

THOMAS: Once upon a time…I thought…when circumstances were right… I'd have the wind stilled when I wanted, the traffic rerouted…so I could think. I'd have restaurants emptied when I desired to be alone. Now circumstances are right and I change nothing. I like things as they are.

HAL: Working conditions in the West Virginia mines.

THOMAS: *(Smiling)* I didn't say that.

HAL: Hitler staring across the Atlantic.

THOMAS: *(Smiling)* No.

HELEN: *(To* THOMAS*)* Once upon a time I was—I may be still—a child, jolted awake, standing barefoot in a doorway, looking at something… center stage—I don't know what—mouth open, eyes dropping out.

THOMAS: Why, Helen, you don't look like that at all. You're a sophisticated woman. It would take something to make those eyes drop out.

HELEN: These eyes aren't the only eyes I have.

HAL: It's true. I've seen the others. There's nothing I can do.

HELEN: Or undo.

THOMAS: Listen to that wind.

(They listen.)

THOMAS: You don't have to go home. You can stay here. The Outer Drive is ice.

HAL: No, we wouldn't want to put you out. Besides, there's....

HELEN: We'll stay.

THOMAS: There seems to be a difference of opinion here. *(Slight pause; to both)* How is the boy?

HAL & HELEN: He's....

THOMAS: *(Laughs, then:)* You first, Hal.

HAL: *(A beat, then:)* I worry. He reads...

THOMAS: Why, that's awful. I'd worry too.

HAL: He reads the same story a dozen times...

THOMAS: Is that it?

(HAL nods.)

THOMAS: Now Helen.

HELEN: There's nothing to worry about. Children do one thing for a while, then they do another.

HAL: I wish I knew where it was all heading.

HELEN: We can't know that.

THOMAS: Nothing *has* happened, has it?

HAL: I have a feeling something will.

THOMAS: You've always had that feeling, Hal. My God, all the things you thought were going to happen. How old were you when Dad died?

HAL: Eight. That happened.

THOMAS: Yes, it did. That would give anyone a sense of...of something waiting in the wings.

(They drink.)

HAL: I sense him...going; perhaps he's just going to go his own way.

THOMAS: That doesn't seem so bad.

HELEN: Hal doesn't think it's good for my son to see me drink.

THOMAS: *(A beat, then:)* Why, you don't drink, Helen. You drink, you smoke. That's the times. You're of them. You're just keeping up with the rest of us.

HAL: *(Raising his glass)* To the rest of us.

(All raise their glasses.)

HAL: May we get home, one way or the other, tonight or tomorrow or the day after. To our hearth fires, our sons— *(To* THOMAS*)* —our nephews, the wind across the lake, a winter's night; ourselves, alive and together; our brothers, our wives...

HELEN: *(Raising her glass higher)* ...our husbands...

*(*HAL *nods, sips; the others follow.)*

THOMAS: That's a hell of a toast, Hal.

HELEN: He's been practicing.

THOMAS: I'm glad my supplies are adequate. It may take more than one drink to do it justice.

HAL: Speaking of fathers... *(Looking at* HELEN*)* ...there's one I've helped home more than once.

HELEN: Now *there's* a drinker for you. Daddy was born with a shot glass in his hand.

HAL: And it's still there.

HELEN: I'm glad he's held onto something.

HAL: Some things, I suppose, run in the blood.

THOMAS: Yes, if only we knew what. Where is your father, Helen?

HELEN: On the road.

THOMAS: Still selling?

HELEN: Still selling.

(Slight pause as they drink)

THOMAS: What did you think of the third act, Hal?

HAL: Well, it was a long time coming.

THOMAS: Precisely.

HAL: And when it got there, not that much happened.

THOMAS: That's it. People expect a third act, but not everything comes in threes, or thirds. In this play there's only before—and after.

HELEN: What about "during?"

THOMAS: Audiences aren't interested in "during," Helen. That's like asking them to watch a rehearsal.

HAL: I think rehearsals are even more interesting than the...

THOMAS: That's you, Hal. And maybe Helen.

HELEN: Yes.

THOMAS: I'm glad you two have something in common.

(HAL *and* HELEN *chuckle.*)

HAL: *(To* THOMAS*)* I've watched yours. I've sat there in the back watching actors change, watching *you* discover...

THOMAS: That's right.

HAL: ...things about your own play, even as I was, only it wasn't my play.

HELEN: No, it wasn't.

THOMAS: *(Reprovingly)* Helen...

HAL: It isn't that my wife thinks her husband is without talent, it's just that she thought he had somewhat more than it turns out he does.

HELEN: I didn't say that.

THOMAS: *(To* HAL*)* Remember what Dad used to say, Hal: "Comparisons, boys, are odious." *(To* HELEN*)* It's *your* talent that ought to matter to you, Helen.

HELEN: It is what matters to me.

(TOM *appears in the doorway, right, dazed from an uneven sleep. He is also dressed for a night in the theatre, though his clothes are a little crumpled now from having slept in them and his shoes have been removed. He has a blanket wrapped around his shoulders.*)

HELEN: *(Not aware of him, lightly)* Without it, I'd still be that child, mouth open, eyes dropping out...

TOM: Dad...

THOMAS: *(To* HELEN*)* Well, if it's any consolation, I'm thinking of a role for you. I'm going to put *you* in my next play, I mean a role written for you, I'm going to put my brother's very talented young wife front and...

TOM: Dad...I can't sleep.

HELEN: *(Her eyes bright)* Thomas, I can't tell you how much...

HAL: *(Holding a hand out to him)* Come here, Tom.

(TOM *walks up to him.*)

HAL: What's wrong, lad?

TOM: I told you.

HAL: You told me. You can't sleep. Right?

TOM: Right. When are we going home?

HAL: We might not be. Listen to that wind.

(*All listen.*)

TOM: I don't care about the wind.

HELEN: *(Gently)* It's there whether you care about it or not, Tom. Listen. Those are real waves breaking across the road, freezing as they break. You can't stand up out there.

TOM: *(Turning to face her)* I can.

HELEN: Maybe you can. I'm the one who can't. You don't want your mother falling down, do you?

TOM: *(A beat, then, very quietly:)* No.

HAL: *(Standing)* Come on, Tom. We'll make you up a real bed and put you in it. How's that sound?

TOM: *(A beat, then, quietly:)* Okay.

HELEN: *(To* TOM *as he and* HAL *leave right)* And then I'll bring you a hot chocolate, Tom. This is a night for a hot chocolate.

(Exit TOM *and* HAL. HELEN *and* THOMAS *sip their cognacs,* HELEN's *eyes still glowing from the offer he has made her.)*

HELEN: *(Perhaps recalling him to the subject)* Me, front and center.

THOMAS: You, front and center.

HELEN: And there won't only be before and after, there'll be during.

THOMAS: It shall be as you desire: There'll be during.

HELEN: That's what you can do for me.

THOMAS: That's what I can do for you.

(Slight pause)

HELEN: What can I do for you?

(They look at each other. After a moment, THOMAS *shakes his head, looks down at the table,* HELEN *raises her hand to her forehead, holds it a moment, lowers her hand.)*

HELEN: Forget I said that.

THOMAS: Forgotten. You were miscued, that's all. *(A large gesture)* Get offstage and come back on when you're supposed to.

HELEN: *(Laughing)* All right. You're a good man, Thomas.

THOMAS: Hal's a good man.

HELEN: The best.

THOMAS: Tom's a good boy.

HELEN: He is.

THOMAS: He's going to be all right.

HELEN: I hope so.

THOMAS: And finally: You're a good woman, Helen.

HELEN: *(Laughing)* All right, so we're all good. What now?

THOMAS: I'll tell you. We all of us have several lives in us.

HELEN: Yessss?

THOMAS: Especially actresses, or actors. Even playwrights. But no matter how many we've got, we only lead one.

HELEN: How boring! What do we do with the others?

THOMAS: *(Standing, taking stage)* Well, a day at the typewriter is a day with the doors shut. A day rehearsing in a cold, half-lit theater is a day the sun doesn't shine. No, we don't live those lives, Helen, we put them onstage. To do anything, as an artist, you learn to sit still, to let life pass in the distance.

HELEN: I'm not sure I can do that, Thomas.

THOMAS: Then it will be hard for you.

HELEN: It already is.

(They look at each other again as HAL *returns with a sigh.)*

HELEN: Asleep? *(Warmly)* Is my boy asleep?

HAL: Not yet. What about that hot chocolate?

(HELEN *stands but isn't able to move immediately.)*

HAL: What's going on? What's happening?

THOMAS: *(Going toward the radio console)* I don't know. Shall we see? It's earlier in New York, earlier still in Europe. *(Tuning the cat's-eye)* You wouldn't believe it: I can get all kinds of places with this thing.

HELEN: *(Leaving right center)* I'll see about that hot chocolate.

(As the light very slowly fades to emphasize that of the radio dial and that which spills from the kitchen where HELEN *can be heard getting milk from the refrigerator, etc, Hitler's voice exhorting his minions fills the room.* HAL *and* THOMAS *face each other for a moment,* THOMAS *turns Hitler down.)*

THOMAS: Well, brother.

HAL: Well, brother.

THOMAS: That's what's happening.

(The brothers look at each other as the light more quickly fades.)

Scene Two

(In the darkness between scenes, the wind off the lake is heard as before, the waves crashing in the distance. As a faint nightlight from the direction of the bedrooms rises, TOM *enters in underwear and socks, the blanket wrapped tightly around him. He goes straight to the radio console, turns it on low, hears dance music of the time,*

leaves it on a moment as he looks around the room at its high ceiling, dimly lit prints and bound books, then turns it off. He goes to a book he knows the location of in the bookcase, takes it to a big chair, turns the floor lamp on low, opens the book, finds his place, reads softly to himself.)

TOM: "The village of Maxley, where, last summer and autumn, these strange events took place, lies on a heathery and pine-clad upland of Sussex. In all England you could not find a sweeter and saner situation..."

(Enter HELEN *in slip and blanket. She has been asleep but has brushed her hair before entering the living room. She speaks softly to awaken no one.)*

HELEN: I thought I heard someone.

TOM: *(His attention in the book)* It's me.

HELEN: I can see it's you. Funny. I woke up, I felt like dancing. *(Walking restlessly around the room, pausing behind* TOM's *chair)* Just you and your terrible tales, I see. What are you reading?

TOM: A tale of the supernatural.

HELEN: Yessss.

TOM: The same one. It's the one I was reading before...about the woman who floats outside the window.

HELEN: It's no night for floating outside the window.

*(*TOM *does not respond.)*

HELEN: I know I'm not as good at this as your father, but would you like me to read it to you?

TOM: *(Looks at her, somewhat surprised, then:)* No, it's all right. I can read it.

HELEN: I'm sure you can. *(Slight pause. She goes to the radio console, stands with her hands on it, turns on the dance music low, moves with it a moment, then faces* TOM.) Would you like another hot chocolate?

TOM: *(Not looking up)* Yes, please.

HELEN: Your wish is my command, sir. *(She begins to leave, pauses for appreciation.)* I said, "Your wish is..."

TOM: *(Not looking up)* Yes, thank you.

*(*HELEN *shrugs, exits into the kitchen.* TOM *immediately turns off the radio, then returns to his reading, comes to a scary part, shudders.* HAL, *in borrowed pajamas that are too large for him, looks in silently; when he looks over* TOM's *shoulder,* TOM *jumps.)*

HAL: *(Speaking softly)* I'm sorry, guy. I didn't mean to scare you.

TOM: You didn't scare me.

HAL: All right, I didn't scare you.

TOM: It was Mrs Amworth.

HAL: Who's Mrs Amworth?

TOM: She's the woman who floats outside the window. *(Pointing to his place in the book)* She's looking in now.

HAL: She is, is she? *(Looking in the direction of the window)* You know, I think I can feel her there, feel her eyes...

TOM: Dad...

HAL: Shall we go look?

TOM: No.

HAL: Shh! Someone might be asleep.

TOM: *(Suddenly standing)* All right.

HAL: All right what?

TOM: Let's go look.

HAL: Okay. Let's sneak up on her.

(As they approach the draped window up right, HAL in a magnified tiptoe)

HAL: You go that side, I'll go this. All right.

(HAL takes a hold of one drape, TOM the other.)

HAL: Ready?

TOM: Ready.

(They yank the drapes apart. THOMAS stands there in silk robe and pajamas, his brandy snifter in his hand. TOM and HAL both exclaim.)

HAL: *(To THOMAS)* Thomas! What the hell are you up to?

(THOMAS shrugs.)

HAL: You nearly scared the life out of us. *(To TOM)* It's okay, Tom. It's your uncle.

TOM: I can see that.

THOMAS: *(Coming into the room)* I'm sorry. I'm not used to other people in my apartment. I couldn't sleep.

HAL: It seems to run in the family.

THOMAS: I thought I heard noises. I checked the door, I poured myself a drink, then I heard someone coming and...and I don't know why, I stepped behind the drapes. It was strange in there, behind the drapes. I forgot all about the room behind me, looking down into the street. I saw a gal down there on the corner waving at cars. Can you imagine—on a night like this? *(Sings briefly, dances with his cognac.)* ...It was on a night like this... I watched until she was... *(Aware of the boy)* ...well, rescued.

HAL: *(To* TOM*)* So, there was a woman out there after all.

TOM: What was she doing, Dad?

HAL: Floating between lives, Tom.

THOMAS: *(Moving into the room)* If not life and death.

HAL: God, that's a reminder, isn't it? Just like Hitler.

THOMAS: Just like the coal miners. It's all around us, isn't it? Some of it's even right here.

HAL: *(A little confrontationally)* What is?

THOMAS: Life, I guess. What did you think I meant?

HAL: Well, I thought it might be a subtle reference to my unemployed status.

THOMAS: Hal, no! I wouldn't say anything like that.

HAL: I know.

THOMAS: I just meant.... I'm used to being alone, you see. I'm just an aging, if successful, playwright. I'm not a husband, or a father, and suddenly it was all here, all those more important things, right inside my door.

HAL: Speaking of wives, I wonder where mine is.

THOMAS: Isn't she with you? I mean... What do you mean?

HAL: I mean you can get a hell of a lot of entrances and exits out of three or four rooms. Who *was* that down there on the corner?

THOMAS: Hal! That's not funny. I'm sure Helen...

(Enter HELEN *with a steaming cup of hot chocolate.* TOM *goes to her, reaching for the cup.)*

HAL: Right on cue.

THOMAS: I couldn't have done it better myself.

HELEN: *(To* TOM*)* Careful, don't make me spill this. I'm not that good in the kitchen, and when I happen to make something right, like this hot chocolate, for instance... Who turned the radio off?

*(*TOM *raises his hand slightly.)*

HELEN: *(To all)* What's going on here? What's happening?

HAL: I don't know. I feel like going home.

HELEN: Hal, the kitchen clock told me a little secret: It's three o'clock in the morning.

*(*HELEN*, dancing a little with* TOM*, who worries about his hot chocolate, singing to him)*

HELEN: ...We danced the whole night through....

HAL: It seems more than one of us is in a dancing mood. However, we're imposing. We're keeping Thomas awake.

THOMAS: No, not really.

HAL: You said you couldn't sleep with other people in your apartment.

THOMAS: I said I wasn't used to it. I can sleep. I'm going to go off and prove it right now.

HELEN: Well, no, if Hal isn't comfortable... Tom, sit down and drink your hot chocolate while the rest of us make a very grownup decision about what to do. *(She looks at* HAL.*)*

HAL: No, it's all right. I'm comfortable. I think I woke up because everyone else was up. Don't blame everything on me.

HELEN: All right, I won't. Who started this? *(Pointing at her son)* You.

TOM: Uncle Thomas was up before I was. He was hiding behind the drapes.

HELEN: Oh, he was?

THOMAS: I was looking down into the street.

TOM: He saw a woman on the corner waving at cars.

HELEN: Oh, he did? You sure she wasn't waving up here?

THOMAS: It wasn't necessary. Another knight in a shining Ford rode off with her.

HAL: Well, folks. Maybe we should all—you know, as in "one, two, three"—go to bed.

HELEN: I think I may be too excited.

HAL: Oh?

HELEN: Yes, I'm still proud I didn't burn the milk in the pan, I didn't burn myself, I didn't spill anything all over the stove. How is that hot chocolate, Tom?

TOM: It's good.

HELEN: You see?

HAL: I see. I'm proud of you, Helen. Maybe I'll let you in the kitchen at home, but for now....

HELEN: Yes. What now?

THOMAS: Well, I could send down for the reviews. *(Slight pause)* Only I'm afraid.

TOM: I'm not afraid. I'm going to bed.

(Exit TOM, *holding his hot chocolate in both hands.)*

HAL: *(As* TOM *leaves right)* Goodnight, guy.

TOM: *(Off)* Goodnight, Dad.

(Slight pause. THOMAS *begins to go right, holding his snifter.)*

THOMAS: My turn.

(Exit THOMAS.*)*

HAL: As I said: one, two, three.

HELEN: One, two... *(Starting off right)* ...threee.

HAL: We should talk.

HELEN: *(Stopping)* About what?

HAL: I don't know.

HELEN: I don't know if I could keep myself awake talking about that. Coming?

HAL: In a minute.

*(*HELEN *nods, exits right.* HAL *looks around at the apartment that isn't his, picks up the still-open book to put it away, becomes interested in the text, sits.)*

HAL: *(Reading very softly as the light fades)* Hm. "In all England you could not find a sweeter and saner situation. Should the wind blow from the south, it comes laden with the spices of the sea; to the east high downs protect it from the inclemencies of March; and from the west and north the breezes which reach it travel over miles of aromatic forest and heather. The village itself is insignificant enough..."

Scene Three

(The next afternoon. Snowbound, the drapes up right open, much of the window plastered with snow, bright with reflected light. A much-thumbed playscript sticks horizontally from the bookcase. HAL, HELEN, *and* THOMAS *are visiting* THOMAS's *friends in 6B.* TOM, *in his dress pants, shiny black shoes and a borrowed sweater much too big for him, sits where* HAL *sat the night before, book open in his lap. He reads. The "in use" light comes on, the elevator is heard stopping at* THOMAS's *apartment.* TOM *waits for someone to come in, then resumes reading and turns a page.)*

TOM: "Then about the middle of August appeared the first of those mysterious cases of illness which our local doctor attributed to the long-continued heat coupled with the bite of these venomous insects. The patient was a boy of sixteen or seventeen, the son of Mrs Amworth's gardener, and the symptoms were an anemic pallor and a languid prostration, accompanied by great drowsiness and an abnormal appetite.

He had, too, on his throat two small punctures where, so Dr Ross conjectured, one of these great gnats had bitten him..."

(A small tapping is heard on the elevator door. TOM *puts down the book, goes to listen at the door, calls through it.)*

TOM: Who's there?

EFFI: I am.

TOM: *(Still calling)* Who's "I?"

EFFI: *(Calling)* Effi.

TOM: *(Calling)* I don't know any Effi.

EFFI: You will. *(Calling)* These places are soundproofed. Push the speaker button.

(TOM *finds the speaker button, pushes it,* EFFI's *voice, somewhat mechanized, continues through it.)*

EFFI: Your parents are visiting my parents in 6B. We're your uncle's friends.

TOM: *(Into the microphone)* So?

EFFI: So, I, well... Aren't you going to open the door?

TOM: I don't know.

EFFI: If you push the "open" button, the door will open. I can close your door from here, but I can't open it.

(TOM *raises his hand to the button, lowers it without pushing.)*

TOM: I don't like buttons. I've pushed enough already.

EFFI: Don't you wonder what I look like?

TOM: Yes.

EFFI: Well, you'll never know if you don't push the button.

(Slight pause. TOM *pushes the "open" button. The door slides silently open,* EFFI *is revealed behind the grating. She is not dressed for the outdoors, but wears a fluffy angora sweater, etc. Very much at her ease, she waits for him to open the grating for her, then, laughing to herself, extends her hand through the grating.)*

EFFI: How do you do? I'm Effi.

TOM: *(Shaking the hand gingerly)* I'm Tom.

EFFI: I know. You know, I could open this grating myself, but a gentleman....

TOM: You might hurt your hand.

EFFI: *(Withdrawing her hand)* You know, Tom, all the cars are stopped, all the buses, all the trains. They're calling this the Great Storm of 1940...

TOM: *(Looking back at his open book)* Are they?

EFFI: ...and I thought, since our parents are trapped in 6B, we might as well be trapped in 4A. We can play...

TOM: I'm not much for playing.

EFFI: I was going to say we can play poker. Or we can call people up and *breathe* into the phone. *(Beat)* All right: We can make brownies and go door to door like Girl Scouts. For this one day—or as long as the Great Storm of 1940 lasts—we can be friends.

TOM: *(A beat, then:)* I don't have many friends.

EFFI: I wonder why. *(He looks at her.)* Do you have any?

(TOM *reaches toward the "close" button.*)

EFFI: Don't push that button.

TOM: Why shouldn't I?

EFFI: I'm not used to having doors closed in my face.

(TOM *pushes the button, the door closes. Silence. He starts toward his book.* EFFI *taps again before he gets there.*)

TOM: *(Not returning, calling)* What now?

EFFI: *(Calling)* Will you open the door if I say I'm sorry?

TOM: *(Calling)* If you say *what?*

EFFI: *(Calling)* "I'm sorry!"

TOM: *(Calling)* You already said it.

EFFI: *(Exasperated)* Tom...!

(*Suddenly* TOM *returns to the elevator and pushes the button, the door opens. They stare at each other a moment through the grating before speaking.*)

EFFI: What are you doing that's so much more interesting than I am?

TOM: I'm reading. I'm reading a good story now.

EFFI: What's it called?

TOM: "Mrs Amworth."

EFFI: Is she a babysitter who murders young boys?

TOM: Very funny.

EFFI: Is she an actress?

TOM: No.

EFFI: Your mother's an actress.

TOM: Yes.

EFFI: That's what I'm thinking of. Someday. *(Beat)* May I come in?

TOM: No.

EFFI: *(Beat)* Why not?

TOM: I don't know. *(Turning back toward his book)* I've seen what you look like.

(EFFI *opens her mouth to speak, then turns to her own row of buttons and pushes one. The door slides shut, the "in use" light comes on though* TOM *doesn't notice.*)

TOM: I didn't mean that. I mean I didn't mean that the way it sounded, but I didn't know how it sounded until I said it. *(Beat)* Effi. *(Turning, calling)* Effi! *(No response. He pushes the speaker button.)* Effi, where are you?

(The conversation continues via the intercom.)

EFFI: *(A small voice in a small speaker)* Going up.

TOM: *(Into the microphone)* You can come in now.

EFFI: If you want to see me, you can come up.

TOM: I don't like elevators.

EFFI: Tough.

TOM: Aren't there stairs? *(Beat)* I said: aren't there stairs?

EFFI: The stairs are scary.

TOM: I wouldn't be afraid. *(Beat)* I said....

EFFI: You said you wouldn't be afraid, but you would, Tom. You'd be terrified.

TOM: You might think so, but I...

(There is a click from the speaker.)

TOM: *(Into the microphone)* Effi? Effi?

(The "in use" light goes out. TOM *returns to his book, sits, finds his place, tries to read, glances at the elevator, looks back at his book, looks longingly at the elevator door, hears sounds, nearly jumps up as the "in use" light comes on, but affects a deep interest in the story of Mrs Amworth. The elevator door opens to reveal* HAL *and* HELEN *in borrowed clothes of* THOMAS's. THOMAS *enters behind them in one of his many expensive sweaters.* TOM *peers around to see if there is anyone else as* THOMAS *closes the grating and the door.*)

HELEN: What are you staring at, young man? You haven't seen a ghost?

*(*TOM *shakes his head.)*

HAL: Mrs Amworth isn't riding the elevator now, is she?

*(*TOM *shakes his head, returns to his book.)*

THOMAS: Well now, listen everybody. I'm just going to read the first scene when they get here.

*(*TOM *looks up, then feigns an interest in his book.)*

THOMAS: I don't like being a one-man show, but the weather makes actors of us all. *(Arranging chairs in a semicircle facing downstage)* Now let's set this up as a bit of a theater, unless of course... *(With a gesture at the radio console)* ...you'd prefer Hitler.

HAL: *(Helping him with the chairs, feigns irresolution)* Well...

HELEN: Hal! We've always liked you better than Hitler, Thomas.

THOMAS: Thank you, Helen.

HELEN: But are you sure you wouldn't rather have me read..?

THOMAS: This isn't your play, Helen. That's to come. In the indefinite future.

(HELEN affects a downcast look.)

THOMAS: We mustn't frighten the muse, you know. Some days I have to get down on my knees and beg just to get her to step off the elevator.

(TOM looks up, then down.)

THOMAS: Besides, who wants a cold reading on an ass-cold day, not that you're cold, Helen, it's just that I know the effect I want, even if I'm not much of an actor.

HAL: You always played the big brother well enough.

THOMAS: That role was natural, Hal. Besides, ten years or more...

HAL: ...made an insurmountable distance. Then, with Dad gone...

THOMAS: Yet I never was your father, Hal.

HAL: No. But I didn't have anyone else to look up to.

HELEN: It's true, Thomas. At first it was always "Thomas this, Thomas that," until he had even me wondering if I wouldn't really rather be... *(Swaggering)* ...Big Tipper on Opening Night.

THOMAS: Big Tipper? You haven't been telling Helen about my tipping habits, have you, Hal?

HAL: It must have been two other fellas.

THOMAS: Well, it's true. *(Rolling out the drinks cart, looking at the coffee service, wondering what to serve)* Since success smiled on me, I have been giving it away. I don't know why. Waiters, waitresses, cab drivers. I don't want them to bow and scrape, I don't want to be big man. But, God—think of what they work for! Think of the hours, the conditions. I haven't got a wife, or children. *(Showing his full money clip)* I can't have this stuff burning a hole in my pocket. I'm not going to be around forever. *(Deciding against drinks, which might stupefy an audience on a snowbound afternoon, returning the cart to its place by the wall)* And it isn't just strangers, Helen, it's family. *(Of* TOM*)* Take our reader here, this young man. If there were ever any problem with his education, Hal, I'm no further away than the phone.

HAL: Thanks, old man. Not just yet.

THOMAS: "Old man." I'm not that old. But wait, I'm forgetting my point. It's this. A writer is, well...at times lent some kind of power...to create worlds that weren't there before. But: has he got employees to be fair to, has he got competitors to be more ruthless to than they are to him? Hal knows: I'm a man of action who sits home all day. However omnipotent on my duff, I stand up powerless. I'd like to stand up Mayor of Chicago. I'd like to pick up that phone and say "Clear the snow." Well, I can say it, but to whom?

TOM: *(Under his breath)* Maybe for fifty cents...

THOMAS: *(As the adults laugh)* And furthermore...

HELEN: Yes, Mr. Mayor, you were saying..?

THOMAS: Oh, damn it, I've forgotten now. But if there's one thing I can't stand at a reading of my latest play, it's snores. *(Heading toward the kitchen)* Helen, will a modern woman help me with the coffee?

HELEN: *(Following)* Oh, I'm not as modern as all that, not in all things.

(Exit THOMAS *and* HELEN, *who will be heard puttering in the kitchen, laughing.* HAL *looks around, sighs, seats himself front and center as audience to the reading of* THOMAS's *new play.)*

HAL: Let the show begin. And may the foolishness that flesh is heir to not overwhelm us this day. May men and women, even the children amongst us, rise above the fears and follies that flood their veins, above the petty jealousies that might rend brother from brother, husband from wife, and fathers from...

TOM: What's that?

HAL: That's a toast, son. Your uncle writes plays, your father makes toasts.

TOM: Dad.

HAL: What is it, Tom?

TOM: What's a muse?

HAL: Ah, those Greeks. Well. Not that I can pretend to an intimate acquaintance, we may not have even met, but as I understand it...

TOM: Should I ask Uncle Thomas?

HAL: *(Beat)* Well, let me try, and then, if you're not satisfied with my definition, you can ask him for his. A muse is a spirit of creation, the Greeks thought of her as female, as seven, or is it nine, sisters, really, who inspire men, at different times in their lives, to attempt the arts. The attempt is... not always successful. And then, we might say, the young lady in question failed to put in an appearance, or...perhaps we saw her passing in the distance, but she didn't smile at us. Does that make sense?

TOM: Can she talk?

HAL: Only to playwrights. For artists she poses. To composers she sings. To screenwriters, I admit, she's sometimes a blur in the background...

TOM: And if she goes away, does that mean you'll never see her again?

HAL: No, son. That means she's sitting on someone else's lap, but if you're patient, if, in your case, you read and read and read, someday, maybe, you'll be ready to write and then she'll sit on yours.

TOM: Sounds good.

HAL: I think it probably is. I think I smell coffee. Do you?

TOM: *(Returning to his book)* Yes.

(The light goes on by the elevator door just as HELEN *and* THOMAS *wheel on a small table with the coffee set thereon.)*

THOMAS: Oh, oh. Here they are. The audience must not be kept waiting. Unless it's an audience of doctors. In which case, the wait should be forty-five minutes, minimum, during which germ-laden magazines will be distributed, magazines which tout capitalism in all its glory, even if the men in white are giving it a bad name.

HELEN: Somebody must have been to a doctor recently.

THOMAS: *(A finger to his lips as the "in use" light comes on)* Shh. I'll tell you later. *(At the elevator, into the intercom melodiously)* Oh, yes! Who's there?

A FEMALE VOICE: *(Harsh)* The Pflaum-Smythes are at the gate.

THOMAS: Ah, the Pflaum-Smythes. Such company I've been keeping since Lady Luck smiled on me.

TOM: *(To* HAL *as the elevator opens)* Is Lady Luck the...?

HAL: *(Nodding)* That's her.

(Enter JACKSON *and* HÉLÈNE PFLAUM-SMYTHE, *followed by* EFFI PFLAUM-SMYTHE. *The last dressed as before, the couple in rich informal day wear.* HAL *stands,* TOM *buries himself in his book.)*

THOMAS: Welcome, welcome to my humble abode.

JACKSON: Ah, well, since you so recently ascended to our humble abode, we saw no difficulty in descending to yours.

HÉLÈNE: *(As* TOM *shrinks)* Ah, and is this the boy genius himself? *(Approaching)* Your parents think the world of you, my boy, especially your father. *(Offering her hand)* Tom, isn't it?

(As TOM *rises to take her hand)*

HÉLÈNE: Named after his famous uncle, I suppose?

HAL: Well...

HÉLÈNE: Why not his father? In my day boys were named after their fathers. Pflaum-Smythes one, two, and three—Jr in some cases—but, as you can see, we only have a girl. Effi, come here. *(To* TOM*)* You needn't cringe, boy. I can assure you Effi is no genius, and her father is not her champion.

EFFI: Thanks, *Maman,* for the charming introduction. *(Holding out her hand)* Well, Tom.

(As the others move to converse and HELEN, *spotting the playscript, snatches it up to read)*

EFFI: I told you we'd be better off on our own.

TOM: You were right.

EFFI: "You were right, Effi."

TOM: You were right, Effi.

EFFI: I'm sorry again. I don't mean to make you jump through hoops. I'm not my mother. I realized after I got out of the elevator, I could still hear you calling my name. I liked the way you said it.

JACKSON: Well, Thomas, do I smell coffee? You're still getting your supplies all right. Have them flown in, I suppose.

THOMAS: Actually, I just get them from a restaurateur I know.

HÉLÈNE: *(Seating herself)* Well, I see the wagons have been drawn into a circle. It must mean the arts are about to show themselves.

HELEN: *(Holding up the script)* What an opening, Thomas!

THOMAS: Now who told you to read ahead?

(As the others choose chairs)

THOMAS: Well, well, get yourselves settled. Coffee, everyone. Make your trip to the facilities, that is, if you haven't already. *(To* TOM *and* EFFI*)* Boys and girls, your attention. If you can't follow this, I've done something wrong. Hal, Helen, are we ready?

HAL: *(Seated at an extreme distance from* HELEN*)* We are. We are the audience you've been waiting for, the one that follows every word, catches each nuance, each glance, gesture, and intonation of the actors; in short, Thomas, the audience in your forehead or the back of your head or...

THOMAS: Actually, Hal, they're right here in front of me and I thank you, all of you, in advance, for being here.

JACKSON: Hear, hear!

HÉLÈNE: That's very gracious of you, Thomas.

*(*THOMAS *walks, script in hand, reads. The lights, responsive to his commands, become more obviously theatrical. As the daylight fades from the window,*

he pictures himself upon the beach and the sea downstage in the auditorium of the actual theater.)

THOMAS: "House lights down. The curtain opens. Stage lights up. A strip of beach, a suggestion of sea, the endless cerulean of tropical sky."

HÉLÈNE: *(To her husband)* Poetic, isn't it?

JACKSON: *(Raising a finger, sotto voce)* Place, mood. Very important. Let him get it.

THOMAS: Thank you, Jackson. "Enter a woman, stage right, thirties, with a suitcase. No, she's not dressed for the tropics. She might still be standing in Midway Airport, wondering where to go. She's out of place, yet adequate to the place. She looks around her, taking command."

TOM: *(Sotto voce, to* HAL*)* Is she the muse?

HAL: *(Very softly)* Shh.

THOMAS: The boy may well be right, Hal. Let's see, Tom.

HELEN: *(Whispered to* TOM*)* Give him a chance, Tom.

THOMAS: "Her eyes are dark, deep, not the blue required to answer to that sky. Her eyebrows are remarkable, bushy, assertive, nearly meeting; her neck fine, yet not too long; her shoulders adequate; her breasts..." I think I'll stop there in deference to the young people.

HÉLÈNE: *(Normally)* Effi knows a woman has breasts, Tom may have noticed.

JACKSON: *(Softly)* Shh.

THOMAS: To paraphrase. Her breasts are important. Her assertion is there, as it is in her straight spine. She is not hiding from the world. And yet... *(Reading again)* "She has come here for a reason. Is it to meet someone? Why that ridiculous cheap suitcase in one hand? In the other she carries her shoes, city shoes, black, circa 1940, entirely inappropriate to this equatorial setting."

HELEN: *(Normally)* Is it my play after all, Thomas?

THOMAS: You may be right, Helen. For the moment, anyway, it is.

HELEN: *(Back straight, breasts asserted)* Then let me read her. I'm almost her already.

THOMAS: I can see that. Patience. *(Reading)* "She sees someone we cannot, approaching stage left, out of the infinitude of that horizon." If I could, I'd have the man minuscule, practically a mirage, before he became lifesize, but that's not possible. So little is. If I could put the sea on stage...

HAL: *(Normally)* Go on.

THOMAS: *(Nodding, reading)* "Enter the man, left. Forties, of medium height. He has not had the good sense to step out of his shoes, though he, too, is dressed for city streets. He, too, carries a suitcase in one hand, and in the other his businessman's hat, circa 1940. It has been said that like attracts like. There may some truth in this."

(*As* THOMAS *reads*, HAL, *straightening in his chair, does assume the characteristics of the man.*)

THOMAS: "Their foreheads are similar, their eyebrows. This too is a person who, we feel, perhaps has not lived, has not lived as he would have liked, who is stepping, he wants to believe, into life only now." (*Cluing his audience in*) That's what all this sea is, this sky. It's the unlived, the scene designer will please note. It's the life that two people, meeting in Chicago well before the midpoint of the century, would like to be able to fly away to, to step into. (*Reading again*) "However, no, they do not drop their suitcases, rush into each other's arms. Instead the man stops at some distance from the woman; the woman..."

(THOMAS, "*seeing*" *the play in the space before him, has stepped somewhat to the side, leaving the center stage of his imagined play unoccupied. Now* EFFI *stands, postured as the character in the play, the "suitcase" almost visible in one hand, her "shoes" almost visible in the other. She speaks without benefit of the script what are obviously the lines of the play, yet no one is surprised and all watch as, before, they listened.* THOMAS, *to the side, occasionally looks up from the script in his hand, also watching.*)

EFFI: I wasn't sure you'd come. It seemed, almost, a promise in another life. It *is* you?

(*At first,* EFFI, *practically entranced, speaks to a point in space; on the last line, the question, that point has moved somewhat in front of* TOM, *who now stands to occupy it, the weight of his "suitcase" in one hand, his imagined "businessman's hat" held by the crown in the other.*)

TOM: I...I think so. I'd like to believe it is.

(*Their eyes now lock as they move slowly, almost as if unaware of it, toward each other.*)

EFFI: Then...you meant what you said?

TOM: I guess I did.

(*Suddenly* EFFI *smiles at the weight of the "suitcase" in her hand, sets it down as* TOM, *in response, sets down his.* EFFI, *coming to life, escaping from the dream, laughs, throws away her inappropriate "shoes."* TOM, *looking at the "hat" in his hand, also laughs, sets it on the back of his head. They stop, very close to each other, their eyes locked. As the somewhat stagy lighting begins to fade toward darkness,* THOMAS *resumes walking and reading.*)

THOMAS: "I wasn't sure you'd come," says the woman. "It seemed, almost, a promise in another life. It *is* you?" she asks. "I...I think so," says the man, "I'd like to believe it is." "Then...you meant what you said?" asks the woman. "I guess I did," says the man.

(No longer reading, but moving at a normal, enthused pace, THOMAS laughs and, with expansive gestures, addresses a captive audience, one that does not appear to hear him as the "lovers" step into a lover's embrace, a lover's kiss, which will not be broken.)

THOMAS: Embrace and curtain. We could end it right there, don't you think?

(Though his audience, spellbound, continues to watch the play, suddenly THOMAS, still amused, moves toward the young couple arms outstretched in a gesture of embrace. His manner is kindly, even affectionate.)

THOMAS: All right you two, break it up.

(Blackout)

(The dial of the radio console lights. "...Bless 'em All, Bless 'em All..." plays very softly, not vocalized, not amplified and occasionally interrupted with static in the split seconds required to clear the stage of THOMAS's furniture and replace it with Tahitian sand.)

Scene Four

(An empty stage, the sound of surf, bird calls from behind the audience. The apartment is gone, the half circle of chairs. Within the world of the play within a play, much is possible that would not otherwise be likely. As, in effect, a tropical sun behind the auditorium rises to bathe the stage in its light, HAL and HELEN are revealed, downstage where TOM and EFFI stood at the close of Scene Three. They are realistically dressed as the young couple imaginatively were: that is HELEN actually carries that cheap suitcase in one hand, her heeled shoes in the other; HAL carries his actual suitcase, his actual hat, their big-city clothing rendering them completely out of place. Their positions are identical to that of TOM and EFFI just before they stepped into the embrace. TOM, in fact, in his bathing suit, though invisible to the couple, sits in the sand left, sweeping up a small mound, if not a castle. Now, instead of the dreamlike, almost mannered motions that characterized the players in the playreading, the gestures of our present couple are relaxed, natural. They simultaneously drop their suitcases, raise their hands to the sky and dance around.)

HAL & HELEN: Whoopie!

HELEN: *(Suddenly serious)* I think, Hal, it might be said that we are here.

HAL: *(As serious)* I think it may be said, Helen, that you are right. *(Looking around)* All right. We achieved the impossible. We quit our jobs. We made it around the U-boats. *(Taking a cigarette, offering HELEN one)* Not to be a spoilsport, but how the hell are we going to feed ourselves, house ourselves?

HELEN: *(After her cigarette is lit)* Thanks. I don't know. *(Looking up)* No coconuts? No thatches for our hut?

HAL: I'll ask at the embassy. There must be something for an American citizen.

HELEN: *(Blowing circles of smoke)* Bogart wouldn't be at a loss. He'd open a nightclub, he'd grease the necessary palms.

HAL: I'm not Bogart.

HELEN: Hemingway'd buy a fishing boat, he'd charter it, he'd keep an eye out for U-boats.

HAL: I'm not Hemingway.

(HELEN *laughs, then* HAL. *Now they step into the embrace* TOM *and* EFFI *assumed at the end of Scene Three.*)

HAL: Ah, you beauty. This is what it's all about, isn't it?

HELEN: Whew! I guess it is. *(Looking around)* Where now? Certainly not here.

(THOMAS *enters right, strolls across the stage. Appropriately dressed for the tropics, linen suit, straw hat, he seems quite debonair as he strolls past reading a dime novel with a lurid cover. The parties do not recognize each other.*)

THOMAS: *(Reading)* "Ah, you beauty," he said, his voice suddenly husky. "This is what it's all about, isn't it?" She gasps for air. "Whew! I guess it is," she says and looks around her. "Where now?" she asks. "Certainly not here."

HAL: *(Approaching* THOMAS*)* Pardon me, sir. Do you speak English?

THOMAS: *(A Vichy accent)* It ees one of ze plaisirs of life to parle another langue, *ne c'est pas?*

HAL: Oh, good, good. My, uh, wife and I are wondering. There wouldn't be a, uh, little hotel around here. *(With appropriate gesture)* Not too, uh...

THOMAS: I see what you mean, monsieur. *Pas trop cher. Mais bien situé,* a view... *(Looking out over a sea of heads here)* ...of the sea, its changing lights, its moods, not to overlook its sounds, forever varying, the sound, some say, of time itself.

HAL: Yes, that's it. That's the hotel we're looking for.

(HELEN *snickers,* HAL *peremptorily gestures silence.*)

THOMAS: *(Having missed nothing)* Ah, there is only one such place on the island, monsieur. The...uh... "The Reaching Arms." How do we say it? *(Laughing at himself)* Ha. *Quelle absurdité.* I have forgotten ze French for it.

HAL: Never mind ze French for it. Just tell us where it is.

THOMAS: Ah, *désolé,* monsieur. It is on the other side of the island. You can't get there from here.

HAL: Perhaps by boat.

THOMAS: No, monsieur. It is on the windward side. The surf is *incroyable*! I wouldn't risk it.

HAL: You wouldn't? What would you risk?

THOMAS: You might try through the Swamp of Desolation, monsieur. There is an outfitter in town. Sun lotion, pith helmets, dugouts, long poles: the works. Native guides. Very reasonable. Mount a little expedition, monsieur. Then you can send for madame. In a week or two.

HAL: We haven't got a week or two.

THOMAS: Take a month. I will look out for madame. When you return, she will speak ze French. She will be doing ze torch songs at Rick's, she....

(HELEN *is laughing outright.*)

HAL: *(His cigarette in the corner of his mouth, taking* THOMAS *by the elbow)* Suppose you and I make a little expedition, monsieur. You and I will find "The Reaching Arms." *(Heading right, to* HELEN*)* I had to do my Bogart. I had no choice.

THOMAS: *(Protesting on the way out)* If you please, sir. S'ils vous plait. This is my beach, monsieur, it is my ocean, my sky...

HAL: Sure, bud, sure.

(*Exit* HAL *and* THOMAS *right to* HELEN's *laughter.* TOM *draws a large. beautiful shell from the sand he has piled, approaches behind* HELEN. *They do not recognize each other, though he may have more of a suspicion than she has that this is a son somehow talking to his mother before he was born or even conceived.)*

TOM: *(100% American)* Excuse me.

(HELEN *jumps, faces him.*)

TOM: Would you care to buy a seashell?

HELEN: Oh, you scared me. A seashell? No, I don't think so. But that is very beautiful. I don't think I've ever seen such a beautiful shell. May I hold it?

TOM: *(Handing it to her)* Yes.

HELEN: *(Feeling its weight, its smoothness)* Magnificent.

TOM: Hold it to your ear.

HELEN: *(Doing so, and much puzzled, she repeats the lines she is hearing; in her own voice.)* "I think, Hal, it might be said that we are here." *(In a rendition of* HAL's*)* "I think it may be said, Helen, that you are right. Not to be a spoilsport, but how the hell are we going to feed ourselves, house ourselves?" *(Holding the shell away from her)* This is a very wonderful shell.

TOM: Yes.

HELEN: And you want to sell it to me?

TOM: If you promise you will listen to it, every day, you can have it. For nothing. *(Stepping back)* It's yours.

HELEN: But why...? I mean, suppose it is magic, supposing *you're* magic, what do I want with this? Why should I want to know what happened a few moments ago?

TOM: Perhaps you will also know what is going to happen. Perhaps you will decide to do something different. Who knows?

HELEN: *(Suddenly tossing him the shell, laughing, moving away, looking after HAL right)* Why should I want to do anything different?

TOM: *(Shaking his head, moving left)* I don't know. Maybe you'll decide to marry somebody else, have a different child; maybe...knowing what's to come...you won't marry at all, won't have children at all, but will devote yourself, wholeheartedly, to you, to your...

(TOM, ignored, withdraws to a spot left, sits in the sand, and, preoccupied, allows handfuls to run through his fingers. HELEN laughs to herself, suddenly kneels to open her suitcase. She withdraws a man's sweater, one THOMAS or TOM wore earlier, obviously one she did not pack. She goes on to find a cigar case and two unbroken brandy snifters.)

HELEN: I thought this was my suitcase.

(Cautiously she withdraws a portable radio that is playing the song that was on the console at the end of the preceding scene, "...Bless 'em All, Bless 'em All..." Almost frightened, standing, HELEN drops the radio in the suitcase, where it continues muffled before it ceases. Enter THOMAS, right, dressed as he was in his apartment, in another of his sweaters, his arms open to embrace her.)

HELEN: Thomas! *(Her coolness stopping him)* What are you doing here?

THOMAS: *(Stopping, lowering his arms)* I was always here, Helen. I was waiting for you. I thought you wanted...

HELEN: *(Backing away)* Never mind what I wanted.

THOMAS: This is your play, Helen. It's also your big chance.

HELEN: I'm not sure I want either.

(Looking from THOMAS to the boy, who ignores her and continues dribbling sand.)

HELEN: Will someone please tell me what's going on here? Where's Hal?

THOMAS: He's buying a small hotel, Helen. He's deep in negotiations with an old gal named Sadie. You're going to be part owner of a wonderfully moldy place, the wood soft and rotting, the sea lapping at the foundations. "Grand Rêve," it's called. That's French for "Reaching Arms."

HELEN: It is not. What's happening? Am I going nuts? How did you get here?

THOMAS: On the P & O Line.

HELEN: But we *flew*! You saw us off at the airport. How could you get here before us.

THOMAS: *(Approaching)* Dear Helen. I'm going to tell you a secret.

HELEN: You can tell it from there.

THOMAS: *(Stopping)* Please. Just listen.

HELEN: All right. If you don't come any closer.

THOMAS: Helen. I've always been jealous of my brother.

HELEN: *You* jealous of *him*! But you're rich, famous.

THOMAS: And he has you.

HELEN: What am I?

THOMAS: *(Strolling along the sea, thinking)* I think, Helen, you are more than an aspiring actress, more even than a character, a role.

HELEN: You're not going to tell me that I'm your...your...

(At the same moment that THOMAS *turns to face her,* TOM *ceases dribbling sand to look at her.)*

HELEN: Thomas, that's ridiculous. That's a lot of romantic—or classical—I don't know what. There are no...there aren't any...

THOMAS: No?

HELEN: Ask yourself. In Chicago as the Great Storm of 1940 closes in, lucky fella finds muse—never mind it's his brother's wife—follows her to Tahiti in a playreading, confronts her on the beach on the wrong side of the island as Hal decides to go into business for himself. Thomas...

THOMAS: Helen, I have no one...

HELEN: Thomas, when you die, the reporters will be at the door as they were for...for...

THOMAS: Sarah Bernhardt.

HELEN: *(With a wave of her hand)* There's nothing like that in this life for me. And your characters, Thomas, they'll all be there at your deathbed, all the characters you ever wrote, doing all the scenes you couldn't let them do, the theater being what it is—as you've so often said.

THOMAS: Helen, when a character steps offstage... Pffft! That's it. Do you think he goes down the street and crosses at the corner? Does he go home to his wife, to his child waiting to be born? Like the playwright who stood up from his work one day and called the real mayor and said, "Clear the streets...!" Click. That's what he gets, that's what's there. "Yeah, sure buddy." Click. And click, click, click! *(Stepping toward her, his arms outstretched)* Helen, you're more. Believe me, you're...

(Enter JACKSON *and* HÉLÈNE *right, appropriately overdressed: shorts, but what shorts; sunhats, but what sunhats; a picnic basket, but what a picnic basket! They converse, oblivious to* THOMAS *and* HELEN *who watch and listen to them, and to* TOM, *who doesn't.)*

JACKSON: Will this war never end? The sea is getting further away every year. It's like a tide going out, taking the beach with it.

HÉLÈNE: Oh, don't be so melodramatic, Jackson. Can't we just enjoy it while we're here?

JACKSON: First Roosevelt, then Hitler. I tell you, Hélène, I can't take it. I can't go on. Did you remember the paté?

HÉLÈNE: No, I just remembered: I forgot it. What difference does it make? The sun still shines. The trades blow. Look, look out there, the little mast...

JACKSON: *(Also looking out to sea)* Little mast..? My God, that's a U-boat, Hélène. They're watching us.

HÉLÈNE: Let them watch. What are they going to see? *(Waving)* Yoo-hoo, sailor! *(Lifting her breasts)* Long time müssen-küssen?

JACKSON: *(Gesturing appropriately without dropping the picnic basket)* My God, Hélène! I didn't know you spoke German.

HÉLÈNE: I don't.

JACKSON: *(To* THOMAS, *without recognizing him)* Once I thought she was some kind of goddess—can you imagine?—some Greek right out of legend, one of the...one of the...

THOMAS: *(Quietly)* One of the muses?

JACKSON: Of the what? Must be, must be. Keep going, Hélène. They're not going to torpedo the beach just to score with you.

(On the last lines as HÉLÈNE *leads* JACKSON *off left,* EFFI *enters right, lovely in a flesh-colored bathing suit. She follows her parents' footprints in the sand reluctantly, her eyes partly covered, as if she is weeping.* TOM *is immediately aware of her even as* THOMAS *and* HELEN, *looking after the* PFLAUM-SMYTHES, *chuckle to themselves.)*

TOM: *(Rising, intercepting* EFFI, *holding his shell out)* Would you care, miss, to buy a seashell?

*(*EFFI *looks up, revealing her tear-stained face.)*

EFFI: No, no. Thank you, anyway. *(Pausing)* It is very beautiful.

TOM: *(Placing it in her hands)* Isn't it? Feel its weight.

EFFI: Yes, it's very smooth.

TOM: Hold it to your ear.

(As EFFI *does so,* THOMAS *and* HELEN *turn to watch the young people. At first puzzled and then with wonder,* EFFI *repeats the lines she is hearing; at first in her own voice.*)

EFFI: "If you push the "open" button, the door will open. I can close your door from here, but I can't open it." (*In* TOM's) "I don't like buttons. I've pushed enough buttons already." (*Her own*) "Don't you wonder what I look like?" (*His*) "Yes." (*Hers*) "Well, you'll never know if you don't push the button." (*Holding the shell away from her*) This is a very wonderful shell.

TOM: Yes.

EFFI: (*Holding it out to him*) It's too good for me.

TOM: Nothing is too good for you.

EFFI: Why do you say that, boy? You don't know me.

TOM: I know you well enough. Why are you crying?

EFFI: (*Shaking her head*) I don't know. I'm not crying now.

TOM: No. (*Stepping back*) You can keep it if you want to.

EFFI: But why...? I mean, suppose it is magic, suppose *you're* magic, what do I want with this? Why would I want to know what happened— or *didn't* happen—in Chicago during the Great Storm of 1940?

TOM: (*Stepping further back*) I think you should know everything.

EFFI: Me? Why me? I'm nobody.

TOM: (*Turning to leave, right*) You're somebody. Oh, maybe not always. But sometimes. (*Leaving*) And when you are, when you have...

EFFI: When I'm who, when I have what...?

TOM: (*Stopping her questions with a raised hand*) Then, when you are, when you have, it's yours to...

(*Exit* TOM *right.*)

EFFI: (*To herself*) Then it's mine to...to what? (*Calling after him, still holding the shell before her*) Boy..!

THE PFLAUM-SMYTHES: (*Off*) Effi...! Effi, this way...

(*Exit* EFFI *left, the shell under her arm. Before she is off, she is covering her eyes as before, possibly weeping.* THOMAS *and* HELEN *face each other.*)

THOMAS: Think, Helen, if such magical children...were ours.

HELEN: Nonsense. I don't even know if I can... We haven't decided. An actress shouldn't have children, should she?

THOMAS: Probably not. (*Looking off right*) Oh-oh. Here comes Hal. I suppose he bought the hotel.

HELEN: I hope so. "Grand Rêve." It sounds so wonderful. May it last! But what if someday it rots and falls into the sea...?

THOMAS: *(Leaving left)* It may well, Helen. It may well. *(Returning to take suitcase)* Oh-oh, that's mine.

(As he picks it up, it briefly, mutedly plays "Bless 'em All," which amuses them both.)

THOMAS: You'll find yours at the airport, my dear. *(Raising his hand to her)* Goodbye, Helen.

HELEN: *(Facing off right, waving casually over her shoulder to* THOMAS *behind her)* Goodbye, Thomas.

(Exit THOMAS *left, enter* HAL *right.)*

HAL: Here I come. What are you waving about? Who was that fellow? Looked like Thomas.

HELEN: What would Thomas be doing in paradise?

HAL: Taking notes for hell.

HELEN: Well, did you buy the "Grand Rêve?"

HAL: How did you know? I've made an offer. She's thinking it over.

HELEN: Sadie?

HAL: That's right. You know a hell of a lot for somebody who's just standing around on the beach.

*(*HELEN *laughs, then* HAL. *Once more they step into that mythical embrace.)*

HAL: Ah, you beauty. This is what it's all about, isn't it?

HELEN: Whew! I guess it is. *(Looking around)* I think, Hal, it might be said that we are here.

HAL: *(As serious)* I think it may be said, Helen, that you are right. *(Looking around)* Not to be a spoilsport, but how the hell are we going to feed ourselves, etc, I mean if this hotel deal falls through...?

HELEN: *(Shrugging)* Eh? Somehow, Hal, somehow. *Plus ça change, plus c'est la même chose.*

HAL: I didn't know you spoke French.

HELEN: I don't.

HAL: Oh, well. I'll ask at the embassy. There must be something for an American citizen. But where's your suitcase? This is no time to start losing things.

HELEN: It's at the airport. I had the wrong one.

(As they leave)

HAL: It looked all right to me.

HELEN: Appearances, Hal.

HAL: *(Eyes wide)* I see.

(They laugh. Exit HAL *and* HELEN, *right. Enter* TOM, *right. He looks down at the evidence of the meeting, of the embrace of* HAL *and* HELEN; *he raises his head, revealing eyes opening wide, mouth beginning to open. Suddenly he is kicking the sand wildly, destroying every trace.)*

TOM: No! No one was here! No one met! No one held anyone else! No one! Magic! There is no magic! *(Stilled a moment, he looks left.)* Effi?

(The sun quickly sets.)

END OF ACT ONE

ACT TWO

Scene One

(HAL *and* HELEN's *similarly arranged, but much humbler apartment. No elevator; cheaper prints on the wall; a ragged, if extensive, library is stuffed in bookcases about four feet in height; a step-in kitchenette right center; the bedroom right; the hall door off left. The window up right, is smaller, dirty on the outside; it cannot be cleaned because it has been nailed shut by the landlord. The very different light of a very different day a week later shines weakly through it. The furniture, similarly placed, though without the semicircle of chairs, is cheaper stuff than* THOMAS *and his guests sit on.* TOM *is seated in the armchair, right, more or less where he was reading in* THOMAS's. HAL *stands at the window, occasionally attempting to see down into the street. He reads to* TOM, *his voice a wonderfully rich one that compels the story. The heat is barely adequate and both are warmly dressed.*)

HAL: "'Then listen, while I tell you about what happened later. I put out all light in the room where the boy lay, and watched. One window was a little open, for I had forgotten to close it, and about midnight I heard something outside, trying apparently to push it farther open. I guessed who it was—yes, it was full twenty feet from the ground—and I peeped 'round the corner of the blind. Just outside was the face of Mrs Amworth and her hand was on the frame of the window. Very softly I crept close, and then banged the window down, and I think I just caught the tip of one of her fingers.'"

TOM: Go on.

HAL: Well, you've read that part, I've read that part...

TOM: Dad...

HAL: *(Once more looking down into the street)* Maybe she got lost.
(Coming back into the room, handing TOM *the book)* I can't right now, Tom. I can't concentrate. But it was good of Thomas, wasn't it? It was gracious of him, to give you that book. Are you still reading "Mrs Amworth" yourself?

TOM: It's better when you read it. I'm on something else, "The Monkey's Paw."

HAL: I remember that one. Something about wishing a son back where he came from.

TOM: Dad...I don't want to know the ending.

HAL: Sorry. It does remind me. Mother or no, we'll have to get you back to school tomorrow.

TOM: I'd rather die.

HAL: And be buried alive, blood dripping from your chin.

(They smile at each other.)

HAL: Tom, it might be all that comes of these days, your education; it might be all any of us has to show. You wouldn't destroy that, would you?

(TOM *shakes his head and returns to his book.*)

TOM: Dad...who's Prometheus?

HAL: Those Greeks again. Prometheus, well, they say he stole fire from the gods and gave it to mankind, the gods didn't like it and...

(Both start as a key is heard in the lock. Enter HELEN, *flushed, happy, sporting a new scarf, bracelet, perfume, her arms full of shopping bags. She faces them.)*

HAL: I thought you were getting something for dinner.

HELEN: I was. I did.

HAL: Well, it ought to be good. It's four o'clock, you left before nine.

HELEN: I ran into Thomas.

HAL: *(Beat)* He's doing his own shopping now?

HELEN: *(Going in and out of the kitchenette, putting away)* Are you? I don't know. His housekeeper forgot something. He was in the checkout line. "Helen!" he said.

TOM: *(Not looking up)* "'Helen!' he said."

HAL: Tom...

HELEN: First read-through, new play. He invited me along.

HAL: With those? I hope the ice cream didn't melt.

HELEN: I forgot the ice cream. The rest he put in his trunk.

HAL: You were driving around with him? It must be nice. Someday we'll have a car.

HELEN: Maybe sooner than you think.

HAL: I'm not accepting any gifts; *you're* not accepting any gifts.

HELEN: I already have, but not a car. Hal...Tom...your wife, your mother, me!, I'm in the play. It's *my* play. I've got the lead.

HAL: How did that happen? It was the first read-through. You weren't even cast as a walk-on. Did you shoot What's-Her-Name?

HELEN: What's-Her-Name fell off the stage.

(As both gape at her)

HELEN: Broke her collar bone. Sure. Honest girl scout. Remember those tremendous "Ahs!" in her famous "listening scenes" when she's giving the other actor all *our* attention...? I guess she didn't know how close she was to the edge. A heel in the footlights. A genuine "Ah!" and it was all over. I had the part. Oh, not while they were carting her off. Someone had to read the part. I did. Afterwards there was a little conference. There was still plenty of time to replace What's-Her-Name, but Thomas spoke up for me and...

HAL: Was that before or after he bought you the scarf, the bracelet, the perfume, the...?

HELEN: It was before. Obviously, Hal, he wants me to be a star... *(Laughing)* I think he called the hospital. I heard him. "Tie her down, keep her there, she always was nuts!" And the rest is history.

HAL: Tom will be reading about it tomorrow in Current Events. *(Clearing his throat)* Miss Smith. *(In Miss Smith's voice)* "Oh, look at this, boys; one of our mothers is going to be a star, one you might have seen at the Homecoming Game, oh, there she is now, the one over there, see, with the paper bag with the little bottle in it..." Oh, to hell with this noise; I'm not going to be a spoilsport.

HELEN: Good.

HAL: *(Kissing her)* Congratulations, my good, my dear, my *talented* wife!

TOM: *(Leaping up to also embrace her)* Congratulations, Mom.

HAL: I believe this calls for a little celebration. It is a *paid* position?

HELEN: Of course. Every two weeks.

HAL: What about the union?

HELEN: I'm in.

HAL: That was fast. As I was saying: a celebration. *(Going to the kitchen, returning with a bottle of champagne)* Just a little something I was keeping chilled...behind the radiator. *(Opening it)* Helen, our crystal, our genuine, imported, lead-content crystal, if you please.

HELEN: *(Stepping into the step-in kitchen)* Oh boy, oh boy, oh boy...

HAL: Frankly, Tom, it was your old man—me—we thought was going to make it first. The phone by that chair of mine you occupy when you're here exists for that sole reason: the call from Hollywood. Did I ever tell you how I was doing an end-run around your famous uncle with...technology?

TOM: Yes.

HAL: Yes! I don't remember that. Yes, the theater is old hat, Tom. I'm the only man who knows it. Look at these hands. Just right for writing "camera dollies up to the star, *soft focus*, etc." Then you'll see it, Tom, my name in lights: "Camera Directions by Yours Truly, Based on a Story by..."

HELEN: *(Back from the kitchen with three ordinary wine glasses she is polishing)* Here we are, my dearest.

HAL: I'd better be your dearest. A whiff of suspicion—my brother, my own brother...!

HELEN: *(Noting* TOM*)* Hal...

HAL: As I said, a whiff of suspicion and I'm out that window—I don't care if the skinflint of a landlord has nailed it shut—and I'm in the air shaft, four stories down. And I don't mean screenplays.

HELEN: Hal... *(Setting up the glasses)* There is nothing to worry about. Nothing.

HAL: Three glasses?

HELEN: Three glasses. It is that kind of occasion, isn't it?

HAL: *(Beat)* It is. Tom. Your first drink. Are you ready?

TOM: *(At attention)* I'm ready.

HAL: Good boy.

(HELEN *is already holding her glass out.*)

HAL: I see I needn't prompt my wife. *(Removing the cork)* Now watch, this is how it's done, even with the cheapest of champagnes.

TOM: Did Thomas teach you how to do that?

HAL: *(Beat)* Thomas taught me absolutely everything I know, Tom.

TOM: I'm sorry. I didn't mean...

HAL: I know, Tom. *(The cork silently removed, pouring)* Now this... I'd better start. Some drinks don't wait for the toast. *(Pouring)* This is, primarily, for one amongst us whose star shines visibly today. It is also for husband and son...

(As they raise their glasses)

HELEN: *(Clinking glasses)* ...whose talents are recognized and deeply appreciated by one who is also wife and mother, even when she's only in the grandstand with a paper bag...

HAL: All for one and one for all!

HELEN: That's the Three Musketeers, Tom.

TOM: I know.

(Her glass empty, HELEN *seizes the bottle, begins by topping up the others.)*

HELEN: I think we intend to finish this.

HAL: I think you're probably right.

(HELEN, *in her eagerness to fill her own glass to the brim, cracks the rim with the neck of the bottle.*)

HELEN: Oh, hell. I think I cracked it. (*Holding her glass up*) Yes, look at that, a crack running top to bottom. (*Bitterly*) Does nothing...?

HAL: (*Taking the bottle back*) No conclusions. No conclusions, Helen, please. The gods are *always* jealous. Think of Prometheus, we were just discussing him. Toss that, Helen. There may be shards, slivers...

(*As* HELEN *discards her glass in the kitchen*)

HAL: Tom, finish your champagne, give your glass to your mother.

HELEN: (*Returning with a juice glass, which she exchanges for* TOM's, *as* HAL *fills all*) I guess I didn't have to throw it out. I could have just stuck it up on that window that never opens to catch the light that never shines. It might have been nice to look at anyway, a kind of symbol...

HAL: Helen, be quiet. Symbol! You think there are symbols in 1940?

(*As they raise their glasses and* HAL *looks at* HELEN *with deep love*)

HAL: Now, once more, for one among us whom, in spite of everything, we cannot help loving; may her talent, her genius, her dark eyes... Enough. Bottoms up!

(*All drink as the light fades.* HELEN, *finishes hers first, lowers it. The others, heads back, still drinking, leave her a moment in which her tear-streaked face is visible. A small table radio comes on in the darkness to play "...Bless 'em All, bless 'em All...", now vocalized.*)

Scene Two

(*Late that night. The empty bottle of champagne and a nearly empty bottle of bourbon are visible in the kitchenette. The old couch is made up with sheet and pillow, but* TOM, *in his pajamas, his blanket over his shoulders, sits alone in his father's chair, a single light illuminating the book* THOMAS *has given him and in which he rereads "Mrs Amworth" softly to himself.*)

TOM: "The moon had long set, but a twilight of stars shone in a clear sky, when five o'clock of the morning sounded from the turret. A few minutes more passed, and then I felt Urcombe's hand softly nudging me; and looking out in the direction of his pointing finger, I saw that the form of a woman...was approaching from the right. Noiselessly, with a motion more of gliding and floating than walking, she moved across the cemetery to the grave which was the centre of our observation. She moved round it as if to be certain of its identity, and for a moment stood directly facing us. In the grayness to which now my eyes had grown accustomed, I could easily see her face, and recognise its features.

(HELEN *appears from the bedroom right in a new and revealing nightgown, a blanket over her shoulders. She has been drinking and still has a heavy glass in one hand. At first she listens unobserved.)*

TOM: "She drew her hand across her mouth as if wiping it, and broke into a chuckle of such laughter as made my hair stir on my head. Then she leaped onto the grave, holding her hands high above her head, and inch by inch disappeared into the earth."

(HELEN *laughs softly,* TOM's *hair stirs on his head. He closes the book, looking at her angrily. Both are careful not to raise their voices.* HELEN *goes to squeeze the last out of the bottle of bourbon into her glass.)*

HELEN: Can't sleep? The couch isn't that bad. I've slept on it. Even your father has. Depending on who stormed out of the bedroom first. So.

(TOM *watches her as she sinks awkwardly into his couch, sets down her drink to light a cigarette, picks up her drink and exhales, her drink in one hand, her cigarette in the other.)*

HELEN: You'll be gone from us tomorrow. Anything special to look forward to back there, a story of yours in the school paper?

TOM: *(After a moment)* I hate you when you're like this.

(HELEN *blinks and looks down. Coming as unexpectedly as it has, and being something she has never heard before, it hurts.)*

TOM: Why do you do it? I hate the glass in your hand, I hate the smoke in your hair. Your eyes... *(Turning away)* I can't look at you.

HELEN: Oh, my dear Tom... *(She sets down her glass, her cigarette in the ashtray. Sliding off the couch, for a moment she is on her knees looking at him as if wondering how she got there.)*

HELEN: It seems...I'm on the floor. So—what else is new?

(She crawls toward him. TOM, *trying not to watch, can't help laughing. She comes to a stop before him, rises to a kneeling position, her hands on his knees.)*

HELEN: My dear Tom. People are a helluva mixture, you know. They're not always what you want them to be, not even what they want to be.

TOM: Couldn't you have waited till tomorrow?

HELEN: Tomorrow—I work. *(A cross-eyed floozy)* "I'm the shtar." I'm sorry, I'm not that drunk.

TOM: *(Withdrawing his knees)* But that's just it: Why are you drunk at all? Haven't you got everything you ever wanted?

HELEN: I have. *(Looking at him)* Absolutely everything. *(Sitting back on her ankles)* And more. It's just that the more was very, very expensive. You don't get anything for nothing in this life, Tom. *(Beat)* Can you forgive me?

(They look at each other. Slowly she kisses his knees, then places her forehead against them and begins to cry. TOM, *horrified at first, softens, caresses her head.)*

TOM: It's all right, Mom. You had to do whatever you had to do. Your acting is everything to you, isn't it?

(HELEN *nods without looking up.)*

TOM: Whatever the price is, you would pay it, wouldn't you?

(She looks up at him, nods; he speaks with quiet authority.)

TOM: Now you just have to keep it to yourself.

(HELEN *glances in the direction of the bedroom where* HAL *sleeps, nods, and, with her weight on* TOM's *knees and a supporting hand from him, gets to her feet. She turns unsteadily, spots drink and cigarette, returns to them.)*

HELEN: I should have been in movies, silent movies, if I'm going to keep everything to myself. Here she is, ladies and gentlemen... *(Posing, her blanket draped off her shoulder)* "Shtinko!" the shilent shtar of shtage and shcreen, and only a little late, for she was never quite at home in the talkies. *(With dramatic pauses)* For thish...was a shtar...with shecrets.

TOM: Don't wake Dad.

HELEN: *(Raising the hand with the cigarette)* Let him sleep, let everyone sleep. Once, Tom, did I ever tell you: Our dream was Hollywood, your father's script... *(With flair)* ...my—whatever. Ironically, it's your uncle's play and...and...

TOM: And your whatever.

HELEN: *(Facing him)* Nobody likes a smart-ass, Tom, especially if he's not quite grown up.

TOM: I'm growing up fast.

HELEN: Whoa! Hold your horses! All childhoods aren't like mine. Yours, for example. For some people, things are going to get more complex, harder than they have been.

TOM: At least I won't be helpless.

HELEN: Am I...helpless?

TOM: No, you're not. Childhood makes us helpless. I'll never be helpless again.

HELEN: That's good. Never be helpless. Down with helpless...ness. Everything under control. *(Looking around her)* The heat, for example. Someday...I am going to control the heat...with a little dial. What do you think of that, Tom? To hell with the landlord!

TOM: *(Quietly, quieting her)* To hell with the landlord.

HELEN: I'll never be cold again. *(Taking space)* I am going to have furniture that does not swallow me alive, fine prints upon the walls, a bed that doesn't squeak...even when my son is away at school. I'm going to change everything! Everything different, that's what I want. Nothing the same. And I want what you want for yourself. I want you to have it. *(Beat)* By the way, what do you want?

TOM: I want to do things the way Dad and Uncle Thomas would if they were one man.

HELEN: One man, with the qualities of, of both?

TOM: Yes.

HELEN: *(Looking at him)* Yes, it's possible: the one's words, the other's heart. But...isn't there anything of mine?

TOM: I want to be...your opposite.

(They stare at each other.)

TOM: Please don't be hurt. It doesn't mean I don't love you....

HELEN: It just means you want to be different.

TOM: Yes.

HELEN: Well, you are. You see, I've done something. I've given you an idea where not to go.

(TOM nods, HELEN gestures expansively.)

HELEN: Stop! Or is it "Shtop?" Do not enter here. This is one helluva dead end, young man. You don't want to grow up to be your mother.

TOM: I want to grow up so she'll be proud of me.

HELEN: Proud that I haven't stopped you where it mattered?

TOM: Proud nothing has stopped me where it mattered.

(A moment in which HELEN laughs)

HELEN: My son...the unstoppable. Well, since you're growing up tonight, would you care for a cigarette, young man, would you care for a drink? *(Vamping it, her blanket nearly off, coming toward him with drink and cigarette extended.)* Would you care to sit your mother on your knee and tell her what she done wrong?

TOM: *(Escaping behind the chair)* No.

HELEN: *(Stopping center)* Don't run from me. Don't you ever run from me, Tom. I've never hit you. I never did anything to hurt you. *(Softening)* You got hurt...incidentally. *(Lowering her hands)* I wish I could have prevented all....

TOM: It's all right. You did your best.

HELEN: I did? *(Again raising her arms dramatically, taking space)* Behold: "Shtinko," the Shtar who could have prevented... *(Correcting herself)* ...who wished she could have prevented...all. *(With finality)* Yes, all. You know, Tom, if, on some tropical island, in some dream of a past your father and I might have had...unless Thomas dreamed it for us... you'd just refused to be conceived, *you* could have prevented all.

TOM: I did my best.

HELEN: Good. That makes two of us. *Et voilà*: the mother and son who did their best. *(Sitting on the arm of the chair, still with drink and cigarette)* One more...speculation, Tom, before you...before you rush into the arms of Mrs Amworth... What is this Mrs Amworth business anyway? Is she the only woman worse than me?

(TOM laughs.)

HELEN: I could have been a vampire, you know. But I wasn't. I hope you'll remember that.

TOM: I'll remember. What speculation?

HELEN: What?

TOM: You said one more speculation.

HELEN: Oh yes. What if...what if...?

TOM: Yes?

HELEN: What if it weren't true?

TOM: What if what weren't true?

HELEN: Everything. Everything I said.

TOM: You mean about how...about how expensive it was?

HELEN: Yes—and everything that preceded that. Earlier, this evening. Today. What if I didn't have to do anything with my...whatever—*and* what if What's-Her-Name never caught her heel in the footlights, never landed on her collarbone, if our shtar never got called upon to read What's-Her-Name's part and never got offered the role she got wined and dined with scarf and bracelet and perfume to play the part of? What if...she even took herself shopping, all alone?

(Slight pause)

TOM: Oh, Mom.

HELEN: Well, I've got to act somewhere. But—what if none of it, none of it happened because...Tom...it's only going to happen now?

TOM: *(Very quietly)* Now?

(They look at each other as HELEN *drains her drink, inhales from and extinguishes her cigarette. Exit* HELEN *silently into the bedroom.* TOM *stands a moment before*

picking up his book and sitting as before. He stares into space a moment before he begins to read.)

TOM: "'Come,'" he said. "With pick and shovel and rope we went to the grave. The earth was light and sandy, and soon after six struck we had delved down to the coffin lid. With his pick he loosened the earth round it, and, adjusting the rope through the handles by which it had been lowered, we tried to raise it. This was a long and laborious business, and the light had begun to herald day in the east before we had it out and lying by the side of the grave. With his screwdriver he loosed the fastenings of the lid and slid it aside, and standing there we looked on the face of Mrs Amworth. The eyes, once closed in death, were open, the cheeks flushed with colour, the red, full-lipped mouth seemed to smile."

(Enter HELEN, right, a woman well dressed for the winter of 1940. When TOM looks at her, she raises a finger to her lips. Her half-smile is loving, she expects understanding, and she doesn't look away from him until she feels she has it. Then TOM almost speaks but doesn't. Exit HELEN silently, left, leaving only her perfume on the air. TOM's eyes return to his book, but he cannot read. The light quickly fades as the table radio comes on with its "Bless 'em All, Bless 'em All," until the light of the dial is the only light.)

Scene Three

(THOMAS's, later the same night. The same tune playing on the radio console, THOMAS, JACKSON, and HÉLÈNE center, all casually dressed, at the folding table; the decanter, three glasses, a whiff of fine old cognac on the air.)

JACKSON: *(Putting down his cards)* I'm sorry. I can't keep my eyes open.

HÉLÈNE: Go to bed.

JACKSON: And leave you to get into trouble. I'd never forgive myself.

HÉLÈNE: I'll never forgive you if you don't.

THOMAS: *(Putting down his cards)* Hm. Well. *(Singing to HÉLÈNE)* "...The night is young and you're so beautiful..."

JACKSON: *(Also singing to HÉLÈNE)* "...beautiful lady..."

HÉLÈNE: *(Very pleased with herself)* Gentlemen, gentlemen, please...

THOMAS: *(Standing)* It's time we all got some shut-eye.

JACKSON: *(Raising his glass)* To shut-eye.

THOMAS: *(Raising his)* I'll drink to that. *(Perhaps with more seriousness than seems warranted)* To shut-eye.

HÉLÈNE: *(A beat, then, raising hers)* Oh, well. To shut-eye.

(They finish their drinks. JACKSON *stands, looks at* HÉLÈNE, *who stands.* THOMAS *escorts them to the elevator.)*

THOMAS: Tomorrow, the first rehearsal. As if I haven't heard it a thousand times already in my head and, indeed, once, yesterday, through the mouths that will finally give it life. And to keep my sanity, you know what I do?

JACKSON: How could we, old man?

HÉLÈNE: Tell us, tell us.

THOMAS: I start a new play. I'll have that in the back of my head tomorrow to keep me from despair.

HÉLÈNE: Despair? What are you talking about?

THOMAS: They can only do it their way, Hélène. I can only help them do it their way. For now, there is no other way. I can't hold them to the way I've heard it through the nights and days. Then, when it's done again, that cast of players will do it their way—only, thank God, I won't have to be there.

JACKSON: Right, right. Clear as mud.

(As the elevator arrives and the PFLAUM-SMYTHES *step in.)*

HÉLÈNE: What do you mean "thank God," Thomas? Why, if I were a playwright hearing my lines...

(The elevator cuts off the rest of her sentence.)

THOMAS: *(Calling through the door)* Goodnight, goodnight! *(Leaning back against the elevator door, smiling)* I couldn't have done it better myself. *(Stepping to the middle of, taking stock of, his apartment, most seriously)* To shut-eye. Wisdom from the mouths of the half-dead.

(He leaves the cards spread on the table, turns off the radio, and proceeds in the direction of his bedroom as the "in use" light comes on behind him. A moment later there is a tapping at the elevator door.)

THOMAS: Damn. *(Going to the elevator door, calling)* Forget something? *(Pressing the speaker button when there is no answer)* Go to bed, Hélène, it's been a long day.

(After a small, feminine giggle on the intercom, patiently)

THOMAS: Even Jackson might notice you're gone.

A SMALL FEMININE VOICE: It's not Hélène, and Jackson never notices when I'm gone.

(After a moment, but with absolutely no curiosity, THOMAS *presses the button and the door slides open.* EFFI *stands there in one of her mother's evening dresses. She raises her crawling fingers as a ghost might.)*

EFFI: Boo!

THOMAS: Go to bed, Effi. Your parents are upstairs.

EFFI: And I'm down here.

THOMAS: *(Pressing the button)* Goodnight, Effi.

(As the sliding door begins to close, EFFI *quickly slides the grating aside and slips in. The doors close behind her.)*

EFFI: You can't get rid of me so easily. I'm not my mother.

THOMAS: I hope not. *(Gently)* What do you want, Effi?

EFFI: I have a proposition.

THOMAS: I'm sick of propositions right now. What can I do for you?

EFFI: Did I ever tell you I want to act?

THOMAS: You've never told me anything, Effi. This is the first time we've spoken.

EFFI: Oh yes, I forgot. Well, may I tell you now?

THOMAS: *(Patiently)* Tell me, tell me.

EFFI: I want to be an actress.

THOMAS: *(Patiently and gently)* Dear Effi...

EFFI: Don't "Dear Effi" me. *(Moving about the apartment)* I know: Everyone wants to be an actress. But there's a difference: I can act. *(Raising* THOMAS's *glass from the table, deepening her voice, dramatizing the lines)* "They can only do it their way, Hélène. I can only help them do it their way. For now, there is no other way. I can't hold them to the way I've heard it through the nights and days. Then, when it's done again, *that* cast of players will do it *their* way—only, thank God, I won't have to be there."

THOMAS: *(Laughing in spite of himself)* What? Is the place wired?

EFFI: *(Pointing at the elevator)* I was right there, listening on the intercom.

THOMAS: I didn't know you could do that.

EFFI: You can't. When my mother got upstairs she said what you said. She's always repeating your lines.

THOMAS: Then maybe she...

EFFI: My mother can't act worth a damn. She does everything badly. You think this little rich girl is so thin because she wants to be? Never mind the catered hot dogs. Having everything, I had nothing. Maybe for you it was different.

THOMAS: It was.

EFFI: *(Earnestly)* Having been handed one life, I had to make another. *(Noting his incomprehension)* You don't understand.

THOMAS: No.

EFFI: It doesn't matter. I know what I'm saying.

THOMAS: I can see that. You have something. I won't deny it. But I have other things on my mind tonight, Effi. I'll have them on my mind tomorrow. *(Reaching back toward the elevator button)* I can't help you.

EFFI: *(Quickly)* You can let me sit in.

(Slight pause)

THOMAS: You mean at rehearsal?

EFFI: I mean at rehearsal. What's wrong with you, Thomas? May I call you Thomas?

THOMAS: I suppose.

EFFI: Why are you so slow talking with me? Usually you're...

(She snaps her fingers rapidly three times. He looks at her a moment, slowly sits at the table.)

THOMAS: I've had some news lately, Effi. It's slowed me.

EFFI: *(Sitting across from him)* Do you want to tell me about it?

(THOMAS shakes his head, EFFI plunges ahead.)

EFFI: Anyway, I want to tell you something. I told you I had a proposition. Don't laugh! I don't like to be laughed at, not even by you. Especially by you.

THOMAS: I'm not laughing, Effi, or, if I am, it's not at you.

EFFI: It better not be.

THOMAS: It isn't.

EFFI: Okay. This is going to strike you as nuts, but here goes.

THOMAS: *(Holding up his hands)* Shoot.

EFFI: Let me watch. Rehearsals. Oh, I'm not an idiot: I don't expect you to make me an understudy—or even to send me for coffee. Let me sit there. For my own reasons. In the shadows. In the dark. In back. *(Standing, walking, eventually arriving behind him)* Can you see me there?

(THOMAS nods.)

EFFI: Can you feel me there—even without looking?

THOMAS: *(Looking straight ahead)* Yes.

EFFI: *(Remaining behind him)* You don't have a wife, do you?

THOMAS: No.

EFFI: Did you ever?

THOMAS: No.

EFFI: And you have no children? Not even a smart-assed, precocious little rich kid?

THOMAS: Not even a... *(Pouring himself a drink)* Come around here where I can see you, Effi. Tell me your proposition.

EFFI: *(Triumphantly coming around, sitting opposite him, one of the remaining glasses in both her hands, leaning forward, getting down to business.)* Thomas...

(The "in use" light comes on.)

EFFI: Oh, Jesus.

THOMAS: *(His eyes following hers to the light)* Oh, Jesus, is right.

(They both listen for a moment to the elevator in use, though it is not audible to us.)

EFFI: Sounds like they're stopping here.

THOMAS: *(Standing)* It does, indeed, sound that way.

EFFI: What do we do?

THOMAS: Play it straight. You came down to make me a proposition. Before you could get it out...

(The elevator door chimes softly.)

EFFI: I have a better idea. *(Pointing at the curtained window up right, she raises her eyebrows in anticipated delight, her fingers already indicating a scramble in that direction.)* I'll just...disappear. It'll be hilarious.

THOMAS: Yes. Later. When you repeat it all verbatim. Meanwhile, your parents will be searching the streets.

EFFI: Are you kidding? Do you believe that?

THOMAS: No.

(The elevator chimes softly again.)

EFFI: Is it a deal?

THOMAS: Uh, let me get this straight. Is this the big one, the proposition?

EFFI: Not yet.

THOMAS: *(A beat, then:)* Okay.

(EFFI, delighted, scrambles, in an exaggerated tiptoe her dress wasn't made for, behind the drapes.)

THOMAS: *(To himself)* It seems I'm to live awhile yet. *(A hand in the direction of the drapes; still to himself, if theatrically.)* The childhood she never had. *(The hand to his chest, realizing something)* The childhood I... Or is it something else? *(To EFFI)* Ready?

(He is answered by a giggle.)

THOMAS: She's ready.

(THOMAS *presses the open button not bothering to ask who it is.* HELEN *stands behind the grating, dressed as when she left* TOM *at the end of Scene Two, her face flushed from excitement and cold.*)

HELEN: Hello, Thomas. *(Beat)* May I come in?

(Beat. THOMAS *sighs and opens the grating for her.)*

HELEN: You look like you've seen a ghost. I guess I am unexpected, aren't I?

THOMAS: One hundred percent.

HELEN: But not unwelcome?

THOMAS: Not a hundred percent. *(Taking her coat)* May I get you something?

HELEN: You know you may. *(Perusing the table)* Seems like a pretty serious game was going on here.

(EFFI *peeks out between the drapes. As her eyes meet* THOMAS's *she raises hers to the ceiling, disappears.*)

HELEN: *(Wondering at the delay in his response)* I said it seems like a pretty serious...

THOMAS: Oh, yes, yes.

HELEN: High stakes?

THOMAS: *(Pouring her, and himself, a drink)* The highest.

HELEN: Life or death?

THOMAS: You might say that.

HELEN: And if I did...? Who won, Thomas?

THOMAS: Death always wins.

HELEN: Does it? I suppose it does. What a chilling thought.

THOMAS: Precisely. *(Beat)* Helen.

HELEN: Yes. Thomas.

THOMAS: Here you are.

HELEN: Yes.

THOMAS: In the middle of the night.

HELEN: In the middle of the night.

THOMAS: Everyone seems to think I have something to give.

HELEN: Who's everyone?

THOMAS: You, the others.

HELEN: Ah, the others. I tend to forget about them. But there must be many...

THOMAS: Thousands.

HELEN: Lucky man.

(Holding her cigarette for THOMAS *to light it, which he does.)*

HELEN: How did the first read-through go?

THOMAS: As well as could be expected. *(Raising his voice somewhat)* "They can only do it their way, Helen. I can only help them do it their way. For now, there is no other way. I can't hold them to the way I've heard it through the nights and days."

(The drapes stir soundlessly, if excitedly, behind HELEN.*)*

HELEN: No. What is it, Thomas? You sound strange. Are you acting?

THOMAS: I...I didn't think so.

HELEN: I know it when I hear it, Thomas. I'm an actress.

THOMAS: And a fine one.

HELEN: Yes, only this isn't my play, it's not the one written for me, is it?

THOMAS: No, Helen. Not yet, it isn't.

HELEN: *(Drinking)* Nothing awful happened today, did it?

THOMAS: No, not today. What do you mean?

HELEN: *(Laughing)* I mean What's-Her-Name—I'm sorry I can never think of the name of your star—

THOMAS: Sarah Bernhardt.

HELEN: Yes, of course. Sarah Bernhardt. Can you never be serious?

THOMAS: No, but I am practicing. I think within a week or two...

HELEN: "Sarah" didn't catch her heel in the footlights and tumble, did she? Somehow I've been imagining all day that that happened.

THOMAS: No, no, it didn't. Though there were moments when I would have enjoyed the spectacle.

HELEN: Ha! Then you realized how miscast that monster is!

THOMAS: I didn't say that.

HELEN: Thomas, you need an unknown in that part. What's-Her-Name—I'm sorry I've lost it again...

THOMAS: Go on.

HELEN: Anyway, she brings too much baggage, too much stardom, a false note...

THOMAS: Helen, is this what you came here to discuss? It's three o'clock in the morning.

HELEN: *(Singing throatily, lovingly to him)* "...It's three o'clock in the morning..."

THOMAS: *(Realistically)* We've danced the whole night through.

HELEN: *(Standing)* Not the whole night, Thomas. Not yet. *(Taking stage, facing him at a distance, acting strongly, genuinely)* Thomas...

THOMAS: What? What is this?

HELEN: *(Briefly giving him his line)* "Helen, I have no one."

THOMAS: *(Beat, then acting)* Helen, I have no one...

HELEN: *(Acting well)* Thomas, when you die...

THOMAS: Yes.

HELEN: ...the reporters will be at the door as they were for...for....

THOMAS: Sarah Bernhardt.

HELEN: Yes, that's right. There's nothing like that in this life for me. And your characters, Thomas, they'll all be there...at your deathbed...

THOMAS: They will?

HELEN: Yes, all the characters you ever wrote, doing all the scenes you never let them do... *(Ending the role; herself again, yet suddenly, unexpectedly even to herself, dropping on her knees)* Oh, Thomas...my dear, my beloved Thomas... just let me sit there in the shadows, in the dark, in back. Oh, I won't spook What's-Her-Name. It will never occur to her I'm understudying...

THOMAS: Of course not. Maybe you can sit there in one of her costumes. I can always tell her, with some truth, that you're my brother's wife.

HELEN: *(Still on her knees)* Thomas, I love you.

THOMAS: I love you too, Helen. I always will. Always, well, for a while anyway.

HELEN: Till tomorrow will be enough. Then, in your play...

THOMAS: You mean in the shadows, in the dark, in back.

HELEN: *(Hanging her head)* Yes. In the shadows, in the dark, in back, you can love me again. Daily, if you like.

THOMAS: Of course. Whenever Equity gives us the okay.

(HELEN, *still on her knees, looks up at* THOMAS, *not sure whether to be hurt or not. A second later* EFFI *sweeps the drapes open theatrically, strides center,* THOMAS's *lines ripe in her mouth.)*

EFFI: "Ah, you beauty," says Hal, his voice suddenly husky. "This is what it's all about, isn't it?" Helen gasps for air. "Whew! I guess it is," she says, and looks around her. "Where now?" she asks. *(Eyeing certain spots on the floor with overlarge eyes)* "Certainly not here." *(Suddenly dropping on her knees)* Oh, Thomas...my dear, my beloved Thomas...just let me sit there in the shadows, in the dark, in back. Oh, I won't spook What's-Her-Name. *(With a peculiar emphasis on the last word)* It will never occur to her I'm understudying...

(Slight pause)

THOMAS: Helen, Effi. Effi, Helen. I believe you've met.

(As HELEN and EFFI look at each other)

THOMAS: I couldn't have done it better myself.

(HELEN attempts to stand too quickly for her condition. EFFI, easily rising, helps her to a chair.)

HELEN: *(Withdrawing her arm, causing EFFI to back away.)* Thank you, Effi. Perhaps if I just sit here a moment, it will all go away.

THOMAS: That is precisely what will happen, Helen. It's the nature of our trade.

EFFI: All *what* will go away, Helen?

HELEN: *(Looking at EFFI)* Tell me you didn't dress her up like this, Thomas.

THOMAS: I didn't dress her up like this, Helen.

EFFI: Are you going to tell us who dressed *you* up, Helen?

HELEN: *(Laughing at herself)* I did it myself.

EFFI: Then no one knows you're here?

THOMAS: Not the costume mistress, anyway. *(Patiently)* Effi, sweet Effi...

HELEN: Sweet Effi!

THOMAS: I was just going to plead with her to behave herself, Helen.

HELEN: It won't work. She's stronger than I am.

THOMAS: Stronger than both of us. I'd hate to think it comes with the territory. *(He gestures upstairs.)* Is that all it takes, Effi, a couple of catered hot dogs and you're ready to crush us all?

EFFI: *(Approaching, her manner changing, to HELEN)* If it makes any difference, I also came here to beg.

HELEN: *(A beat, then:)* Welcome to the party. *(Offering her a seat at the table, which she accepts)* What did you come here to beg for?

EFFI: A place in the shadows, in back. I just wanted to learn....

HELEN: Well, you're learning. So you dressed yourself up like this?

EFFI: Yes.

HELEN: Well, it's very attractive. It works.

EFFI: Thank you.

HELEN: Tell me. *Did* it work? Have you got your place in back?

EFFI: We were just discussing it when you made your entrance.

HELEN: Don't let me interrupt the negotiations.

EFFI: *(Laughing)* This is fun.

HELEN: I'm glad somebody thinks so.

THOMAS: *(Sitting across from EFFI)* Well, let's hear it, young lady. Your proposition.

EFFI: Oh, it doesn't seem to make much sense now.

HELEN: No, really, Effi, we want to hear it.

EFFI: It made sense when I had it going, it made a lot of sense. Let's see if I can remember...

HELEN: Somehow I'm sure you can.

EFFI: All right. *(Standing, taking stage, ending up behind THOMAS, slowly getting it back)* Just let me sit here, Thomas.

HELEN: *(Softly)* Thomas!

EFFI: *(Ignoring her)* For my own reasons. In the shadows. In the dark. In back. Can you see me here?

(THOMAS *nods.*)

EFFI: Can you feel me here—even without looking?

THOMAS: *(Looking straight ahead)* Yes.

EFFI: *(Remaining behind him)* You don't have a wife, do you?

THOMAS: No.

EFFI: Did you ever?

THOMAS: No.

EFFI: And you have no children?

THOMAS: None.

EFFI: *(Her voice changing, behind him, her hands on his shoulders)* And something's wrong, isn't it? Something you haven't told us, something you haven't told anyone?

(THOMAS *opens his mouth when the "in use" light goes on. Noticing both women watching it, he turns his head just as the chime chimes.*)

EFFI: Ladies and gentlemen, the Pflaum-Smythes. Contrary to expectations, they have arrived to reclaim their... *(Enunciating, and asserting her breasts)* ...errant teen.

THOMAS: Then you get it, Effi. You can make your proposition to me in writing tomorrow. *(To HELEN as EFFI goes to the elevator)* The Girl Who Knew Everything answers the door.

HELEN: *(Concerned for him)* What is everything, Thomas?

(EFFI *pushes the button, the door slides open.* HAL *stands behind the grate, which he immediately slams open. He marches in, walks left and right across the room, ends up looking at the table.*)

HAL: Three glasses. Where have I heard that before? (*Looking from the card game to* HELEN *to* EFFI *to* THOMAS) What the hell is going on here?

THOMAS: Less than you might think. Or more.

(*Beat*)

HAL: What's wrong, Thomas? You look horrible.

THOMAS: I'm glad somebody noticed. Sit down, Hal, and I'll tell you— that is if Effi doesn't beat me to it.

HAL: *(Not sitting)* What's Effi got to do with it?

THOMAS: Less than nothing.

EFFI: That's what you think.

HELEN: She just knows the future.

EFFI: And the past. I have an incredible memory.

HAL: I'm glad to hear it. Have you thought of becoming an actress?

EFFI: I...

HAL: Suppose you tell me, Thomas. I'd like to know what's wrong. I mean it. I can deal with my wife myself.

HELEN: I don't need dealing with, Hal.

THOMAS: It's true. Helen can take care of herself. Effi can. You can. I'm the problem. Sit down, Hal. Effi.

(HAL *and* EFFI *join* THOMAS *and* HELEN *at the table.*)

THOMAS: *(Standing)* This is going to sound ridiculous.

HELEN: Tonight nothing sounds ridiculous.

HAL: Helen.

HELEN: Sorry.

THOMAS: *(Coming downstage)* It seems we're going to learn the truth of that idea of yours, Helen, that a playwright's characters gather at his deathbed, performing all those ordinary, if torturous, moments that would be too slow, too quiet for the theater....

HAL: What is it, Thomas? Your heart, your lungs.

THOMAS: My liver.

HAL: But...

THOMAS: That's right. I hardly touch the stuff.

HELEN: It ought to be me, my liver. Sometimes, when I look down, I'm afraid I see snakes.

THOMAS: Well, I'll be seeing them when I look up. Along with the ants, the grasshoppers, the crickets. Or a piece of glass, an old toothbrush. God knows what else.

HELEN: *(Attempting to raise spirits)* God knows!

THOMAS: Well, may they do it on my grave. May they enjoy it. May they be fruitful and multiply.

HAL: How long have you known?

THOMAS: About a week.

HAL: And how long...?

THOMAS: That one I can't answer. They couldn't answer it for me. I'm going to get me a big calendar, and a set of darts, and I'm going to stand here and...

(Suddenly EFFI rushes to THOMAS wrapping her arms about his waist.)

EFFI: Oh, Thomas!

THOMAS: *(Holding her)* What's this? What's this? You hardly know me.

EFFI: *(Holding on)* I know you through and through.

HELEN: Anything's possible. She's not acting.

THOMAS: She's not acting.

HAL: Is there anything we can do?

THOMAS: You have nothing to do, but receive, Hal.

HAL: I don't want that. *(Suddenly stricken, hardly knowing he's standing)* The earth will be empty without...

THOMAS: *(Moved by HAL's emotion, though he had intended not to be moved by the relating of these facts)* Hal, Hal... *(Still holding onto EFFI)* I'm not being crass, believe me. I don't know where the next play was coming from. Yours, Helen. I don't think I have it in me. Why not get this over with before I blow it all...on what? Showgirls?

HELEN: My play doesn't matter, Thomas. We want you.

THOMAS: *(Releasing EFFI, who droops in place)* Tom finishes school. Hal gets years at his screenplays. I think, Helen, that you had it right in the first place, when you married him. That's where the big role lies. And you can do it. Can't you?

HELEN: Yes.

THOMAS: Enough, enough. I'm exhausted. Will everybody please go home. Then I'm going to disconnect the elevator. *(Getting coats)* I'll see you tomorrow, Hal.

HAL: Yes.

THOMAS: And Helen and Tom too. Time to go home, Effi.

(HAL *and* HELEN *are in the elevator. As* THOMAS *raises his hand to them, and they theirs to him,* EFFI, *recovered, pushes the button that closes the door.*)

THOMAS: Effi.

EFFI: They're going down, I'm going up.

THOMAS: It's possible.

EFFI: And then, there's my proposition.

THOMAS: Tomorrow.

EFFI: It is tomorrow.

THOMAS: All right, it's tomorrow. If I can sell my soul, Effi, it's a deal.

EFFI: It's not as bad as that. Here it is. Simply.

THOMAS: Simply.

EFFI: Let me sit in the back and watch. You'll know I'm there.

THOMAS: Yes.

EFFI: And somehow, I don't know how, it will be...all for me.

THOMAS: All for you. The rehearsal?

EFFI: The rehearsal, the performance. I'll be audience, and actresses and actors, and you, I'll be you. And I'll be the play, this play and the next, even if it's the last, even if...it remains unwritten. All this, and wife and daughter too. (*Questioningly, perhaps thinking of her own*) And mother?

THOMAS: Leave my mother out of this. My mother...

EFFI: You wanted to be her opposite.

THOMAS: Now what gave you that idea?

EFFI: I don't know. It just came to me. I will be a mother.

THOMAS: (*Pushing the elevator button*) You are going to be everything.

EFFI: A fine mother.

THOMAS: An excellent one.

(*The elevator arrives,* THOMAS *opens door and grating.*)

EFFI: But for now we're leaving her out of here. For now, I am... Well, you know who I am, you know what I am, don't you?

THOMAS: (*Guiding her into the elevator*) Yes, I believe I do.

EFFI: (*In the elevator*) Goodnight, Thomas.

THOMAS: Goodnight, Effi.

(*The elevator door closes.* THOMAS *turns back into the apartment.*)

A SMALL VOICE IN THE INTERCOM: Is it a deal?

THOMAS: *(Laughing)* We'll see, Effi, we'll see.

(He turns the lights out and heads toward the bedroom, hesitates, and returns to the table, picking up a rough sheaf of paper on the way. Moving a small lamp to the table, he sits down to write as the lights, indeed, fade. In this darkness there is only the sound of scribbling.)

Scene Four

(Late afternoon. The PFLAUM-SMYTHES, *dirty, deeply tanned and in rags, sit upon the beach.* JACKSON *is trying to make something out of a bit of old tire and a length of dead rope,* HÉLÈNE *is eating the remains of a melon without benefit of utensils.)*

JACKSON: Sometimes I wish we'd never bought that damn hotel, Hélène. If you hadn't fallen in love with paradise...

HELEN: It's hard not to fall in love with... *(Slurp)* ...paradise, Jackson.

JACKSON: But we were so superfluous down here, Hélène. What did bed and breakfast have to do with the war effort?

HÉLÈNE: So why did we buy that damn thing, Jackson? Couldn't you see the first big wave that came along...?

JACKSON: I was blinded, Hélène, blinded by—I hate to say it—the competitive urge. I knew I could outbid an unsuccessful screenwriter and his bride-to-be. I bid. I won. I watched him drag his suitcase back to the airport.

HÉLÈNE: Anyone would think you were in a dime novel, Jackson.

JACKSON: Look at it this way, Hélène: We've read Chapter 11. We're unlikely to buy "Grand Rêve" again, should it come on the market.

HÉLÈNE: Jackson, clear your mind. "Grand Rêve" fell into the sea. We watched it go, through the peephole of the hurricane cellar. We gasped. We sniffled. "*Scheisse*," we said.

JACKSON: "*Scheisse*?" I didn't know we spoke German.

HÉLÈNE: We don't. We dried our noses. We stepped out into the dawn of a new day. The storm had passed. We took stock of the situation. We decided to become beach bums.

JACKSON: That's it, Hélène. That's our story. And here we are. *(Looking left)* On the wrong end of the beach, I might add.

HÉLÈNE: True. Very little manages to wash up here, besides us. Jackson?

JACKSON: What is it now, Hélène?

HÉLÈNE: Didn't there used to be three of us?

JACKSON: Three? Aren't two of us enough?

HÉLÈNE: I suppose you're right. What is that you're making, Jackson?

JACKSON: I don't know, Hélène. All I've got is this bit of rope, this bit of old tire. I thought something might come of it.

HÉLÈNE: Great things have come from less, my dear. *(Looking left)* Oh-oh.

(Both watch with dread as THOMAS *approaches left. Enter* THOMAS, *in his bathing suit, the sheaf of papers and pencil still in his hand, a folding beach chair under his arm. He sets up his chair, places his paper and pencil on it, then strides up to the seated* PFLAUM-SMYTHES *and wildly kicks sand at them.)*

THOMAS: I warned you! Out, out, off, off, and away.

(The PFLAUM-SMYTHES *beat a ragged retreat.)*

HÉLÈNE: Oh! Oh! I can't stand it. To be driven off by the Big Tipper himself.

JACKSON: I say, old man, you might have a little...

THOMAS: Compassion? I've none to spare. Out, out, off, off, and away!

JACKSON: *(Dashing back to retrieve them)* If you please, sir! That's my bit of string, my tire! I was making something!

THOMAS: Take it and begone. *(To himself)* Making something.

(The PFLAUM-SMYTHES, *clutching their miserable few possessions and raising their arms defensively as if they were in some old painting, are driven off right.* THOMAS, *alone, exhausted by the effort, smooths the beach.)*

THOMAS: *(To himself)* That my last effort should be mindless farce...is probably something the gods can live with. *(Suddenly he puts his hand to his liver.)* Maybe not.

*(*THOMAS *sighs and sits down in his beach chair, raising pencil over paper. The sun is slowly sinking.)*

THOMAS: I think I was going to have a tanned and healthy Hitler cross right to left here, smiling to himself.

*(*TOM *enters left, attired as in Scene Two, in his pajamas, carrying his book. Though, in fact, still thirteen, he's much older. For some time it is unnecessary for* THOMAS *to look at* TOM; *he knows he's there.)*

THOMAS: Forget something?

TOM: *(Keeping his distance)* I had...a wonderfully weighty shell last time I was here.

THOMAS: A wonderfully weighty shell.

TOM: Yes. Have you seen it?

THOMAS: *(Returning to his papers)* I saw a bit of old rope and a piece of tire, but they've been claimed.

(TOM *sits in the sand well behind* THOMAS *and opens his book;* THOMAS *returns to his paper and pencil.*)

THOMAS: *(Still not looking at him)* It makes me nervous to have people reading when I write.

TOM: *(Not looking up)* Tough.

THOMAS: "Tough?" Where have I heard that one? Or, on second thought, have I? *(Attempting to look at* TOM *but finding it uncomfortable to do so)* Who are you?

TOM: *(Reading)* Your nephew.

THOMAS: My nephew. Hal's boy.

TOM: That's right.

THOMAS: What are you doing here?

TOM: I'm the understudy. "Oh, Thomas, can't I just sit here...in the shadows, in the dark, in back?"

THOMAS: I had no idea Hal's son was such a pest. *(Over his shoulder)* Why don't you just go away?

TOM: You'll be gone before I will.

(Slight pause)

THOMAS: That reminds me. Some Indians, in the Americas, had the custom of passing the crown, or whatever, not to the son, but to the nephew. I've always wondered about that. About the reasoning. About the reality. I think it was the Aztecs, or the Incas.

TOM: It was the Aztecs.

THOMAS: You've read that.

TOM: I think so.

THOMAS: Does it make sense to you?

TOM: It makes sense to me.

THOMAS: *(Holding his head a moment)* It seems I've taken, or come near to taking, quite a bit from your father.

TOM: It seems that way.

THOMAS: Would he mind, Tom, the crown on your head?

TOM: *(Looking right)* Why don't you ask him?

(*Enter* HAL *right, dressed to kill in a priceless tropical suit, straw hat, decorative cane, etc,* HELEN, *in equal splendor for the tropics, at his side.*)

HAL: *(To* HELEN, *laughing)* Washed away by the sea! Can you imagine? Lucky we lost the bidding on that one. Wonder what happened to that clotheshorse who bought it.

THOMAS: I think I can answer that one.

HAL: Don't bother. I can imagine. Clotheshorse to ne'er-do-well in one easy lesson. *(Recognizing him)* Thomas, is that you?

THOMAS: *(Finding himself too weak to rise from his beach chair)* It's me, Hal. What are you doing here?

HAL: Well, Helen and I...

HELEN: Hello, Thomas.

THOMAS: Helen.

HELEN: Thomas, I've been thinking. That may have been my play ages ago, before, passing in the distance.

THOMAS: That may well be, Helen.

HELEN: And so...

HAL: So Helen and I came back to look at the spot we almost bought for a song, for a dream, years ago.

THOMAS: And how was it?

HAL: You won't believe it, Thomas. The "Grand Rêve." Twenty rooms, ten with ocean view. Gone. The foundations washed by the sea.

THOMAS: I believe it. And your work, Hal?

HAL: Well, Thomas, as, I believe, you can see: I've sold one.

THOMAS: A screenplay.

HAL: A screenplay.

THOMAS: *(Overjoyed for him)* Well, I'll be, kid!

(They make a few boxing motions at each other. HAL almost goes to him, THOMAS almost rises.)

THOMAS: *(Sitting back)* Ah, well, then you don't need anything from me.

HELEN: *(As HAL nods)* Your understanding, Thomas, your tolerance, your love. No, that's asking too much. You've given us so much.

THOMAS: What have I given you?

HELEN: I think I'd call it a sense of scene. We know when a scene is over, Thomas. We know what to do then.

HAL: *(Guiding HELEN left)* We leave. We take a plane somewhere. We go back and start over. It seems I'm always starting over, Thomas. From nothing. A blank page.

THOMAS: I know what you mean.

(As they leave)

THOMAS: Oh, Hal. The boy. How's the boy doing?

HAL: Fine. Better. I think he's going to be all right.

THOMAS: Good. Good.

(HAL *begins to go.*)

THOMAS: Hal.

(HAL *stops.*)

THOMAS: How would you feel if...if he took after me?

HAL: *(Deeply moved, with a slight bow)* I'd be...most deeply honored. *(With a slight wave)* So long, brother.

THOMAS: So long, brother.

HAL: Until next time. Hold on.

THOMAS: I will, Hal. I promise.

(HAL, *leaving, turns back to give the thumbs-up sign,* HELEN *waves most gently. Exit* HAL *&* HELEN.*)*

TOM: *(Silently reading, not looking up)* Now you know.

THOMAS: *(Weakening, his hand to his side)* Now I know.

TOM: *(Reading aloud)* "'One blow and it is all over,' he said. 'You need not look.'

"Even as he spoke he took up the pick again, and, laying the point of it on her left breast, measured his distance. And though I knew what was coming I could not look away...

"He grasped the pick in both hands, raised it an inch or two for the taking of his aim, and then with full force brought it down on her breast. A fountain of blood, though she had been dead so long, spouted high in the air, falling with the thud of a heavy splash over the shroud, and simultaneously from those red lips came one long, appalling cry, swelling up like some hooting siren, and dying away again. With that, instantaneous as a lightning flash, came the touch of corruption on her face, the colour of it faded to ash, the plump cheeks fell in, the mouth dropped." *(He reads a moment silently, then moves closer to* THOMAS, *though staying behind him.)* Mind if I ask you a question?

THOMAS: One question is usually allowed.

TOM: What's the difference between a muse and a vampire?

THOMAS: *(Puzzling, still not looking at* TOM*)* Between a muse and a vampire...

TOM: Don't tell me you've never thought about that.

THOMAS: I don't believe I have.

TOM: It's time to think about that.

THOMAS: *(Feigning a little worry)* Is it?

TOM: These might be your thoughts anyway.

THOMAS: They might be.

TOM: So think. The vampire takes your life's blood, and you give it, unconsciously, in your sleep; the muse wants you to sit still, awake and willingly, while life passes in the distance.

THOMAS: Or behind me. Since you, evidently, have thought about it, perhaps that means I don't have to.

TOM: It means what you want it to mean.

(TOM *moves downstage to throw his book into the sea.*)

THOMAS: Tom!

TOM: What?

THOMAS: Never destroy a book.

TOM: It's behind me.

THOMAS: Soon, sooner than you think, everything will be behind you. *(Looking at* TOM, *now that he can be seen)* You don't look much like Hal.

TOM: *(Keeping his book)* I don't look much like you either.

THOMAS: Give it fifty years, more or less. *(Beat)* You know, it remains to be seen.

TOM: What does?

THOMAS: What you're going to do. If you don't do it, it isn't there.

TOM: Maybe, when you've done it, it isn't there either. *(Looking around)* It isn't here, I don't see it. And if it isn't here, it must be somewhere else. *(He moves away left.)*

THOMAS: Tom!

(TOM *pauses, looks back, but* THOMAS *has nothing to say.*)

TOM: *(Leaving)* So long, uncle.

THOMAS: So long, nephew. (TOM, *extreme left, without stopping turns back to give* THOMAS *the thumbs-up sign, exits left.*)

THOMAS: His father's son. I think I would have done that differently, yes, I'd have given him a little something more to say... *(In pain, his hand to his side)* ...something encouraging.

(THOMAS *writes "enter* EFFI *right" as he speaks the words and* EFFI *enters right, empty-handed, in bathing suit; though thirteen, unlike* TOM *she is now somehow younger; she has stepped back, temporarily, into childhood.*)

THOMAS: *(Writing)* "Enter Effi right...with shell." *(He turns, with difficulty, to look at her.)* Where's the shell?

EFFI: What shell?

THOMAS: Didn't I... *(Correcting himself)* Didn't Tom give you...a wonderfully weighty shell?

EFFI: Who's Tom? I wouldn't take anything anybody gave me. Who are you?

THOMAS: You're Effi.

EFFI: *(Cautiously)* Yes?

THOMAS: Hm. Yes. *(Finding it difficult to speak)* That's a...that's a diminutive, I suppose?

EFFI: *(Coming somewhat closer)* A what?

THOMAS: A nickname, isn't it? What's your real name, the one they put in writing.

EFFI: *(Hesitantly)* Ephemera.

THOMAS: Ephemera. That's a lovely name. Did I give it to you?

EFFI: *(Stepping back)* What are you talking about?

THOMAS: I'm sorry. Sometimes I get confused. *(Making an effort at clarity)* Effi, when we're not here...I live downstairs. In 4B. You and your parents live upstairs. In 6A. I believe you want to be an actress.

EFFI: Me? I haven't thought about it.

THOMAS: Well, think about it. Wouldn't you like to be? The theater needs... *(How to say it)* ...the theater...needs...

(EFFI, *apparently in response, opens her mouth, but nothing comes out.*)

THOMAS: *(Seeing)* What's wrong?

(EFFI, *having lost her poise, closes her mouth, shakes her head; to himself.*)

THOMAS: Little muse, I see you weeping.

EFFI: I never cry, but I can't be an actress because...I have no memory, I can't remember anything...

THOMAS: *(To himself)* No memory.

EFFI: ...and...I don't know why I'm telling you this...

THOMAS: *(Gently)* Tell me.

EFFI: I'm... Well, here goes. I'm afraid.

THOMAS: Afraid? Of what?

EFFI: I have no confidence. I can't stand up in front of people.

THOMAS: Neither can I, but sometimes people get over that. Wouldn't you like to sit there, in the shadows, in the dark, in the back of the theater, gaining confidence?

EFFI: No.

THOMAS: Maybe, sitting there, you'd find your voice, and then...

(She laughs.)

THOMAS: *(Encouragingly)* That's a lovely laugh.

EFFI: I'm laughing at myself. When I stand up in front of people, I stutter. I st-st-stutter! What kind of actress would I be?

THOMAS: A stuttering one. *(Almost to himself)* You'd ruin the lines. The ones you can't remember.

EFFI: Yes.

THOMAS: Oh, Effi! You must remember me.

EFFI: I do not.

THOMAS: Effi, my name is Thomas, I write for the theater. When I learned my days were numbered, I thought of putting up a huge calendar, throwing darts at it, but never mind that. You hated, though you didn't know me very well, you hated to think that I... You ran toward me, you threw your arms around me. You said, "Oh, Thomas!" I held you. I said, "What's this? What's this? You hardly know me." You held onto me. You said, "I know you through and through." Helen said...

EFFI: Who's Helen?

THOMAS: My brother's wife. Listen, will you? Try to remember. Helen said, "Anything's possible. She's not acting." I had you in my arms, Effi. Effi, I knew. You were holding me up. I said, "She's not acting." *(He looks at her intently, but she crosses left behind him.)* Effi?

EFFI: *(Very cautiously)* What?

THOMAS: *(Softly)* Don't run off. Not like that. I won't ask you to remember anything else. Listen, Helen, my brother's wife, Helen told me the end would be a crowd scene, all my characters would be there, doing the things they couldn't do in the theater—oh, not what you're thinking, just the little things there isn't time for, not only the before and after, as Helen so wisely put it, but the during. *(Touching the corner of his eye with his next to little finger, looking at it)* Removing something from the corner of your eye, for example, looking at it...

(EFFI *is steadily backing away left.*)

THOMAS: *(Panicked)* Effi! *(Calming himself)* Effi, if you must go, take a message. Tell them Helen was wrong. Tell them... Tell them I'm alone. Tell them I can't get out of my chair. Tell them...

EFFI: *(At a distance, her voice very small)* Tell who?

THOMAS: *(Correcting her)* Tell *whom*, Effi, tell *whom*.

EFFI: Don't make me jump through hoops.

THOMAS: There, that's my old Effi talking. My old Effi. Why, tell anyone. Tell those ridiculous parents of yours. I thank God no one like them ever existed. I thank God you can't remember what fools I've made of others, what a fool I've made of myself. Tell anyone, Effi. Anyone real. Grab 'em, Effi, send 'em this way, tell them an old fool's dying on the beach and he wants a crowd scene. Haven't I got the same rights as any shark victim, any poor drowned bastard? I want a crowd!

(She is almost gone.)

THOMAS: Effi, Effi...you know who Sarah Bernhardt is?

EFFI: Does she live in 5C?

THOMAS: Effi! *(More calmly)* Yes, Effi, that's her. The gal with the little dog. How she walks him with that one leg of hers I'll never understand. But she does, she makes it to the deli on the corner, as we all know, comes back munching a corned beef on rye, walking that disgusting little dog, and hopping like a vulture. Effi, when Sarah Bernhardt died, her last words, more or less...

EFFI: *(Nearly off)* Sarah Bernhardt's not dead.

THOMAS: You know, you're perfectly right. But when she is, if she ever is, just before, she's going to ask...

(Exit EFFI left.)

THOMAS: *(More quietly, knowing she's gone)* She's going to ask, "Tell me, tell me: Are the reporters at the door?" Ha-ha-ha-ha. *(More quietly)* I hope you enjoyed that one, Effi, as much as I did. *(Raising his voice slightly in the direction of her departure)* And I hope, when you return, you'll have that goddamn shell. *(To the empty beach, more quietly)* You may be wondering why I called you all here today. I want a crowd scene! *(Yelling both ways on the beach)* Hey, crowd! Crowd! Over this way, there's a man, seems he's all alone! *(Writing furiously)* "Enter Helen left." *(He waits, looks left, writes again.)* "Enter, Helen, left." *(Not writing, tossing his sheaf of papers to the wind; then lightly:)* ...dressed for the tropics; her lovely figure, which I have never seen...though it may not be too late...I raise an eyebrow...I pick something from the corner of my eye and... *(A Romeo gesturing at a HELEN spread before him on the sand)* Ah, you beauty! This is what it's all about, isn't it? *(Looking left, a despairing cry)* ENTER! HELEN! LEFT! *(Looking over his shoulder)* Enter Hal from behind tree. MY BROTHER! Enter the Pflaum-Smythes and their charming daughter. Exit my brother's son. And...all the others. *(Looking straight before him)* Take your liver.

(Pause; and as the sun sets or the lights obey, which pleases him, THOMAS gives his final stage direction.)

THOMAS: ...light...fades...

(The sun quickly sets.)

END OF PLAY

www.ingramcontent.com/pod-product-compliance
Lightning Source LLC
Chambersburg PA
CBHW061304110426
42742CB00012BA/2046